Promoting Regulation and Flexibility in Thinking

This concise guide introduces the importance of executive function for social and emotional well-being and effective learning. It clearly explains the research that underpins important topics such as working memory, organization, self-regulation, attention and cognitive flexibility, and how they apply to the real-world settings in which we work with children, adolescents, and families. This engaging book offers knowledge and strategies for improving executive function together with an understanding of its relevance for diverse populations.

The authors use the most current research to provide an overview of what executive function is, how it develops, and how it works in coordination with other developmental factors to promote regulation and flexibility in thinking. Chapters contain detailed information about the biological and physiological foundations for brain development and emotion regulation, as well as advances in cognition, emotion, and social relationships. Making the research accessible to all with evidence-based writing and theory-to-practice applications, the book provides applications with career contexts and interviews and case studies that bring the book to life.

Designed to introduce professionals, advocates, and parents to the importance of executive function in human development, this book is for all those working with children and young people. It will also be of interest as an introductory text for those new to the field or as a way to learn to apply developmental principles in practice.

Kristen M. Weede Alexander is a Child and Adolescent Development Professor at California State University, Sacramento. She received her Ph.D. in Human Development from the University of California, Davis in 2002 and her current research interests are in stress, coping, and memory in context.

Karen M. Davis O'Hara serves as the Executive Dean of Sierra College (Nevada County Campus), having formerly been a Professor of Child Development and administrator in the College of Education at California State University, Sacramento. She received her Ph.D. in Human Development from University of California, Davis, and her research focuses on emotion regulation.

Applying Child and Adolescent Development in the Professions Series

Editor: Kimberly A. Gordon Biddle, Emeritus Professor of Child and Adolescent Development, Sacramento State, California, USA

The field of Child and Adolescent Development is being recognized and legitimized more and more as good preparation for a variety of careers in various fields such as; psychology, education, allied health, non-profits, and social work. As more theories are created and research is conducted, more attention and recognition is given to the field of Child and Adolescent Development.

This series takes core and current topics in the field of Child and Adolescent Development, defines the topics, describes the topics as they develop in children from infancy to age 25 or describes how the topic impacts children from infancy to age 25, and then applies them to careers in five main fields, psychology, education, allied health, non-profits, and social work. Various application strategies and techniques are shared. The core topics addressed in this series of books are as follows; attachment, motivation, social and emotional competence, executive function, and MultiLingual and MultiCultural Development. The current niche topics represented in the series are these; transformative frames for anti-racism, socio-cultural deprivation, and growth mindset for transformative thinking. The writing level is accessible and engaging for students in high school and the first or second year of college. However, the information may be useful for graduate students, too. These books are excellent for early, mid, and late career professionals, too. Employee training and professional development can be enriched with the books of this series.

It is the intention of the book authors that the volumes are helpful to all people who work with and care for children. Indeed, the topics explored in Applying Child and Adolescent Development in the Professions Series move the field forward.

Inspiring Motivation in Children and Youth
How to Nurture Environments for Learning
David A. Bergin

Promoting Regulation and Flexibility in Thinking
Development of Executive Function
Kristen M. Weede Alexander and Karen M. Davis O'Hara

For more information about this series, please visit: www.routledge.com/Applying-Child-and-Adolescent-Development-in-the-Professions-Series/book-series/ACADP

Promoting Regulation and Flexibility in Thinking

Development of Executive Function

Kristen M. Weede Alexander and Karen M. Davis O'Hara

Routledge
Taylor & Francis Group

NEW YORK AND LONDON

Designed cover image: © Kristen M. Weede Alexander

First published 2024
by Routledge
605 Third Avenue, New York, NY 10158

and by Routledge
4 Park Square, Milton Park, Abingdon, Oxon OX14 4RN

Routledge is an imprint of the Taylor & Francis Group, an informa business

Library of Congress Cataloging-in-Publication Data
Names: Weede Alexander, Kristen M., author. | Davis O'Hara,
Karen M., author.
Title: Promoting regulation and flexibility in thinking : development of executive
function / Kristen M. Weede Alexander, Karen M. Davis O'Hara.
Description: 1 Edition. | New York, NY : Routledge, 2023. |
Series: Applying child and adolescent development in the professions series |
Includes bibliographical references and index.
Identifiers: LCCN 2023033418 (print) | LCCN 2023033419 (ebook) |
ISBN 9780367673673 (paperback) | ISBN 9780367673697 (hardback) |
ISBN 9781003131052 (ebook)
Subjects: LCSH: Thought and thinking. | Cognition. | Emotions. |
Developmental psychobiology.
Classification: LCC BF441 .W44 2023 (print) | LCC BF441 (ebook) |
DDC 153.4/2–dc23/eng/20231026
LC record available at https://lccn.loc.gov/2023033418
LC ebook record available at https://lccn.loc.gov/2023033419

ISBN: 978-0-367-67369-7 (hbk)
ISBN: 978-0-367-67367-3 (pbk)
ISBN: 978-1-003-13105-2 (ebk)

DOI: 10.4324/9781003131052

Typeset in Galliard
by Taylor & Francis Books

To Brian, my partner in everything, and to Sydney, Brooke, and Trent who have unquestionably been my best teachers of human development

–KWA

To my children, Aily and Nolan who confirmed everything I didn't even know I knew about child development

–KDO

Contents

Figures

Boxes

Series Editor Foreword

The field of Child and Adolescent Development is in infant stages of development, but it is steadily maturing. It is time for it be recognized and legitimized. As the theorizing and conduction of research in the field become more solid, complex, and applicable to life; recognition comes that the field is for people in a variety of professions. The traditional education and psychology fields are enriched with the knowledge obtained from the field of Child and Adolescent Development. Additionally, allied health, social work, and non-profit fields are improved with knowledge of how to apply Child and Adolescent Development in the workplace setting. Everyone who works with or cares for children from birth to 25 years will benefit from reading and applying the information from the books in this series. Collectively, the authors have created books rich with foundational information and application techniques and strategies. Thematic boxes of interviews, case studies, and research and theory into practice run throughout all the books. These books help to answer some of the most important questions concerning children and their development. All who love and care about children should read every book in the series.

The excellent writing team of Dr. Kristen Alexander and Dr. Karen O'Hara present *Promoting Regulation and Flexibility in Thinking: Development of Executive Function*. This book is truly a monumental one that pushes the field of Child and Adolescent Development into the future. Executive function and the relationship it has to traditional cognitive development is presented in a reader friendly and digestible manner. The book begins with defining executive function, relaying its theoretical and biological foundations, and describing its processes. There are also explanations of how it impacts and interacts with emotions and social cognitions. The last two chapters apply the concepts to settings of children. One chapter covers direct, micro settings and the other focuses on indirect and advocacy settings. A key setting mentioned is mental health professional settings and the role and usefulness of executive functioning in these settings. One key concept that is not to be missed is the bi-directional nature of executive functions. They impact the child and the child's environment.

However, the child's environment and the child also impact executive functions. This book is necessary reading for all adults in all settings that interact with children from birth to age 25. It can be especially enlightening for parents and all professionals.

Dr. Kimberly A. Gordon Biddle

Preface

This book has but two authors and yet a community of support made this book possible. With unprecedented quarantine in the early stages of this process, it has been an interesting journey. Kimberly Gordon Biddle brought up the idea one day that she was editing a book series and the idea for this book was born. Thanks to her for her ideas, patience with multiple and not-necessarily-timely drafts, and encouragement in this process.

Kristen will start with a shout out to her village: I give a special thanks to my family—to the family that raised me, Jean, Dave, Holly, and Todd, the family that welcomed me into theirs upon marriage, Beth and Dale, and the family that has poured into me every day, Trent, Brooke, Sydney, and Brian (who has picked up the slack during this process, and pretty much always)—you all provide me with the constant support, ongoing encouragement, and unconditional love that makes me feel safe in this world and able to think I can accomplish big things. This also includes my beloved Grandma and best-ever aunt and uncle. Thanks also to my friends-who-are-family—I hope you know who you are. My life and thoughts would not be same without my Pumalo Posse, Lat Lab team, Quaranteam, and BFFs, along with my supportive colleagues at Sac State, my church family, and those I get to celebrate holidays and vacation with, who understand why I sometimes steal away to work. You have walked with me through the years and encouraged me every step of the way. I am overwhelmed with gratitude. Thanks to our great God who put this all into motion, gave me the skill to do this work, and put the people in my life that supported my own development of executive function used to complete this task. And thank you to my brilliant co-author, who I am also privileged to call my friend.

Karen would like to thank and honor her children, Aily and Nolan, who make me very proud to call them mine. They give me inspiration to be a better, stronger and more worthy person every day. I want to thank my parents, Gary and Susie for giving me life and love and for supporting everything that I do, no matter how random it may seem at the time. Who knew that packing up and moving to the Sierra foothills without a plan would end up in the most exciting and fulfilling job I have ever had. My best friends, Amy, Rochelle, Kim and Lori, for loving me even when I vanish for months on end and for being my biggest cheerleaders for the past 40-odd years. And for all the professional mentors and colleagues along the way, including the Child Development and College of Education faculty at Sacramento State, the Lat Lab team including Rosemarie Kraft, and the hundreds of students who have challenged my thinking and pushed me to always be learning. Thank you, Kristen, for this opportunity to collaborate and always gently pushing me forward. You are such an inspiration to me—you are kind, tenacious and brilliant, and I am honored to be your co-author and most importantly your friend.

And a big shout out to those who directly contributed to stories, images, and interviews contained in this book. Thank you for sharing your insight and vulnerabilities so that the rest of us can learn from your experiences: Abigail Colwell, Aily O'Hara, Bronwyn Murphy, Brooke Alexander, Erika Molina, Holly Blagg, Jackson Mank, Julia Gladding, Marcus and Audrey Wiggins, Mark Colwell, Mesara Jayalath, Mia Gladding, Mia Murphy, Leia Murphy, Sarah Siverling, Sydney Alexander, Tarin Varughese, Trent Alexander, and Vy Tran. Other familiar names have been used in fabricated stories—thank you for letting us use your names to tell our story.

Introduction

Promoting Regulation and Flexibility in Thinking: Development of Executive Function

We experience executive function in action every day. As adults, we have competing demands for attention and choose what to listen to or think about or pay attention to. When we have that annoying interaction with a classmate or co-worker, we try to hold back our automatic reactions like rolling our eyes or saying something unprofessional, and we may pause for a few moments to plan our response. All humans have these experiences to some degree, and changes develop over time due to the development of such underlying skills as controlling attention, emotion, and behavior, remembering events and people, and planning for actions.

Executive function (EF) is a complex set of skills that can be difficult to understand for those not immersed in scientific research. Even more challenging might be applying that understanding while working with or in advocacy for real children, adolescents, and families. And yet, understanding EF is critical for thinking about how individuals with different abilities, resources, and experiences can think, understand, and act on the world in different ways. EF affects how we remember, organize information, regulate thinking, control emotion and behaviors, and focus our attention. Because there is considerable change in how well humans exert cognitive control between infancy and adulthood, EF has important applications to how children of all ages form relationships, understand and express emotion, and interpret and act on their knowledge and experiences. Understanding these developmental changes and the contexts in which they occur can help professionals, parents, community members, and child advocates support children and families to succeed.

As you read this book, you will learn about how the science of EF can be applied in many careers. The first chapter provides an in-depth overview of the various psychological and biological processes involved in EF. Typical patterns of development from infancy through adolescence and adulthood, theoretical approaches, biological underpinnings, and sources of diversity and individual differences in developmental patterns are described using the most current scientific evidence. Different ways in which professionals in child and adolescent development can promote social, emotional, and cognitive development are discussed with a focus on leveraging assets.

The next three chapters cover some of the major developmental milestones in cognitive, emotional, and social growth. Chapter 2 examines theories and research in cognitive development and how EF and complex thinking are intertwined. Chapter 3 details the foundations for emotional development by focusing on how EF guides and is guided by self-regulation, attachment, and temperament. Chapter 4 takes a more outward orientation, focusing on the role of cognition, emotion, and EF in the development of social cognition, considering such topics as self-awareness, self-control, perspective-taking, and empathy. All of these content chapters highlight the critical role of biology, individual differences, and social and cultural context in order to make clear the importance of parents and professionals in supporting individuals to optimize their developmental outcomes.

The final two chapters provide applications of the understanding of EF development within specific career contexts that support human development. Chapter 5 lays out a theory of ongoing interactions between the person and their environment to focus on professions that involve direct interactions with children, youth, and families in fields such as education, psychology, law, and healthcare. Chapter 6 further elaborates on levels of context and how they differentially influence human development, concentrating on careers that center children, youth, and families through indirect pathways, such as policy, administration, and advocacy. This final chapter also underscores the role of EF in developing humans working to create change in their own environments.

Chapter I

Executive Function and Human Development

Control, Biology, and Regulation

Executive function helps us adapt to our surroundings as we reflect, plan, and move beyond instinct to engage in intentional and effortful behaviors. It guides how we think, what we think about, how and when we act, and how we regulate our emotions and behaviors. Central to executive function is a set of both biological and psychological functions that develops substantially between birth and adulthood, and so the development of executive function is tied to many of the changes we see in other domains of human development, such as learning, memory, relationship-building, abstract thinking, and emotion regulation. Differences in biology and context create variation in executive function (EF) and affect how individuals adapt to and thrive in various contexts, such as the classroom or family settings. Understanding what executive function is and how brain development and the environment contribute to changes in EF is important for professionals interested in serving children and families in order to create appropriately supportive environments and design suitable curricula to meet the goals of diverse communities of children and families.

Source: Shutterstock.

DOI: 10.4324/9781003131052-1

What is Executive Function?

Executive function (EF) allows humans to intentionally control their emotions, thoughts, and behaviors. Although its precise definition may vary slightly according to which publication you read (Müller & Kerns, 2015), there is general agreement that it allows us to engage in top-down processes, such as planning, problem-solving, and thinking about abstract ideas (Diamond, 2013). **Top-down** processes are those in which our thinking and higher cognitive functions guide our thoughts and behavior and allow us to use the big picture to understand smaller parts. Figure 1.1 illustrates how this can be contrasted with **bottom-up** processing that is driven more by our sensory responses to the environment and smaller pieces that need to be assembled to lead to a bigger idea or more organized behavior. Humans have a limited number of psychological resources available to engage in top-down processing because of the interplay of conflicting sensory and cognitive inputs all coming in at the same time, and executive functions organize the person's ability to control and manage these inputs (Welsh & Pennington, 1988). For example, you may want to scroll through your social media, but know that you should be studying for a test. EF will help you delay the gratification of watching a show to engage your top-down conscious self-control with studying for that test. Executive functions are thus effortful processes we use to facilitate cognitive control and engage in goal-directed behavior (Hendry et al., 2016).

Executive function is very important not just for behavior and performance in general, but has been identified as one of the six major neurocognitive domains in the Diagnostic and Statistical Manual of Mental Disorders (5th edition; DSM-5), the book clinicians use to identify and diagnose a variety of mental health challenges (American Psychiatric Association, 2013). As such,

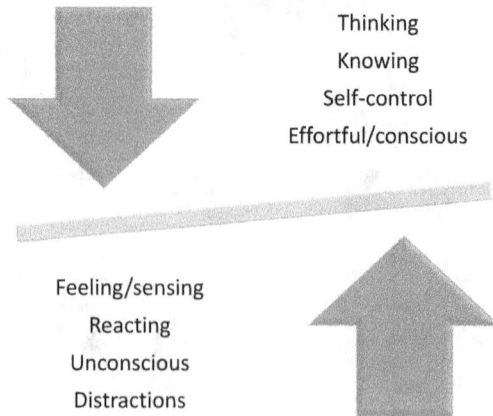

Thinking
Knowing
Self-control
Effortful/conscious

Feeling/sensing
Reacting
Unconscious
Distractions

Figure 1.1 Top-down and bottom-up processing.

EF is factored into all neurocognitive diagnoses, with clinicians examining planning, decision-making, working memory, feedback response, inhibition, and cognitive flexibility to diagnose and treat their clients. Therefore, understanding and supporting the development of EF from infancy is important in the establishment and maintenance of emotional and psychological health.

For our purposes and consistent with research in the field, EF can be divided into three main categories of skills that promote higher-order thinking: inhibition, working memory, and cognitive/attentional flexibility (Diamond, 2013; Zelazo et al., 2008). These early core functions develop substantially during early childhood to create the foundation for higher-order skills such as planning and goal-setting in middle to late childhood, resulting in complex regulation of behavior and emotion that emerges in adolescence and beyond. That is, whereas infants and young children tend to be more impulsive and rigid in their thinking, adolescents and young adults are typically able to control their behavior and be more flexible in their thinking. In fact, as we will describe throughout this book, all areas of EF improve dramatically between infancy and adolescence, with cognitive flexibility displaying the most extended period of development (Diamond, 2013). Moreover, tasks involving the coordination of multiple aspects of EF together may develop well into adolescence and beyond (e.g., Müller & Kerns, 2015). Figure 1.2 illustrates the overarching concept of executive function promoting higher-order thinking.

Let's imagine a preschool classroom full of 3-year-olds. There is only one musical drum to play with and Shawna currently has it. Dante wants it. Dante has his goal of obtaining the drum, but how can he achieve it? Read on to see how different EFs can play a role in how Dante might think about how to reach his goal.

One effective solution may be for Dante to immediately grab the drum. Depending on the relationship he has with Shawna, the classroom climate and current social setting, and numerous other contextual factors, this may work. But did Dante consider these factors before engaging in his solution? Grabbing the drum may encourage Shawna to play with something else, depending on her general demeanor and how she feels at the time. Or it may entice her to react by grabbing it back, screaming, or telling the teacher that the drum was unfairly taken from her without her permission. Insofar as Dante and Shawna are allowing themselves to consider multiple options, they would be using executive function; however, given their age, it is less likely their EF would be engaged than in older children or adults, and the preschoolers may be more likely to react without engaging in this top-down thought process.

Inhibition

To consider his goals and avoid an automatic or impulsive reaction, Dante would need to engage his inhibition. **Inhibition** is an EF that involves

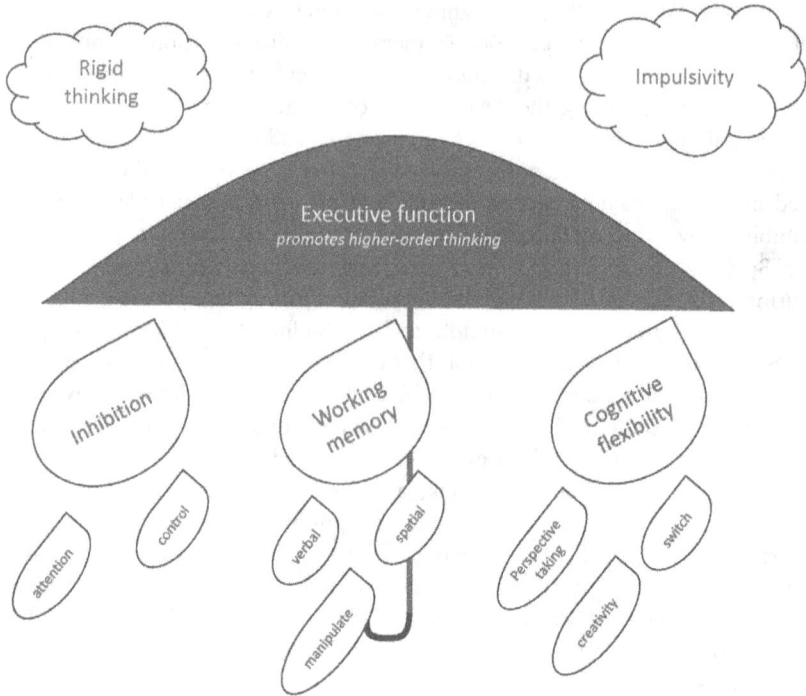

Figure 1.2 Executive function umbrella: when engaged and fully developed, this umbrella can allow the individual to choose to avoid rigid thought and impulsivity.

effortfully putting aside the impulse for immediate gratification and can require executive functions such as self-control, perseverance, attention, and regulated action. Inhibitory ability increases substantially during early childhood, emerging during the first year in simple forms such as *restraint inhibition* to stop a behavior by direction of the caregiver (Kochanska et al., 1996). A different kind of inhibition—*interference control*—advances through preschool between ages 3 to 7 and involves a greater ability to stop irrelevant information from interfering with the task at hand (Diamond et al., 2013). Although the bulk of inhibitory development occurs before middle childhood, inhibition continues to gradually increase in some ways into adulthood (Müller & Kerns, 2015).

Now, let's turn back to our preschooler who wants that drum from his classmate. Dante may realize that he has a goal but must stop himself from acting immediately in order to allow himself to consider options. In order to regulate his behavior, Dante needs to engage in *self-control* by *inhibiting* the impulse to take the toy immediately. To do so, he may use inhibitory skills such as paying *attention* to what is happening around him and *regulating action* by pausing to *plan* his behavior. It may take *perseverance* to engage in this behavior consistently or for extended periods of time. Regardless of the action implemented, if these processes occurred, EF was actively engaged.

Working Memory

Another EF is **working memory**, which is the term used to describe how we store and manipulate information that is currently on our minds. Information is held in working memory primarily in verbal/linguistic or visual-spatial patterns (Baddeley, 2002). As was discovered decades ago and remains true, working memory is limited in capacity and duration; we can only hold five to nine items in mind at a time (Miller, 1956) and only for 20 to 30 seconds at a time if we are not effortful (Atkinson & Shiffrin, 1968). Although working memory functions early in development, there are apparent increases in capacity (Spencer, 2020). Researchers do not agree on the source of these capacity increases, and it is possible that more items can be held because of **chunking** (Cowan, 2016).

Chunking involves combining multiple pieces into a whole, such as remembering a series of letters as a single word instead of a long series of separate letters or recalling the layout of a chess board as a whole rather than 32 separate chess pieces. Moreover, the duration of working memory can be extended by using **strategies**, which also increase in number and effectiveness with age (see Chapter 2 for more). Further, depending on a person's biological predispositions (e.g., temperament) and experiences involving language, vision, and proprioception (i.e., sensation of the body in space), many people tend to be better at holding and manipulating information in one of the formats: verbal/linguistic versus visual-spatial information (Baddeley, 2002).

Let's think about Dante again. If Dante inhibited his natural tendency to achieve immediate gratification, he would then have the opportunity to hold in mind multiple aspects of the situation, such as his relationship with Shawna, his perception of the classroom setting, and any ideas he has for achieving his goal, such as grabbing it, asking for it, or sitting nearby to wait until Shawna is done. Each of these takes space in working memory. Other working memory space may be occupied by the sound of the drum, the way it makes him feel not to have the drum, and additional details not relevant to the current situation (e.g., that he is hungry). Based on any remaining working memory space and cognitive resources, he can think through solutions using language, by talking himself through various scenarios, or spatially, by imagining the actions taking place. These potential solutions also take up working memory space. Because working memory capacity develops extensively along with other EFs during the preschool years, it would be reasonable to expect Dante's working memory to be overwhelmed.

Note the connection here between the executive functions of inhibition and working memory. Dante must inhibit his immediate action and attend to the most relevant details while blocking out distractions. This increases the

Source: Shutterstock.

availability of his working memory for task relevant details. Likewise, Dante must hold and manipulate ideas to solve his problem, and it is through his newly generated ideas and solutions that he can engage in renewed effortful control over his thoughts and actions.

Cognitive Flexibility

The third major component of EF is **cognitive flexibility**, which allows individuals to consider alternative perspectives, think creatively, and switch between tasks (Diamond, 2013). Cognitive flexibility often involves shifting from one rule, perspective, or object feature to another rule, perspective, or object feature. For example, sorting toys by color and then switching to sorting by shape is difficult without cognitive flexibility. Cognitive flexibility increases extensively during the preschool years in the form of shifting between features of objects or rules for sorting (e.g., Perner & Lang, 2002), and changing rules and switching tasks continues to improve through adolescence and early adulthood (Ferguson et al., 2021; Zelazo & Carlson, 2020). These abilities are expected to support higher-order thinking as characterized by novel, abstract and flexible thought used to plan, solve problems, and weigh more personally variable ideas such as morality and ethics (e.g., Diamond, 2013).

Although our preschooler is in a phase of relative immaturity and yet rapid development of cognitive flexibility, he may still see multiple aspects of the problem and rules by which to solve it. That is, while inhibiting, his working memory may be generating new ideas: Dante may consider Shawna's perspective of the situation; he might decide to find an alternative object to drum with; or he may decide to engage in a completely different activity. These solutions all require creative thinking and potentially adapting his goal. In this situation, Dante's inhibition of impulse and distractions makes available space in working memory to engage in flexible thinking. The cognitive flexibility exhibited in the manipulation of potential solutions and taking on multiple perspectives occurs in his working memory space.

Developmental Change

Importantly, changes in these three major components of EF are associated with some overarching developmental shifts. For instance, speed of processing has been linked to improvements in inhibition and working memory (McAuley & White, 2011) and how fast infants process information predicts later EF (Rose et al., 2012). Other links to EF across development are made with improvements in the use of strategies in problem solving and self-regulatory behaviors (Müller & Kerns, 2015). Much of this book will elaborate on EF as related to changes in relationships, emotion regulation, and thought that occur throughout childhood and adolescence.

Theoretical Approaches and the Role of Executive Function in Human Development

Along with other developmental researchers and professionals, Lerner (2006) argued for developmental science to take an asset-based approach to understanding and supporting positive developmental outcomes across diverse people and contexts. The work of these developmentalists has promoted a paradigm shift in practice from a focus on deficits and weaknesses (e.g., how to "fix" things) to an emphasis on strengths and assets (e.g., how to effectively engage personal and community resources). By looking for the strengths of individuals, families and communities, professionals can better understand their place in supporting individual or collective development. This approach is particularly critical for People of Color (e.g., Yosso, 2005) and minoritized groups (e.g., Garcia Coll et al., 1996), and can be used to support children and adolescents in a variety of settings to leverage their personal and contextual strengths as they strive toward their developmental aspirations. That is, rather than focusing on perceived problems, practitioners can use a **strengths-based approach** (or **asset-based approach**) to focus on fostering healthy development using tools within individuals and their communities. The image of holding hands gives us a reminder of the cultural asset provided by generational wealth.

Source: Shutterstock.

We can take an asset-based approach to our work with children, adolescents, and families while using a variety of theoretical approaches to understand the mechanisms underlying change. Some theories are more obviously compatible with the asset-based approach to working with children and families, and yet as practitioners we can draw from the ideas of various theories to guide our approaches to identifying and building on strengths as we promote child, adolescent, and family development. A theoretical perspective can be thought of as a lens through which we view the research and practices; knowledge of different theories can help practitioners draw on different ideas about how change occurs to best serve children and families.

In this chapter, we will introduce two theories that define development more broadly. These two theories were chosen because of how they present different ways of viewing EF: one theory situates EF as *the* regulator and the other includes EF as one of *many* regulators. The first is based on a computer model, in which executive function can be seen as a controller of information as it flows from the environment into memory, where it is eventually represented for use in current or future thinking and behavior. Another theory situates EF as one part of an intricate web of developmental systems with bi-directional influence on relationships, emotions, and thoughts. These different theoretical perspectives are not opposites, but rather they represent different sets of assumptions about how EF changes and the role it serves within developing humans. These theoretical perspectives are explored further next.

Information Processing

Information Processing theory was designed to explain how we take in information from the environment to store it indefinitely, and it was initially designed to explain how adults think. Atkinson and Shiffrin (1968) proposed a model that has continued to guide research, theory, and practice in specific areas of cognition and development (e.g., memory, social behaviors; Atkinson & Shiffrin, 2016). In this model there are three primary systems: sensory register, working memory (although the original theoretical model called this short-term memory, which described a place to temporarily hold information in consciousness, current models recognize the information is not static and can be operated on and manipulated, thus making the term working memory more appropriate here (Baddeley, 2002)), and long-term memory. Each of these systems operates as the term dictates, such that the **sensory register** (also sensory memory) is designed to take in large quantities of information for only a fleeting moment; working memory holds fewer items but for several seconds and allows for a mixing of old and new knowledge; and **long-term memory** is thought to be unlimited in the amount of information and length of time it can store information. And yet it is not this simple because which information makes it through these systems into long-term memory is governed by control processes, which include EF (Atkinson & Shiffrin, 1968), and all develop systematically throughout childhood and adolescence (e.g., Kail & Bisanz, 1982).

For example, think about the last person you saw and try to recall the color of the shirt they were wearing. Try it! If you are like most people, you cannot recall the color of the shirt. You must have noticed they were wearing a shirt, right? This means you took in this information at some point, but your information processing system deemed it unimportant and so it rapidly disappeared. If the color of the shirt caught your attention, it may have moved from the sensory register to the next system in the information processing network—working memory. You may have thought about the shirt, integrating it with prior knowledge by recognizing that it matches the one you thought about wearing today. Or you noticed that you really liked (or didn't like) that shirt they were wearing. You still could forget the color a few minutes later because working memory, as the receptacle of information you are currently thinking about, is limited in the amount of information it can hold and it generally removes that information when it leaves your current thoughts. But if the color of the shirt was meaningful enough that your information processing system spent the time and resources storing it away in long-term memory, it may be stored indefinitely (see Figure 1.3).

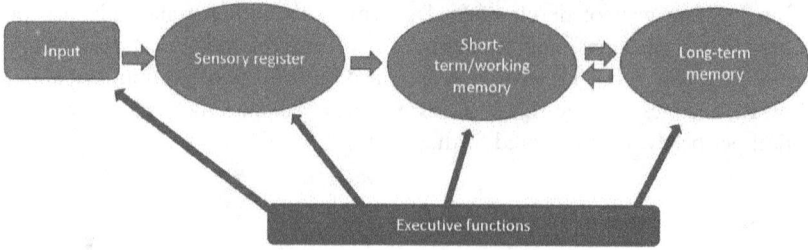

Figure 1.3 Information processing model with EF regulating the flow.

Note the previous example involved some automatic processing, but also some conscious, intentional thought. It required control to move the information through the information processing system to the next step. That control is regulated by EF. Inhibition (focused attention, self-control, perseverance, regulating action), working memory (verbal and visual representations), and cognitive flexibility (perspective taking, creativity, shifting ideas/attention) regulate the flow of information through this system. Given the massive amount of information inputted to the sensory register (literally everything you see, hear, touch, smell, taste) and limitations of working memory, consider the inhibition required to focus attention on specific details, the regulation necessary to hold and manipulate information, and the flexibility required to manipulate and fit new information into old ideas. Without executive function, information cannot effortfully move through the system. These ideas will be elaborated on in later chapters to consider how these assumptions might help practitioners identify and maximize individual and contextual strengths to promote positive development.

Systems Theories

An alternative theoretical perspective focuses on the **softly assembled structures** of humans and how each part of the human is best understood within the context of the whole being. Note that assuming humans are *softly assembled* does not mean they are squishy, rather it refers to the dynamic, flexible adaptation humans make in context and the assumption that they are malleable or changeable (Lerner, 2006). Also, *structures* in this context does not refer to literal physical entities, but they are more like sets of skills or organized ways of seeing the world that coexist in the body and mind. Systems theory uses the term "systems" to refer to structures as organized sets of actions, behaviors, or emotions that interact with one another over time. Thus, although humans grow and change in adaptation to the context, we do so in an organized manner that integrates various parts of the whole human (e.g., Cantor et al., 2018). As one element of the system changes, it offsets the equilibrium of the systems and so each system adapts to reach equilibrium again and works with other systems in an organized manner (Fischer & Bidell, 2006).

Systems theories are often illustrated by webs or concentric circles to display the multiple domains and various connections each part has with the others (e.g., Bronfenbrenner & Morris, 2006; Fischer & Bidell, 2006; Lerner, 2006). Figure 1.4 shows this by using gears inside and outside of the human—as one gear shifts, all gears must shift to accommodate the change, resulting in a changed person. In such models, theorists emphasize the importance of time, the process by which the individual engages with the environment, and the bidirectional nature of connections among person and context. As people interact with contexts, they are changed. And yet, as the individual interacts with these contexts, the contexts themselves are also changed. This "dance" between different aspects of individuals as well as the contexts in which they grow and adapt continues throughout the lifespan and will be expanded on in Chapters 5 and 6.

The role of EF in Systems theories is critical because new behaviors, ideas, and actions emerge as a result of multiple systems interacting and self-organizing over time (Thelen & Smith, 2006). As a critical system in the developing human with an elongated period of development, EF is an important driver of development. Importantly, understanding the existence of multiple systems within individuals and their contexts and their interactive effects can help practitioners better understand and identify assets that may operate together to promote positive development. Systems theory will be used in further chapters to consider the interactive effect of context, biology, and EF.

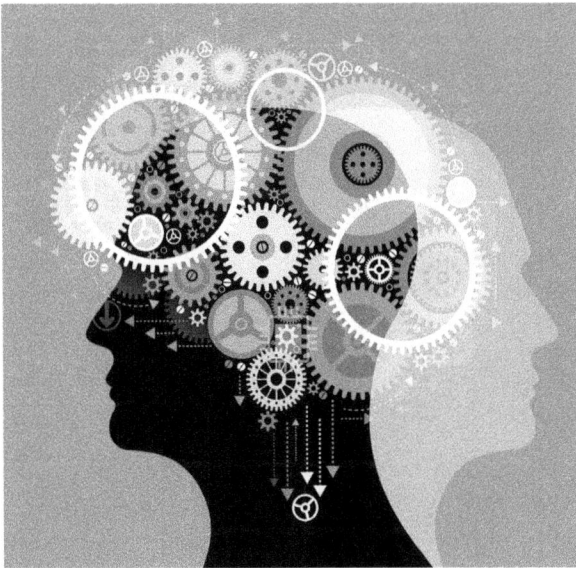

Figure 1.4 Illustration of Systems theories using gears.
Source: Shutterstock.

Biological Foundations of Executive Function

Executive function is regulated, in part, by the brain regions it uses to function. Brain development is defined and regulated by genes and so the unfolding of genetic material over time and the way in which the brain develops form foundations for EF. The next sections describe some of the terms and processes that are used to explain how genes work and contribute to EF, as well as how brain cells organize into a functioning brain and how these processes influence EF. These biological foundations are elaborated further throughout the next chapters.

Genes and Executive Function

General Terms

Genes provide the instructions for development from conception through death. They are contained in the nucleus of every cell in your body, as parts of strands of **deoxyribonucleic acid (DNA)**. DNA is made up of different combinations of chemical bases that are used to "code" for all changes in structure and function in the human. Human DNA contains approximately 22,000 **genes** (small portions of the DNA strand) that provide the code for your body to combine amino acids in a specific way to create a specific protein sequence (International Human Genome Sequencing Consortium, 2004). An illustration of genes can be found in Figure 1.5. **Amino acids** enter the body through

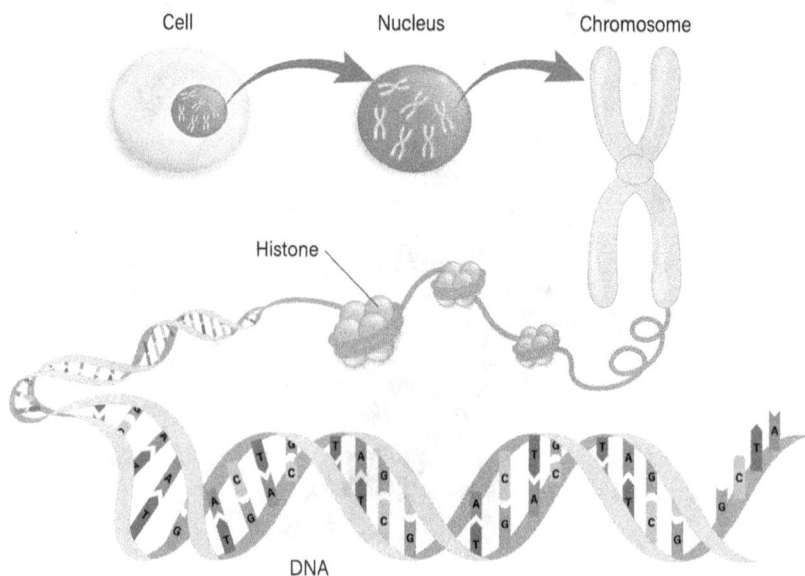

Figure 1.5 An image of how DNA is situated within every cell of the body.
Source: Shutterstock.

nutritional sources (e.g., food), to provide the building blocks of protein that the genes work with. A lack of amino acids can lead to problems with gene expression and protein building, and an excess of certain amino acids can lead to toxicity and crowding out of other needed amino acids. (DNA contains additional genes that serve a more regulatory or stabilization function (Storz, 2002).) It is important to note that not all genes are expressed; that is, the code for a specific gene will not result in protein production if regulatory functions turn a gene "off" or the body does not support creation of that protein (e.g., necessary amino acids are not present in the body or body temperature is high). **Gene expression** will be revisited in more detail in later chapters, but for now it is important to know that it is the *function* of genes that causes human development, and function is defined by organization of the genes themselves plus the biological context in which they are expressed.

DNA sequencing is established prior to birth based on the parents' DNA and does not change with development. And yet, the DNA in every cell of your body is identical. How do some cells know they need to turn into the brain while others become skin? Why can one identical twin (with identical DNA) be diagnosed with a fatal disease while the other is healthy? A critical explanation for differences despite identical DNA was more recently discovered, and it highlights ways those genetic instructions can be modified in an enduring way.

The long DNA strands of instructions wrap around special structures called histones, and those histones can be modified by different enzymes attaching (or not) in ways that prevent or promote access to the DNA portions they are near (Jenuwein & Allis, 2001). **Histone codes** thus modulate gene expression and can cause some genes to be "on" (i.e., result in protein production) and others to remain "off." These codes resulting from histone modifications can be passed on by parents to their offspring (i.e., hereditary), but are not as permanent as the DNA sequence because histone codes can be altered based on environmental factors (Jenuwein & Allis, 2001). Depending on the location of the cell and its function, histones may be modified in different ways that moderate how genes are expressed and thus affect human development (Day & Sweatt, 2011).

Some changes to how genes are expressed can be due to gene mutations, cell location (i.e., cells secrete chemicals that guide further development within that region), or connections with other cells. These effects can occur in one individual and may be temporary or isolated to a specific area of the body in which it occurred and not be passed on to offspring in the DNA. **Mutations** occur when the DNA is making a copy of itself and makes a mistake by adding or deleting genes or portions of genes. Some mutations are genetically preprogrammed to occur, and many occur spontaneously and are thus not passed down from parent to offspring. Such mutations can cause neurodevelopmental disorders such as Rett's syndrome because of changes to the expression of key genes for brain development (e.g., Day & Sweatt, 2011), and thus they can impact EF.

Genetic Contributions to Executive Function

Examining EF at the level of genes has resulted in findings suggesting that genes play a strong role in EF skills. Specifically, EF has a high heritability (Friedman et al., 2008). **Heritability** represents the estimated contribution of genes (in contrast to environmental factors) to individual variation. In other words, when individual differences exist in EF, is it because of genes (high heritability) or because of environment (low heritability)? Given the previous discussion about the role of genes as the blueprint for development, a high heritability may make you think that EF is entirely innate and immutable (unchangeable) like our DNA, making much of this book useless to us as individuals wanting to learn more about EF to promote positive outcomes in children, youth, adults, and families.

This is not true! Importantly, heritability estimates in research are based on a particular group of people at a specific time, without reference to factors of influence before or after the measurement (Miyake & Friedman, 2012). It does not apply to individuals, but rather to a population of individuals. For example, if identical twins who share the same DNA have different outcomes, it might be assumed this is due to environment because they share all of their DNA. And yet, remember histones and the importance not only of having the genes, but of expressing them? Studies looking at performance of EF skills rely on the *expression* of genes, which is intimately tied to environmental influence (and histones and mutations).

What, then, can we make of this strong heritability of EF? One idea comes from work suggesting that the heritability of EF increases with age (Engelhardt et al., 2015) and that genes may predispose individuals to select specific people and places to be around and elicit specific reactions from others based on behaviors, thus making it appear that the environment did not have an effect (Scarr & McCartney, 1983). In fact, studies show that environments with greater physical resources (e.g., more activity options, educational experiences) afford more diverse opportunities and resources and yield higher heritability ratings (Tucker-Drob et al., 2013). If high heritability meant "unchangeable" and "due to genes," these findings could imply that having more resources actually changes our genes, which we know not to be true. Instead, it means that despite any lack of flexibility in the structure of DNA, gene expression can be modified if we identify and support strong networks for medical care, education, and learning experiences and materials in the home and care setting. Such supports of diverse needs may best facilitate healthy EF development in a variety of contexts.

Brain Development and Executive Function

Neurons

Development and effectiveness of executive function is closely tied to systematic changes in the brain throughout infancy, childhood, and adolescence. To best explain this, a few terms and ideas need to be introduced and these are illustrated in Figure 1.6. The brain is composed of millions of **neurons**, which are the cells of the brain that are responsible for communication within the brain (Stiles & Jernigan, 2010). Neurons have a cell body, and on one side are branch-like extensions (i.e., **dendrites**) that receive communication from other neurons. From the other side of the cell extends a long arm (i.e., **axon**) that branches out to allow the neuron to send its message to other neurons. The mechanism by which neurons send messages is electrical impulse, which travels through the axon to transmit the message and typically responds in an all-or-none manner. For the electrical impulse to travel through the axon to efficiently transmit the message and fire, it needs to be insulated by **myelin**, which is a fatty substance that serves a function similar to the cover we place on electrical cords.

The cells of the brain are organized in different structures and areas of the brain, each responsible for different functions (Stiles & Jernigan, 2010). The **cortex**, the bumpy pink structure that epitomizes the brain, is where much of our conscious and effortful thoughts occur. The areas beneath the cortex, or "subcortical" areas are primarily responsible for more automatic actions and those necessary for survival, such as breathing. The cortex has been further divided by theorists and researchers to understand how different areas of the cortex contribute to different functions. For example, if you've ever hit the back of your head really hard, you might have seen "stars." That is because the rear of the cortex is the occipital lobe or visual cortex and when stimulated, those neurons fire and send a message that communicates visual stimulation and light (i.e., the "stars"). Most relevant to the development and function of EF is the **frontal cortex**, and particularly the **prefrontal cortex** located directly beneath the forehead (Diamond, 2013).

Synapses

How do neurons communicate to cause thoughts and behaviors? Interestingly, neurons do not touch to transmit the electrical impulse directly but rather, the impulse causes the axon to release tiny chemicals (i.e., **neurotransmitters**) into the **synapse**, which is the space where neurons "connect." The dendrite of the next neuron takes up those neurotransmitters to continue the message by generating an electrical impulse that travels through the cell and down the axon to cause new neurotransmitters to be released. This continues in a "telephone-like" fashion until the message is carried out, halted, or dissipates. Some neurotransmitters "excite" other neurons, triggering them to keep the communication going, while other neurotransmitters "inhibit" other neurons, triggering them to stop the communication. This complex interplay of turning neurons on and off develops over time in a way that becomes a finely tuned instrument that organizes itself. Figure 1.6 shows different aspects of this process.

The way neurotransmitters work might be likened to an Olympic relay race in track and field. As one runner approaches the next, they must pass the baton to signal to the next runner that they can continue the race. Passing the baton does not involve direct touch between the runners but involves one delivering

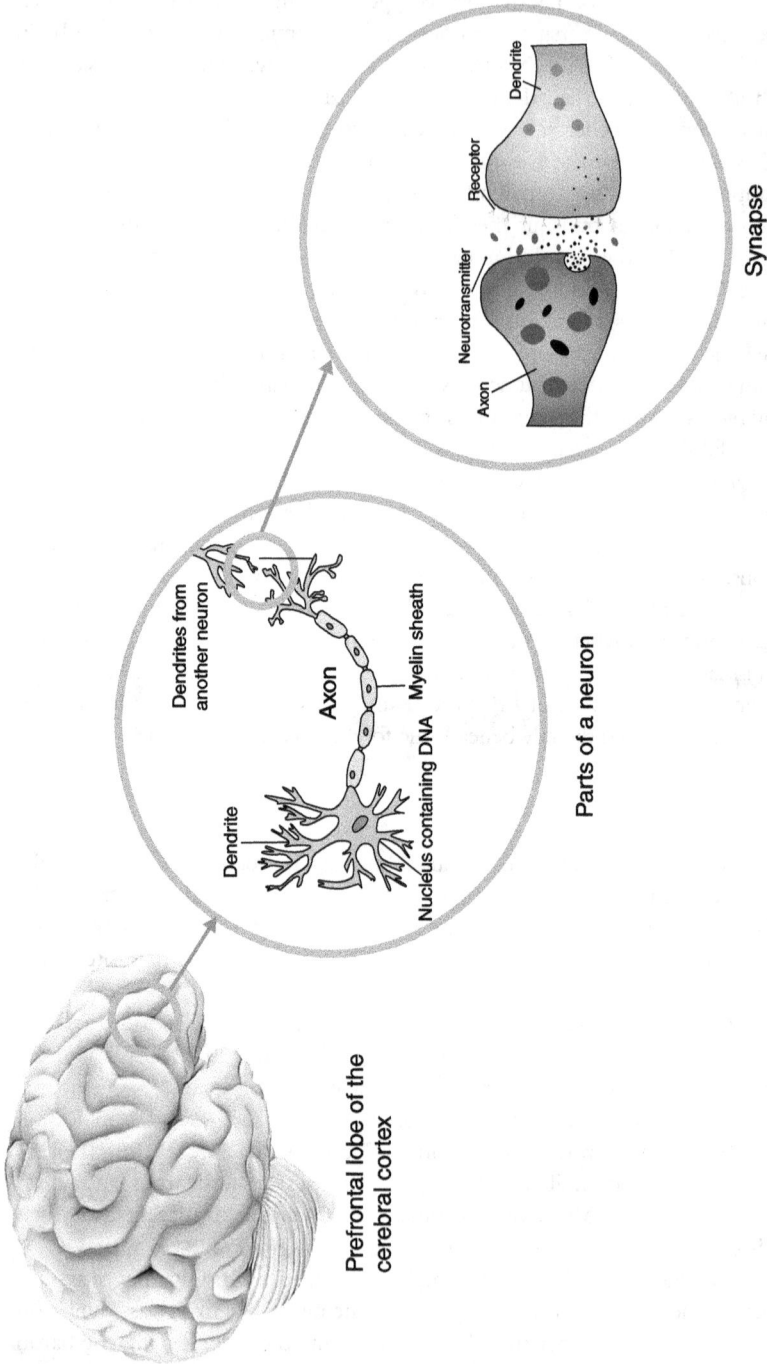

Figure 1.6 Beginning with the prefrontal cortex, then zooming in on a neuron and its parts, and finally the synapse, where neurotransmitters are released from the axon terminal and taken up by the dendritic receptors of another neuron to continue the electrical signal.

the baton and the other being prepared to receive it. This process is technical and, if not completed correctly, could lose the race for the entire team. Similarly, within a synapse, one neuron must release neurotransmitters that are effectively passed to the next neuron for the signal to continue. The neurons do not touch, but rather, within the synapse the neurotransmitters are released and must be taken up by the next neuron in order for the signal to continue on to reach its destination (the finish line). Note in our relay example that the training and strength of the runners and the way in which they work together is still vital to successfully complete the race. Similarly, the growth and development of neurons is critical to effective transmission of neuronal signals to effectively move impulses from source to destination to reach the goal.

EXPERIENCE-EXPECTANT SYNAPTOGENESIS

Synaptogenesis occurs according to varying developmental timelines depending on the area of the brain that is critical to that function. At times, in expectation of certain universal experiences that generally happen for all individuals, **experience-expectant synapses** are rapidly overproduced in a specific area of the brain. (The area in which this occurs varies depending on the experience and connections being generated.) This more frequently occurs in sensory and motor systems; for example, the visual cortex experiences rapid overproduction of synapses right before visual experience is expected to begin (Greenough et al., 1987). These synapses are genetically programmed on a basic structural level, but then they are refined through pruning based on experience in such a way that tailors connections to experience and eliminates unused connections (Greenough et al., 1987). This type of brain development is thought to contribute to **sensitive periods** of development; times during which an experience is expected to occur and without that experience, it is difficult to develop that function. For example, experience-expectant synaptogenesis occurs in the visual cortex and if visual stimulation is eliminated or prevented, connections are lost and recovery of function is difficult or limited (e.g., Hubel & Wiesel, 1962).

Because synapses are generated prior to experience occurring, they provide a "head start" and make possible rapid learning. Most experience-expectant synaptogenesis occurs earlier in life to aid with such universally human experiences such as vision or language comprehension and the prefrontal cortex is no exception. Some argue for a sensitive period in the development of the prefrontal cortex during the first six months of life and possibly multiple sensitive periods for various EFs (Thompson & Steinbeis, 2020). There is evidence for an overproduction of synapses in the frontal lobe so that synaptic density peaks around two-years, at which time toddlers have 50% more synapses than late adolescents and adults, and those synapses are not as efficient or well-developed as adults' synapses (Huttenlocher, 1979). Between two years of age and the teen years, the frontal cortex gets rid of unused neuronal connections through natural processes such as pruning to refine synaptic connections, to a great extent based on experience, and this is the time during which we see marked increases in EF.

EXPERIENCE-DEPENDENT SYNAPTOGENESIS

Not all learning is anticipated or universal among all humans. The brand-new connections you are making while you read this book (e.g., learning) are due to the brain's continued plasticity referred to as **experience-dependent synaptogenesis**, because they form in *response* to or resulting from experience (Greenough et al., 1987). It is an element of your context that your genes would not anticipate, can occur at any time in life, and can be evidenced through learning and memory. Note that the learning that generates experience-*dependent* synapses is generally slower or more effortful than experience-*expectant* synaptogenesis because of the biological process of connections being made beforehand versus during/after. (Consider how difficult it can be to learn new words or languages as adults, whereas toddlers pick up language at what seem like impossibly rapid rates.) Most scientific writing about the development of the prefrontal cortex focuses on experience-expectant synaptogenesis; however, the prefrontal lobe relies on both types of synaptogenesis, particularly in cases when the environment does not provide the expected context (Kolb & Gibb, 2011).

Development of the Prefrontal Cortex

As has been stated earlier in this chapter, the prefrontal cortex has an extended period of development from birth through young adulthood (Sowell et al., 1999; Stiles & Jernigan, 2010) and a sensitive period for early synaptogenesis and organization (Thompson & Steinbeis, 2020). As the brain grows, there is also development in different regions of the cortex, increased thickness of specific cortical areas, and stabilization of structure and function (Stiles et al., 2015). Multiple factors can contribute to growth and functionality in the frontal cortex, and four discussed here are:

1 functionality of neurotransmitters;
2 changes in gray matter;
3 increased white matter; and
4 connectivity of brain regions.

FUNCTIONALITY OF NEUROTRANSMITTERS

In order for connected neurons to communicate, the functionality of the neurotransmitter system is vital. Before infants are born, their neurotransmitter pathways are being formed (Herlenius & Lagercrantz, 2004), and researchers have identified changes in prefrontal neurotransmitter pathways even into adolescence (Markant & Thomas, 2013). Variations in genes and how they are expressed play a role in this formation (Diamond et al., 2004; Logue & Gould, 2014), and the pathways continue to be refined, connected, and myelinated to support a maturely functioning EF system in adulthood.

Further, EF is supported by changes in the availability of specific neurotransmitters within defined areas of the prefrontal cortex. For example, inhibition is heightened by the presence of neurotransmitters *norepinephrine* and *acetylcholine* as well as increased activity in receptors for the neurotransmitter, *serotonin* (Logue & Gould, 2014). Attention and cognitive flexibility also rely on norepinephrine and acetylcholine, with the addition of *dopamine* (Logue & Gould, 2014). Some of what we have learned about the importance of neurotransmitters in EF comes from studies of EF skills in individuals with Phenylketonuria (PKU). Because of a specific gene mutation, people with PKU lack the enzyme to break down the amino acid, Phenylalanine into the substance needed to make the neurotransmitter, dopamine. Because people with PKU are not able to convert the Phenylalanine to this needed substance, and despite early treatment, there is a direct impact on dopamine function in the prefrontal cortex, which limits executive function (Dyer, 1999), as shown with indicators of working memory, response inhibition and cognitive flexibility (Diamond et al., 1997).

CHANGES IN GRAY MATTER

The cell bodies, dendrites, and axon terminals of neurons make up the content of the brain called **gray matter**, and the volume of gray matter in the prefrontal lobe increases from infancy through pre-adolescence (Samango-Sprouse, 2007). Neurons are some of the only cells in the body that do not get replaced when they die, and therefore humans are born with more neurons than they will ever have again during their lifetime. Because of this, we know that the growth of gray matter is due to the development of dendrites and synapses in the frontal lobe during infancy (Huttenlocher, 1979) and continued growth in dendrites (Huttenlocher, 1990). For example, evidence for increased numbers of **synaptic spines**, or the growth and proliferation of the dendrites receiving signals in the synapse, has been found until approximately ages two to five years, after which synaptic spines in the prefrontal cortex maintain levels and begin to decline around puberty (Petanjek et al., 2011). In adolescence, this decrease in gray matter reflected in a loss of synapses is thought to indicate greater organization of neural pathways.to allow more efficient function (Fuster, 2002).

To put this in less technical terms, because humans have limited cognitive resources, over time the brain adapts to the environment by refining and reducing neural connections, which serves as a foundation for higher-level activities such as EF (Edelman, 1987). In fact, the frontal regions have been argued to be the most efficiently connected areas of the brain with each other and with other brain regions important for higher-order thinking (Fuster, 2002). Figure 1.7 shows the difference between gray matter and our next topic of discussion: white matter.

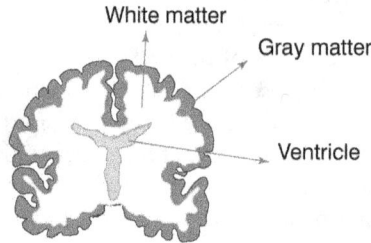

Figure 1.7 Gray matter outlines the cortex, whereas white matter fills the cortex. The ventricle is an open space filled with fluid.
Source: Shutterstock.

INCREASED WHITE MATTER

In a different pattern, white matter increases well into adulthood (Sowell et al., 2001). **White matter** refers to the content of the brain composed of myelinated axons (which appear white), and so the increase in white matter is thought to be driven by *formation* of myelin, as the prefrontal cortex is theorized to be the last area of the brain to be myelinated (Yakovlev & Lecours, 1967). Although the patterns of development of gray and white matter in the cortex differ, there is ultimately an increase in the volume of the prefrontal cortex from birth through young adulthood (Fuster, 2002), with some areas of the prefrontal cortex reaching maturity up to ten years after puberty (Gogtay et al., 2004). As with other areas of the brain, increased myelin results in increased functionality of those areas. Specifically, studies show that myelination in adolescence is associated with increases in inhibition, working memory, and attention shifting (Goddings et al., 2021).

CONNECTIVITY OF BRAIN REGIONS

Although the cortex is divided into regions both anatomically and functionally, these areas must have an effective network of connections to communicate. Ultimately, it is the network of connections related to the prefrontal cortex that underlie the most important aspects of EF development. That is, as the previously described brain structural development occurs, the way different areas of the prefrontal cortex communicate with one another also changes. Importantly, refining and insulating neural connections may be critical to developing a coherent brain structure; however, the strength of connections among brain systems may drive improvements in EF (e.g., Edin et al., 2007).

The developmental change observed in these networks seems to show a change from more localized function to more distributed organization across brain regions (see Müller & Kerns, 2015 for a review), as might be expected as these discrete regions of the prefrontal cortex become better able to communicate with one another.

Contextual Foundations of Human Development

Individual Differences

Although we can describe general developmental patterns and relations, the way these patterns function and change in any specific individual varies. In other words, the *average* human actually does not exist—the average is an indicator of the middle, with half of all people below that and half above on any particular measure of skill or function. As indicated thus far and further elaborated in the rest of this book, each skill or function can follow a different developmental timeline and its expression may differently depend on contextual influences, making someone above average on inhibition in some areas and below in others and other people strong in mathematical skills but struggling with verbal skills. Regardless of individual differences, these unique characteristics all work cooperatively to utilize the person's available resources to allow them to most effectively adapt to the environment (Osher et al., 2020).

Importantly, effective adaptation depends on the context in which it occurs, both environmentally and culturally. Optimal development has typically been defined according to Eurocentric characterizations (Joseph et al., 1990), leaving some individual differences that may be a positive adaptation to certain contexts marginalized (Witherspoon et al., 2020). As discussed previously, a strengths-based approach helps us to identify assets and better understand how individuals positively adapt to their surroundings. To illustrate this point, Box 1.1 provides an example of individuals who have perfectly adapted to their environment by capitalizing on their strengths. In fact, viewing these individuals with a deficit model would make it appear we needed to "fix" a problem that, after taking a different perspective, we realize does not really exist.

Box 1.1 Theory to practice

Setting the Stage

Some innovative studies of newborn vision have shown that newborns are legally blind! That is, when measured by adult standards, newborn infants have such poor distance vision that they cannot make out distinct shapes across the room. However, if we consider an asset-based approach to these results, we might

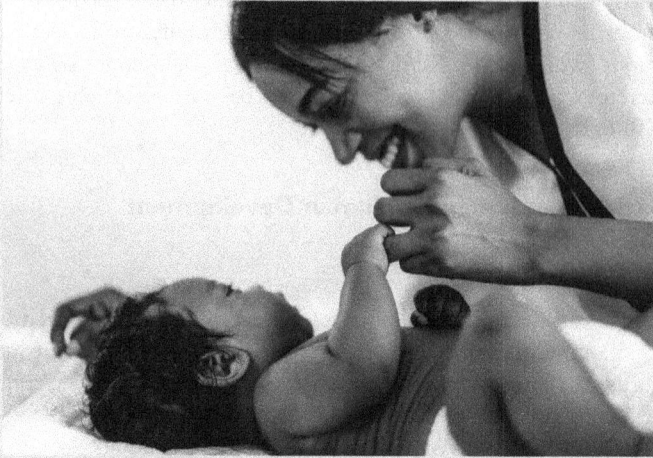

Source: Shutterstock.

shift our focus to the infants' strength—they can generally see quite clearly at a distance of about 8 to 12 inches, and this is just the distance of a caregiver for feeding or caring for the infant (Bjorklund & Causey, 2017).

Application

Think about the developing prefrontal cortex and executive function (i.e., inhibition, working memory, control) of the newborn and how overwhelmed the systems might be if they took in all information in the environment. Instead, the newborn is perfectly adapted for that situation by having a biological system that takes in the critical information and prevents overwhelming input. If compared to adults, infants would be identified as having impoverished vision; however, a focus on their visual strength allows us to capitalize on their assets (e.g., close vision), and a focus on these assets reveal their vision is ideally functional for their needs and in their context.

Reflection

1   Consider what you know about human development. Are there other adaptive skills that humans may have that are considered limitations?
2   Think also about the community in which the human is developing—are there adaptations communities make that increase adaptation and growth but may appear as limitations to others?
3   How might professionals reframe these ideas?

In sum, having individual differences allows for a wide range of human strengths to emerge, making all individuals unique in their contributions within their community. Considering a systems approach, we can be mindful that development in one area should always be viewed within the intertwined context of the whole human adapting to their environment. A perspective focusing on strengths in EF might note a child's strong inhibition and regulation of behavior and emotions in the family context while also noting the absence of this regulation in the school context. Such a focus on the strength in the family context might help practitioners identify characteristics of the family context that support strong inhibition, and those supports might be drawn upon in the school context as needed to help the child adapt. Alternatively, a focus on deficits might only document the low inhibition at school, which could have a variety of detrimental effects on the child, such as being labeled negatively by the self and others, lowering expectations, and ultimately even spilling over into the family context to create negative developmental outcomes. Because individual differences in EF are all the result of genes being expressed in adaptation to a specific environment (Waddington, 1942), with an inextricable link between individual and context over time (e.g., Bronfenbrenner & Morris, 2006), the remainder of this chapter will focus on environmental factors.

Some individual characteristics pose challenges in specific contexts, and it is important to identify assets within the individual or context that may ameliorate such challenges to promote healthy development. These individual characteristics may relate to genes, how those genes are expressed, or lasting results from an experience or set of experiences. For example, genetic variation has been associated with differences in both prefrontal activation and performance on EF tasks (Senzaki et al., 2020). Further, specific developmental diagnoses may present challenges for EF development and thus, obstacles to meeting socially expected relationship, emotion regulation, and cognitive milestones. There are several diagnoses commonly associated with a different pattern of EF development, including Autism Spectrum Disorder (ASD), Attention Deficit Hyperactivity Disorder (ADHD), Down's Syndrome, and traumatic brain injury.

Executive Function Applied: Autism Spectrum Disorder Research and Advocacy

To better understand how EF development is related to resilience and healthy development, we will use ASD as an example of how biology and context shape EF outcomes and how a focus on strengths can facilitate healthy developmental outcomes. Children and adults with ASD may exhibit a variety of characteristics, but the official diagnosis listed in the DSM-5 requires individuals to meet these two criteria: a) Persistent deficits in social communication and social interactions across multiple contexts, and b) Restricted, repetitive patterns of behavior, interests, or activities, as manifested in more than one manner (American Psychiatry Association, 2013). These characteristics can become overwhelming for the individual with autism.

Source: Shutterstock.

There has been an historical focus on deficits associated with autism, and much of the scientific research documents delays as measured using standard psychological or cognitive tasks. Autism is associated with different patterns of growth in the prefrontal cortex during childhood and early adolescence, with more neurons and weight (Courchesne et al., 2011) in addition to a disproportionately large increase in white matter in the prefrontal cortex during childhood (Herbert et al., 2004). Autism is also related to structurally different development of the cerebellum, an important brain structure involved in coordination of sensation and thinking (D'Mello & Stoodley, 2015). It is possible, taken together these neurological differences create "noise" in the prefrontal cortex and thus tax the limited resources of the prefrontal cortex (Herbert et al., 2004).

In fact, although strengths-based research has been increasing slightly over the years, over half of recent articles take a deficit approach to ASD research (Burnham Riosa et al., 2017). Findings show that this diagnosis can be associated with limited or lack of verbal skills, reduced eye-contact, and immature sensorimotor skills (Park et al., 2016). Some studies suggest that children with autism have executive *dys*function, with delays in shifting and planning as compared to same-age peers with learning difficulties or no diagnosis (Ozonoff et al., 1991). Children with autism tend to exhibit less emotion regulation, which directly predicts lower EF as measured by inhibition, working memory, and cognitive shifting (e. g., Tajik-Parvinchi et al., 2021). However, there is inconsistency in these conclusions, as other studies show preschoolers with autism exhibit equivalent inhibitory control to their typically developing peers (Zhou & Wilson, 2020).

Further, there may be problems with the methodology and conclusions of some of these studies. For instance, using Information Processing theory, some researchers have argued that the way individuals with autism take in new information and organize it may simply be *different* from that of typically developing peers, and so it may need to be accessed differently in research situations (Williams, 2018). That is, maybe there is a problem with how *we* conduct our research and measure skills and abilities in children with autism.

And yet, identifying strengths can help us provide building blocks for optimizing EF and more effectively work with children, youth, and families experiencing ASD. Because of the overwhelming use of deficit approaches and inappropriate or inconsistent measurement, child and family advocates must be critical as they apply research to practice. We also need to learn more about ASD: Burnham Riosa and colleagues (2017) reviewed over 1000 published study topics to suggest several assets that should be further researched to better understand ASD (e.g., self-determination, motivation, and character), all of which have ties to EF.

Assets and Protective Factors

In addition to a focus on strengths in adaptation, it is also important to note that challenges do not create insurmountable obstacles. **Protective factors** are characteristics of the individual (e.g., temperament, linguistic experiences) and/or context (e.g., emotional support, cultural tools or resources) that provide the human with a buffer from challenges and provide potential support or strength to achieve positive development. Protective factors facilitate **resilience** in children and youth, which means protective factors help them adapt and "bounce back" even in the face of biological and/or environmental challenges (e.g., Masten, 2018; Ungar et al., 2013). In fact, some argue that strong EF skills can actually promote resilience in children and youth with ASD (Johnson, 2012). Further, there are genetic and contextual strengths (e.g., positive parenting, inclusive schools) that promote positive developmental outcomes in individuals with ASD (Szatmari, 2018). After this focus on individual differences in EF in humans, we will turn to how these differences interact over time with the contexts of development.

Box 1.2 Chatting with a Parent of a Child with Autism Spectrum Disorder

Setting the stage

Leigh is the mother of third-grade boy Amari. As you read this interview, consider how Amari's challenges and strengths relate to specific features of EF (i.e., inhibition, working memory, and cognitive flexibility) and how those caring for Amari use their knowledge of his EF and other strengths to promote his well-being. And while taking in Amari's story, keep in mind that this is his lived experience and that it does not represent the experience of all people with autism. In the words of Dr. Stephen Shore, an autistic professor who has spent his career advocating for and teaching about autism: "If you've met one person with autism, you've met one person with autism."

Source: Shutterstock.

Interview

DR ALEXANDER: Tell us about Amari's education and background.

LEIGH: Amari was diagnosed with speech and language delay when he was 3 and then with Autism about 6 months later. Then he was diagnosed with ADHD a year after that and then anxiety/depression at age 9. He's had an IEP [Individualized Educational Plan] since beginning preschool and has been in an inclusive educational setting since preschool. Currently, he is treated with regular social skills-oriented therapy and medication. (Individualized Educational Plans are created for children who are eligible under the Individuals with Disabilities Act. To be eligible, a child must be diagnosed with a specific disability that poses significant challenges to their academic achievement. The IEP lays out the plan for services and adaptations to be made in collaboration with professionals and caregivers that allows for the least restrictive educational environment for the child.)

DR ALEXANDER: Children with autism can struggle with some things that require a lot of control or perspective-taking. Where is Amari strong in these regards?

LEIGH: He does best playing games and engaging in activities with clear and predictable outcomes.

DR ALEXANDER: Are there situations that are more challenging for Amari?

LEIGH: He struggles in novel and unfamiliar social situations and situations without clearly delineated social roles and expectations.

DR ALEXANDER: Have you seen a change as he gets older?

LEIGH: He has improved with age and maturity, but these skills lag behind his peers. As he has gotten older, he's been more aware of how his peers behave and also how he might be perceived by his peers. This has resulted in an increased desire to try new things, but also higher degrees of social stress.

DR ALEXANDER: Can you tell me more about Amari's relationship strengths and challenges?

LEIGH: Amari is more at ease with people he knows well and trusts, and will initiate conversations, engage in turn taking, and is able to have longer, more positive social interactions with his "safe" people. He seeks to spend quality time with those people and seems at ease and comfortable. He really likes learning important details about those he trusts and loves making those people feel special by celebrating birthdays, holidays and important milestones with them.

DR ALEXANDER: How have you seen Amari grow in how he handles emotion?

LEIGH: As he has grown, his emotional regulation has improved substantially. Most of the time, Amari is able to appropriately express his feelings verbally, but he does need some coaching at times when he becomes flooded with emotion. Recently, he has been more readily able to communicate his feelings before he gets flooded and has been observed to make a plan before being overwhelmed. For example, he will ask for space or downtime.

DR ALEXANDER: Does Amari like to learn?

LEIGH: He is very interested in learning about topics that pique his interest. He enjoys learning facts and details about his topics of interest, and will spend a great deal of time reading and discussing these topics. He enjoys learning about the world around him and what he can do to make the world better for others. He finds comfort in knowing facts and details about the world and the people in it—I think it helps him give order to a chaotic world. He is drawn to topics involving history, social justice, animals, people he loves, and science. He appreciates the opportunity to explore preferred topics in great depth.

DR ALEXANDER: How does Amari share his knowledge and interact with others?

LEIGH: His preferred method of communicating his knowledge and mastery of a subject is in conversation. He is able to communicate quite a bit orally in informal situations, but struggles to communicate knowledge and mastery in written form or in a more formal assessment situation. He connects well with people who reciprocate his interests and will seek them out for further discussion.

DR ALEXANDER: What professionals have you worked with that have supported Amari and your family in this journey?

LEIGH: Many! Speech and Language Pathologists, Occupational Therapists, Educational Specialists, Resource Specialists, Inclusion Specialists, School Counselors, School Psychologist, Social Skills Trainer, Developmental Pediatrician, General Pediatrician, Psychiatrist (for medication management), Paraeducator Professional, General Education Teacher, Education Related Mental Health Provider

DR ALEXANDER: Is there a story you might share of a time when Amari overwhelmed you with his amazingness?

LEIGH: He is very observant and remembers details about people he loves and trusts. He will often spend days planning a birthday surprise for a friend or family member and is an incredibly thoughtful gift giver. He sees to it that people he loves and trusts are appropriately celebrated and desires to share in the celebration with them. He also is very interested in learning about marginalized populations and enjoys reading about issues pertaining to social justice, participating in social justice initiatives, and forming friendships with those who society has marginalized.

Application and Reflection

Now that you know more about Amari and his journey with ASD, what do you think? Consider these questions:

1   Consider the EFs of inhibition, working memory, and cognitive flexibility. For each of these three, find an example in Amari's skills, abilities, and/or experiences and explain how it shows that specific aspect of EF.
2   If you were in the role of one of the professionals working with Amari, what strengths might you have identified? How might you use those strengths to support his adaptation to various contexts, including home and school?
3   What questions would you like to ask Leigh to learn more about Amari and his experiences? Reflect on each question and how it might inform you as a professional while drawing on biological, contextual, and theoretical knowledge from this chapter.

Context: Families, Communities, and Culture

Regardless of the biological contributions of the individual, the context in which developing humans find themselves remains critical to the development of EF. Executive function draws on and contributes to social, emotional, and cognitive growth across contexts, including the earliest environment of the home to later settings such as schooling, recreation, medical care, neighborhood, and the larger society. Contextual influences on EF development include the social and emotional influences from the people in our lives as well as physical environmental factors such as access to adequate nutrition, exposure to environmental toxins, or having adequate medical care. Differences in the environment across development, from the prenatal days through death, interact with personal characteristics to create individual differences in the development of EF across the lifespan (e.g., Bronfenbrenner & Morris, 2006).

Importantly, culture is an overarching setting that provides children and adolescents with values, tools, education, and family interaction styles (e.g., Bronfenbrenner & Morris, 2006; Vygotsky, 1978). Within some cultures, the people value collectivist over individualistic ideals, in which case the sense of self and others is construed differently and the tools available for thinking and feeling may differ. In collectivist, or interdependent cultures, the self is seen as intertwined with that of other members of the culture, whereas in independent or individualist cultures, the self is construed as separate from others.

In research on the impact of these cultural differences on EF, Sobeh and Spij-kers (2013) tested children in Syria (collectivist) and Germany (individualistic). Although there was an improvement with age across tasks and cultures, they found German children were generally faster and more accurate than their Syrian counterparts on a formal test battery of inhibition, working memory, and flex-ibility. Of note, the test battery was developed based from Western values and thus may be designed in a way to highlight individualistic skills. In support of this idea, the authors of this study noted that one Syrian child asked about the purpose of these tests, pointing out the lack of utility these tests brought to this group of children. Another set of researchers has been investigating cultural differences in EF with similar conclusions: How we test EF is critical and in cultures where uti-lity of actions and knowledge is highly valued, our Western laboratory tasks do not capture EF adequately (Gaskins & Alcalá, 2023). Nonetheless, this research provides an example of how the social and cultural context can shape the expres-sion and therefore measurement of executive function.

Varying cultures often use different ways of teaching in their formal educational systems. For example, families emphasize education and independent learning more in East Asian nations than in Western nations. Studies show that Western children performed consistently worse on EF tasks than their East Asian peers (e.g., Wang et al., 2015), although results are different when parent or teacher reports are examined instead of examining children's behaviors (Schirmbeck et al., 2020). Further, a culture valuing multilingualism may support increased EF (Palomino & Brudvig, 2022; Schirmbeck et al., 2020). These cultural differences need to be further examined to understand the specific factors of the environment and available tools, how it is most beneficial for individual and group adaptation to that context, and where strengths grow from these differences. Therefore, as you consider how to work with infants, children, and adolescents with varying levels of executive function, keep in mind how critical it is to know their background, cultural assets and values, and individual expectations and environment.

Source: Shutterstock.

A plethora of ever-changing contextual, cultural, and social factors can present challenges to healthy EF development, including experiences of lacking material or psychological resources, and experiences of stress and trauma (e.g., Bos et al., 2009). Traditionally, these youth and communities have been termed "at-risk," highlighting the potential for failure through obstacles; however, contemporary work uses language to reframe our approach to serving youth in these contexts, and the term "at-promise" is now used to signify that despite challenges, the strengths of these individuals maintain promise for success (e.g., Swadener, 2012). This approach does not diminish the challenges such individuals face, but places the focus on the assets that individuals may draw upon within themselves and their communities to pursue their success. Understanding strengths in children, youth, families, communities, and cultural values and practices can allow us as youth and child advocates to best support healthy EF development.

Wealth

To elaborate on this idea, poverty-related environmental challenges to EF development will be discussed, followed by factors associated with resilience. Poverty alone does not create challenges to EF, but findings consistently show monetary wealth as a protective factor. For example, childhood poverty, or low income-to-needs, has been related to less sustained attention in infancy (Brandes-Aitken et al., 2019) and overall EF function, and these effects can persist into preschool and throughout elementary school (Brandes-Aitken et al., 2019; Hackman et al., 2015). Importantly, when family income increases, these income disparities are reduced in EF development, specifically for children's planning ability (Hackman et al., 2015). These results are not limited to Western samples. In a Cambodian sample, children benefitted from wealth-related effects on EF performance, with children from wealthy families outperforming those in less wealthy families, and these EF differences increased over the preschool years (Berkes et al., 2019).

Wealth in and of itself does not provide benefits, and wealth need not be defined solely financially. Yosso (2005) argued that **cultural wealth** can provide assets on which children and youth draw to thrive in various situations. That is, families and communities, regardless of income and availability of physical resources, convey knowledge, serve as networks, and teach the use of tools while providing emotional support and instrumental support in navigating social systems. Through these contributions, families and communities can encourage empowerment, hope, perseverance, skilled communication, strong values, self-esteem, and a sense of belonging (Yosso, 2005).

To illustrate this point, we will discuss another cultural asset that Yosso (2005) labeled "linguistic capital." **Linguistic capital** refers to the benefits many People of Color may experience because of cultural values of storytelling and oral history, experience communicating in a variety of ways and with diverse audiences, and the ability to speak more than one language (Yosso, 2005). In fact, studies consistently show bilingualism is a benefit for EF across cultures, with preschoolers and school children speaking more than one language exhibiting greater EF than their monolingual peers (Palomino & Brudvig, 2022; Schirmbeck et al., 2020). Placing these results in the historical context of marginalizing second-language learning and multilingualism emphasizes the idea that societally defined success is not always consistent or accurate, and it underscores the importance of the multiple aspects of context that can promote positive development. Multilingualism provides linguistic capital, a type of cultural wealth that can be exciting and open new opportunities.

Nutrition

Recognizing that poverty itself is not an unbeatable challenge, researchers have worked to identify factors outside of income alone that impoverished families might experience. Because the prefrontal cortex has a long developmental period, through the preschool and childhood years, adequate nutrients, such as long-chain polyunsaturated fatty acids (present in breastmilk and modern infant formulas), folate (often found added to cereals and maternal supplements), and iron (added to most table salt), are necessary from conception to birth and throughout the early years of brain growth. Because EF relies so importantly on the prefrontal cortex with its protracted period of development, EF is particularly vulnerable to early nutritional deficits.

Nutrients support early gene expression and formation of critical connections in the prefrontal cortex necessary for optimal EF (Cusick & Georgieff, 2016). Children without adequate iron during infancy can have lasting alterations in the function of their neurotransmitters (Lozoff et al., 2006). Iron deficiency in infancy was associated with inattention and sluggish cognitive tempo at age 10, and young adults who experienced iron deficiency as infants evinced lower EF (East et al., 2021). Importantly, these effects do not need to be permanent, and studies show biological resilience in that nutritional supplements provided to preschoolers can cause significant improvements in EF in children who had experienced previous iron deficiency (Roberts et al., 2022).

Importantly, availability of nutrients in addition to beliefs and practices surrounding food (e.g., foods that are healthy and how to prepare and eat them) can be context and culturally driven (e.g., Monterrosa et al., 2020). In areas where nutrients are difficult to acquire, the natural properties of breastmilk can be especially important for early brain development (e.g., Daniels & Adair, 2005). Illustrating the value of cultural wealth, despite identified barriers, low-income mothers across 19 countries were generally dedicated to breastfeeding their infants, a result contrasting with studies of higher income mothers in developing countries (Balogun et al., 2015).

Household Stability and Parenting

The climate of the home can also be affected by poverty. Regardless of the warmth and affection the caregiver has for the child, living and employment situations of the caregiver(s) may prevent devoting the desired time, energy, and material resources to child-rearing that would promote EF. For instance, if caregivers work all day or hold multiple jobs to maintain housing, they may not have the capacity to also monitor consistency in the home routine, control safety in the neighborhood, provide enriching material resources, or help with academics. In cultures fostering "familial capital," working may alternatively result in positive outcomes for children spending more time with extended family and feeling a strong sense of familial and community belonging (Yosso, 2005). On the other hand, if such situations result in neglect, children can experience alterations in brain development and negative outcomes for executive function, especially if neglect occurs in early childhood (DeBellis, 2005). Importantly, even if social deprivation occurred, infants can optimize development of EF when provided with intentional interactions later in infancy (Bos et al., 2009).

Source: Photograph by author KWA.

Prenatal stress or early chronic or severe stress can result in changes in the circuitry of the prefrontal cortex (e.g., fewer connections; Kolb et al., 2012). In fact, evidence shows that household instability and disorganization are significantly predictive of lower EF (Andrews et al., 2021). Because EF relies on a limited set of cognitive resources, extended periods of fatigue can also contribute to deficits in EF, as shown with both cognitive fatigue (when someone has been intensely engaging in thought; Persson et al., 2007) or inadequate sleep (Holingue et al., 2021). Even with these potential challenges, specific strengths of the home can create resilience in EF development. Specifically, responsive parenting, as will be discussed more in-depth in Chapter 3, and enriching home environments are related to more advanced EF (Sarsour et al., 2011). Illustrating that these findings cross borders, research from a Cambodian sample shows that positive early nutrition and parenting strategies are two factors that appear to create and counteract wealth discrepancies in EF performance (Berkes et al., 2019).

Valuing the role of the parents and extended family is an asset of some communities (Yosso, 2005) and may encourage members to utilize educational opportunities. For example, parents who were motivated to engage in coaching to learn more about responsive infant parenting and how to provide nurturing care provided support for positive developmental patterns in their children's EF (Korom et al., 2021). Further, the presence of a supportive other (e.g., responsive, consistent caregiver early in life; peers, teachers), and positive connections with the neighborhood, community organizations, and/or school can buffer negative effects and bolster the resilience of the individual (Hostinar & Miller, 2019). Support can also be provided directly to children, as research shows that reinforcing children's development of strategies for emotion regulation advanced their EF (Tajik-Parvinchi et al., 2021).

Using Executive Function to Understand Human Development and Real Humans

EF has far-reaching implications for the outcomes of human development, with relations to mental health, physical health, academics, job success, and relationships. As has been illustrated, both biological and contextual factors contribute to EF development (e.g., Diamond, 2013; Waddington, 1942). Thus, understanding changes over time in the links between EF and relationships, emotions, and thought across development is critical to serving developing humans. Remaining chapters in this book will focus on cognitive, social, and emotional development as related to EF, including details on research, theory, and real-world application. It is important to note that the organization of this book creates the appearance of a division between social/relational, emotional, and cognitive development, and yet these domains of development are inseparable. For instance, emotions are only experienced by interpreting (thinking about) how one feels, and such experiences are most frequently displayed in, result from, or affect social interactions. The way we think and remember is shaped by our previous experiences (e.g., Craik & Lockhart, 1972) and the past and present emotional and social context shapes how humans feel and think about one another (Crick & Dodge, 1996). Please consider these connections as you continue to read.

Careers and Fostering Executive Function in Children and Adolescents

Thus far, this chapter has primarily focused on what EF is and how it develops similarly and differently in diverse populations. To develop to their full potential, humans need to adapt to their environment using self-regulation, planning, organization, and flexibility.

Knowledge of how executive function unfolds across the lifespan directly informs policy and practice in sensitively supporting human development. Creating and supplying tools and resources to children, youth, and families ultimately relies on this understanding of the needs and developmental processes. Appreciating the *what* (regulation, control, organization, planning, focus), *how* (transactional processes), and *why* (biology, environment) of EF is thus necessary to make informed decisions to work with and for children, youth, and families.

Specific Applications of this Knowledge to Careers Serving Children, Youth, and Families

1   Knowing the challenges to EF of growing up in a low-physical-resource setting, *program directors, policy-makers, and governmental advisors* can create, advocate for, and write grants to earn funding for governmental

Source: Shutterstock.

programs such as providing supplemental nutrition, support for parenting, and strategies for individual coping. The most effective and sustainable supports can come from within the community and in partnership with the community, involving community members, leveraging community voices, and responding to community-identified needs rather than imposing a pre-determined structure (e.g., Lo & Cho, 2021).

2   Understanding average milestones of EF development can help *teachers, school personnel, recreation leaders, and curriculum developers* to have appropriate expectations for behavior and learning in the classroom and on the playground; develop quality programs for emotional, physical, social, and cognitive well-being of infants, children, teens, and parents; and create standards of performance that emphasize strengths rather than focusing on weaknesses.

3   Appreciation of individual differences in EF, and the biological and contextual factors that contribute to those differences, provides an opportunity for *administrators, educators, and policy makers* to advocate for inclusive practices that allow for participation by individuals with varied skill levels, and for *those working directly with children, youth, and families* to uniformly implement inclusive practices.

Summary

Executive function involves a host of cognitive control skills, including inhibition, working memory, and cognitive flexibility. EF undergoes a great deal of developmental change from birth through adulthood and in fact, is a set of skills that has one of the longest developmental trajectories. Many theories can be used to understand how EF develops and influences different domains of human development. Information Processing theory takes a process-oriented approach to understanding how humans regulate the flow of information into memory and how we manipulate it at any given time. Systems theory takes a more holistic approach to human development, arguing for a self-organizing system of skills that use genetic and environmental input to create stability in development.

Because of the extended development of EF, it is critical to understand contributions made by genes and gene expression as well as brain development, including neuron growth, connectivity, and neurotransmitter availability. Notably, not all children, youth, and adults develop EF in the same way or at the same time. Differences in developmental patterns can be due to individual characteristics, contextual influences, and protective factors. Parents and professionals who understand EF development and learn to identify individual strengths can provide services and resources to children, adolescents, and families within fields such as education, government, psychology, and healthcare.

Further Resources

Diamond, A. (2013). Executive functions. *Annual Review of Psychology, 64,* 135–168. https://doi.org/10.1146/annurev-psych-113011-143750

Doebel, S. (2018, December). How your brain's executive function works and how to improve it. [Video]. TedX Talks. www.ted.com/talks/sabine_doebel_how_your_brain_s_executive_function_works_and_how_to_improve_it

Institution of Medicine and National Research Council. (2000). *From Neurons to Neighborhoods: The Science of Early Childhood Development.* Washington DC: National Academies Press. https://doi.org/10.17226/9824

Chapter 2

Thinking, Learning, and Development of Executive Function

Cognitive development involves growth in thinking, learning, and memory and is essential to, and dependent upon, EF development. Beginning at birth, infants must learn, adapt, and remember, and the complexity with which they must use these skills increases as they change and experience new and larger environments. The role of EF in these cognitive processes is critical to allow for focused attention, use of strategies in thinking, flexibility in taking on new ideas, and integration of old and new knowledge.

This chapter is devoted to how thinking develops, how it relies on and promotes EF, and how we can use knowledge of these connections to serve children and families. First, specific areas of cognitive development are introduced with a focus on how this development is embedded within EF. Theoretical perspectives will be revisited, and individual differences in people and their environments will be discussed. Finally, we will examine specific applications of this knowledge to working with infants, children, adolescents, and adults to support healthy development. Importantly, ideas presented in this chapter are foundational for EF across contexts, and subsequent chapters will also use concepts within cognition to explain emotional and relational development.

What is Cognitive Development and How is it Related to Executive Function?

Perhaps the most logical link between executive function and human development is with cognition. Cognitive development involves increased capacity to take in and manipulate information effectively; that is, to think and make sense of the surroundings. Executive function relates directly to cognitive development in that cognition relies on allocation of limited resources to attend to people and objects, access prior knowledge effectively, create links between new and old information in transformative ways, and switch tasks, topics, and perspectives (Kail & Bisanz, 1982).

DOI: 10.4324/9781003131052-2

Source: Shutterstock.

Humans Play an Active Role in their Cognitive Development

The hypothesized mechanisms driving the connection between EF and cognitive development depend on the theoretical perspective adopted. Most current understandings of cognitive development view the child as an active participant in thinking and learning (e.g., Miller, 2016). There are two primary ways humans are active in their cognitive development: 1) by exploring, adapting, and biologically attuning to the environment (Piaget, 1954), and 2) by directly controlling the information taken in and how it is interpreted (Kail & Bisanz, 1982).

Classic theories of human development suggest that the way humans adapt to their surroundings depends on the tools they bring within themselves (Piaget, 1954) as well as cultural and contextual supports and challenges (Vygotsky, 1981). Further, the choices humans make in where to allocate their attention, time, and energy shape the information that is available (e.g., Scarr & McCartney, 1983). Finally, even in the same situation, different people learn and remember and think in different ways because of their previous adaptation and their current social, emotional, and cognitive tools (e.g., Crick & Dodge, 1996). All of these factors make the human an active contributor to their own thinking.

How does this relate to changes in executive function? As you might have guessed, development of attention, working memory, and flexibility in thinking are critical to support the active role of humans in cognition through infancy, childhood, and adolescence. Rather than an environmentally-driven process, even from the initial phases of development humans actively engage with the world, for example by controlling gaze and attention and integrating prior and new knowledge to affect how new information is interpreted. Systems theories argue that the infant is born with the ability to self-organize incoming information, to be motivated to alter systems in response to changes in other systems, and to work toward homeostasis (Lerner et al., 2006). This human-driven processing would imply a dynamic being playing an active role in their cognitive development.

Taking the theoretical approach of Information Processing theory might appear to imply a passive role of humans in receiving information, much like a computer simply records information. However, it could be argued that the effortful processing that occurs through EF, namely inhibition of distractions and impulses, manipulating information in working memory, and task shifting and flexibility, requires an active human controlling the flow of information into and out of the processing system (e.g., Miller, 1956).

Cognitive Development Can Change Both Abruptly and Gradually

Another theoretical consideration is whether changes in cognition occur abruptly, with a new way of thinking about the world emerging (i.e., qualitative or **discontinuous change**), or gradually, with steadily increasing effectiveness in cognitive (i.e., quantitative or **continuous change**). Although theories of EF development support both patterns of change, many clearly state whether they posit that change occurs discontinuously, or in a step-wise manner (e.g., Piaget, 1954) or continuously with a gradual, linear pattern (e.g., Kearsley & Royce, 1977). Figure 2.1 shows how these two approaches compare.

As with many contemporary theories, both Information Processing and Systems theories acknowledge both of these patterns of change in cognition, albeit in different ways. Information Processing theories might argue that the

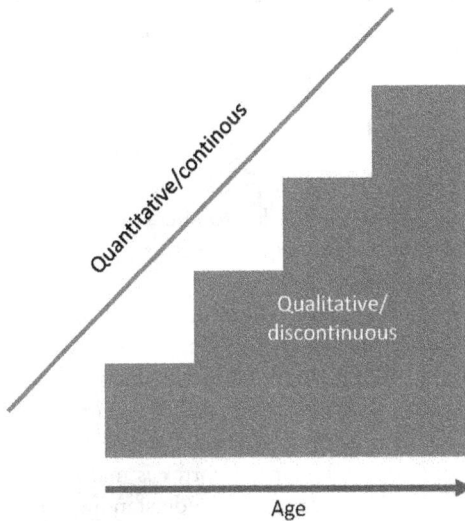

Figure 2.1 Depiction of development as qualitative versus quantitative change.

level of analysis dictates the type of change one observes; that is, observing steadily increasing, quantitative changes in attentional skills of executive function might lead to sudden, qualitative shifts in the strategies one uses to effectively recall information (Kail & Bisanz, 1982). Systems theories might instead focus on how gradual, quantitative improvements in the attentional system cause an overall reorganization of EF systems and memory systems to create qualitative shifts in thinking (Fischer & Bidell, 2006).

Biology, Executive Function, and Foundations for Development

As was just highlighted, EF development depends on the interplay between the human and their biology within a context. This section provides detailed explanations of biological terms and concepts, including genes and brain, that will be used in this chapter and throughout the remainder of this book to explain how EF development relies on and creates biological change and how parents and professionals can use this knowledge to support biological development.

Gene Expression

A critical foundation for cognitive development is the contribution of genes and how they interact with the environment to form the brain. As discussed in Chapter 1, genes provide the plans for the brain to develop; however, it is also necessary to have the materials and resources to implement these plans. In other words, genes are critical, but *gene expression* is what dictates whether, when, and how those genetic plans are actually implemented.

Brain Development

Humans generally develop in utero for about 270 days before being born (Clancy et al., 2001), and their brains grow from a single cell into a functioning system during that gestational period. Genes provide the blueprint for brain development, although brain development is characterized by **plasticity**, or adaptability. With age, plasticity decreases as the brain tissues and cortical areas become increasingly specialized based on the needs and biological resources of the human they serve (Johnson, 2011). For example, as the prefrontal cortex develops from conception through early adulthood, it becomes more specialized and efficient in supporting higher-order thinking, and the neurons become less flexible at adapting to the environment (e.g., it is more difficult to recover from damage to the prefrontal cortex after adolescence).

Recall again from Chapter 1 that the cortex is made up of neurons, and so how those neurons develop is critical to understanding how the cortex functions. Neural development includes four major processes, most of which occur prenatally, and all of which have implications for later development and EF:

proliferation, migration, differentiation and synaptogenesis, and myelination. To contextualize this chapter's discussion, these brain developmental processes are briefly described next, with a particular focus on neurons in the cortex, or what we might think of as the outer covering of the brain—that pink surface full of hills and valleys—in which higher order thinking resides.

Before embarking on the technical explanation of neural development, let's consider the example of a forest of redwood trees as a metaphor for how neural cells move, become rooted, grow, and share resources. First, consider a barren land with no trees. Perhaps one seed was dropped by a bird and a tree grew. On that tree grew many cones filled with more seeds. Rather than placing all of the seeds directly beneath the tree, nature has a way of distributing those seeds from the cones across the forest—squirrels pick up the cones and move them; birds and other animals eat the seeds and drop them elsewhere; and wind blows the seeds that have a tail-like coating to help them fly farther away. So, although the seeds are all generated at one source, they spread throughout the forest with support, some built into the seed and other support from the environment. Once the seed arrives at its final destination, it needs to sprout roots to stabilize and gather the nutrients it needs to grow and survive. Some seeds will never germinate and will just die depending on the context. Other seeds will sprout, but not be able to get enough sunlight or water and thus will die, but in doing so, they may make the soil richer. And still other seeds will flourish and grow, and all of those seeds, the cones on which they grew, and the wind and the animals that distributed them are critical to the formation of this forest. Important to the redwood forest, though, is that its roots spread out and connect with the roots of neighboring redwoods, providing strength for individual trees against forces of the environment. Neural development undergoes a process that can be likened to this forest.

Proliferation

The first step in brain development is the formation of support cells that are designed to help with a variety of functions, including creation of new neurons. The process of forming new neurons is called **proliferation** or neurogenesis

Source: Shutterstock

and it is much like the seed in the forest example above. Proliferation occurs increasingly rapidly from gestational week 7, with peak production in the cortex occurring around 15 gestational weeks (Clancy et al., 2001). When a genetic error occurs, the neurons may not be told to stop producing and so neurons continue to proliferate, the brain is enlarged, and EF deficits ensue (Nelson et al., 2006). Proliferation results in billions of neurons being formed after less than four months post-conception (Stiles et al., 2015). Specifically, the area of proliferation for neurons destined for the prefrontal cortex is larger and further from the final destination than for other brain areas (Rakic, 1995). Although new neurons can be generated in some regions of the adult brain (Eriksson et al., 1998), we do not generally produce or replace neurons after birth. That is, if you skin your knee, your body has mechanisms to heal it and new skin cells will replace the old; whereas, if damage occurs in the brain that causes neurons to die, those neurons are not regenerated (Nelson et al., 2006).

Importantly, we have more brain cells at two months before birth than we ever have again in our lives because of the process of **apoptosis**, or programmed cell death. Don't worry—it's a good thing! Even in our previous forest example, if every single seed sprouted and grew, the forest would be too dense for all trees to thrive. In fact, apoptosis is part of healthy brain development. Some of those billions of neurons and support cells have lasting uses within the brain, and yet others serve their purpose and are no longer needed. Those that are not needed would only take up space and resources to maintain, and given the limited biological resources of the human, it is most adaptive and efficient to eliminate those cells. There is an early overproduction of neurons and support cells prenatally, and so apoptosis begins before birth and continues as the brain develops and refines structure and function (Stiles et al., 2015).

Migration

Proliferation occurs deep within the developing brain so new neurons need to move to their permanent location for further development. In our forest example that began this section of the chapter, migration of the pine seeds can occur in the wind or with the help of animals. Neural **migration**, or the movement of neurons to their intended location, can occur in two primary ways: 1) formation of new neurons pushes those previously developed further away, or 2) new neurons move along a support cell to a programmed location (Johnson, 2011). The cortex is made up of six layers of cells, and in order to create organized layers that function optimally, neurons must move to their precise genetically programmed location (Stiles et al., 2015). Migration generally occurs once neurons begin proliferating and continues through 24 weeks gestation (Nelson et al., 2006), although it continues in some areas until around birth (Markant & Thomas, 2013).

Differentiation and Synaptogenesis

Once neurons reach their destination, if they are not eliminated via apoptosis, they will need to become part of the cortical region in which they lie and begin to function as part of that system, which is called **differentiation**. As our seeds establish themselves in the soil and begin to germinate, those seeds transform. Neural differentiation involves neurons growing in size, forming an axon and dendrites, and reaching out to other neurons for connectivity, and differentiation begins early but occurs primarily in the cortex during the latter third of the gestational period, with programmed synaptogenesis continuing into adolescence (Nelson et al., 2006). Chemicals guide dendrites to increase the number of spines (i.e., branches) and reach out to axons. As you might expect, more dendrites result in the increased chance of neurons being connected to one another. In the first six months of life, there is extensive growth in the length of dendrites in the prefrontal cortex (Webb et al., 2001).

Recall from Chapter 1 that a **synapse** is that space where the axon from one neuron communicates with the dendrite of another neuron. The neurons communicate with one another as the axon releases tiny chemical neurotransmitters into the space and dendrites take those chemicals up to receive a message that may be either excitatory or inhibitory (Nelson et al., 2006). If the signal is excitatory, it will create an electrical impulse that can result in the message continuing through multiple neurons until the message (neurotransmitters) dissipates. This means **synaptogenesis**, or the formation of synapses, is critical for the brain to function and send effective messages (or stop thoughts or behaviors). Synaptogenesis happens at different rates and times in different areas of the brain, which can be tied to **sensitive periods** in development related to experience-expectant or dependent patterns of synapse growth. The prefrontal cortex experiences a peak of synaptogenesis after many other areas, between approximately 15 months and 42 months of age (Huttenlocher & Dabholkar, 1997; Petanjek et al., 2011).

As the brain develops, synaptic **pruning** occurs such that some synapses are eliminated to allow for those resources to be used for more effective or useful pathways. Pruning allows for the human to adapt to the context in which they are growing, and extensive pruning occurs in the prefrontal cortex from infancy through adolescence (Hodel, 2018). This indicates that the prefrontal cortex has a much longer period of influence by the environment, indicating that **neuroplasticity** of this neural region remains high, and therefore able to be shaped by the environment and modified by experiences throughout the first decades of life.

Myelination

Another developmental process that contributes to effective brain function is **myelinization**. This process is critical for development of neuronal communication, as it insulates the **axons** of the neuron, increasing the speed, and therefore efficiency, of electrical impulses (Waxman, 1980). Like synaptogenesis, myelinization does not develop in a linear fashion around the brain regions, but instead each region, and therefore its underlying function, develops at different times and rates. Important for our focus on EF, myelinization of the prefrontal cortex has a protracted period of development, from the first few weeks of life and even into late adolescence (Hodel, 2018), following patterns of the development of its function in supporting EF. Additionally, myelin is formed, develops, and can be modified throughout life according to neural firing, availability of the material to make myelin, and functional needs. Thus, based on environmental demands, myelin may form only along a portion of the axon, increase or decrease in thickness, or be "remodeled" to best support functional needs (Williamson & Lyon, 2018).

Figure 2.2 shows how the different aspects of brain development interplay and overlap in different brain regions. Through a complex interplay of synaptogenesis and myelination, neuroplasticity and development continue well into young adulthood in the prefrontal cortex (Buyanova & Arsalidou, 2021). This gives rise to progressively adaptive improvements in control of behaviors, thoughts, and emotions by engaging increasingly effective EF.

Specific Domains of Cognitive Development

To explain cognitive development in more detail, we will overview the developmental processes for the areas of perception, representation, memory, and language. The way in which EF and brain development support changes will be explained, with relevant examples and applications to clarify ideas.

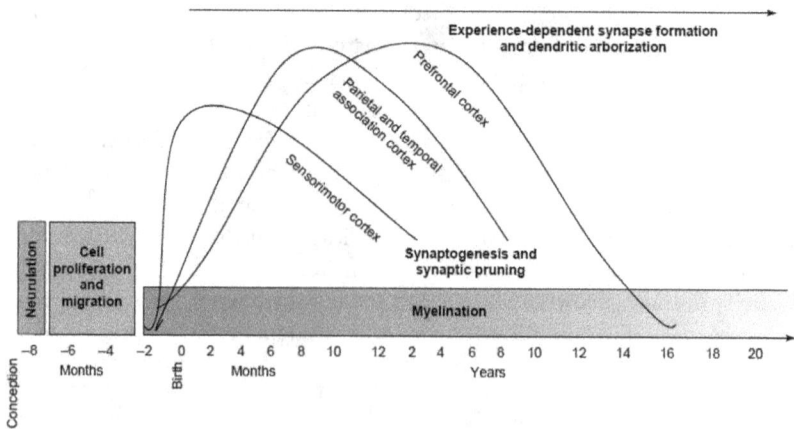

Figure 2.2 Brain development in response to experience.
Source: Casey et al. (2005), used with permission.

Perception

Perception is thought to guide all that we know. For all senses, environmental information must be detected, encoded, and interpreted through biological systems that are refined through experience. Perception involves the ability to organize incoming sensory information, thus relying on and contributing to cognitive systems. Although an objective reality exists in the environment, the way an individual perceives that sensory input is dependent both on the functioning of their sensory systems as well as their interpretation of incoming information based on prior knowledge and current state (Bornstein et al., 2011). Perception is perhaps the earliest cognitive system to develop, which continues throughout childhood and maintains relative stability until middle-to-late adulthood (e.g., Kearsley & Royce, 1977).

Infants use their perceptual skills (along with motor skills) for their earliest interactions with the world (e.g., Piaget, 1954). Their initial actions are reflexive, meaning they occur automatically and without effort. Despite a relative lack of effort, EF begins to function right away to help infants regulate attention (Johnson, 1990), inhibit focusing on distracting stimuli (Diamond, 2013), and begin to soothe themselves (Rothbart & Derryberry, 1981). For example, one of the earliest regulatory skills that infants exhibit is redirecting gaze when the view is overstimulating or disturbing, which slows or stops the flow of information from the overwhelming visual environment. Further, once the cortex is exposed to environmental patterns and refines its connections, EF is critical to organization and interpretation (Proctor & Proctor, 2021).

Most senses are relatively mature by birth (i.e., touch, taste, smell) and functioning even prior to birth, with hearing improving in specific ways throughout childhood, and vision developing extensively from birth through the first years of life (Bornstein et al., 2011). So that the visual system can become attuned specifically to the infant's environment, synapses form prenatally in an experience-expectant manner, with rapid production of connections until 6 months of age, when infants have more synapses in the visual cortex than they ever will again (Huttenlocher, 1990). Critical to the development and refining of the visual system are automatic or innate processes as well as effortful control of attention at the level of perception (Diamond, 2013).

Executive Function and Perception

Although many of the early phases of perception are automatic, EF plays a critical role in directing voluntary attention (Diamond, 2013). Thus, as infants gain motor control and are able to direct their bodies more effectively, we begin to see the role of EF in their regulatory behaviors more clearly (Rothbart & Derryberry, 1981). This active role played by humans in their perception can move from simple control mechanisms such as directing gaze to more complex and effortful actions, like moving toward or away from an object and making choices about what to reach for and touch. Even newborns begin to effortfully inhibit attention from irrelevant,

Source: Shutterstock.

overwhelming, or redundant information by choosing where to direct their gaze, and they show a preference to scan faces and areas with visual contrast (Bornstein et al., 2011), presumably refining neural connections to better represent their environment. These seemingly automatic attentional biases may be controlled by EF through the visual perceptual system's lower-level functions such as spatial scanning (Kearsley & Royce, 1977). In fact, all developing perceptual systems are refined as a result of changes in the brain, context, and the engagement of early executive functions (e.g., Squire, 2004). This provides an excellent illustration of the Systems theory, in that change in one of these areas begins a cascade of changes in the other areas as the individual actively re-organizes the information into a new, coherent whole (e.g., Bronfenbrenner & Morris, 2006).

Intersensory Integration

An added complexity is the integration of these different sensory systems to work in collaboration to support human development. Our perceptual combination of input from sight, smell, touch, balance, taste, and hearing is often experienced as a single event, such as watching someone's mouth while they speak and expecting the sound to match the movements of the mouth (have you ever watched a performance when the prerecorded sound doesn't match the performers and it is difficult to watch?!). Similarly, our senses of vision and touch are integrated when we reach out to pick up a large, smooth rock, and we expect it to feel solid and smooth. We would indeed be confused if it slid through our fingers like water. In this example, the visual stimulation would lead us to expect a specific tactile (i.e., touch) sensation based on our experience with and knowledge of rocks (e.g., most rocks are heavy and solid).

In fact, even newborns can integrate senses in crucial ways, such as matching faces to vocalizations (Lewkowicz, 2010). This integration is so seamless that we often fail to recognize the separateness of the systems sensing those pieces (Lewkowicz, 2010). Using creative methods to test infants during the first month of life, researchers have established that infants prefer looking at a pacifier that matches the shape of the one they had in their mouths earlier (Meltzoff & Borton, 1979). Experiencing the same event in multiple modalities may support executive functions and help infants take in information and more effectively focus attention on the relevant stimuli and inhibit distractions, thus allowing for more complex perceptual and cognitive processes (Bahrick et al., 2004). Furthermore, multimodal perceptual experiences promote formation of more advanced neural circuitry (Stein et al., 2014).

As children develop socially, emotionally, and cognitively, more sophisticated sensory integration thus becomes apparent. Imagine seeing two children wrestling in the grass. If that sight is accompanied by laughter, you may not be alarmed; however, if that sight was accompanied by cries for help, a different feeling altogether would arise. Combining the sensations may lead, ultimately, to a different interpretation of the event. Now imagine that you aren't able to put this multimodal experience together and you are only able to rely upon the first idea that came to mind as you decide to act. Or, imagine that you have so much information coming in from each sensory system that your head feels foggy and full. Typical development involves growth in the ability to inhibit impulsive responses and seemingly hold more in working memory. However, in some situations, these experiences may feel unavoidable and overwhelming, especially for individuals with autism spectrum disorder (ASD), attention deficit hyperactivity disorder, or sensory processing disorder.

CHALLENGES TO INTEGRATION

Sensory processing difficulties may be associated with a number of different diagnoses, most of which involve a complex interplay of biology and environment. Sensory processing disorder (SPD) or sensory issues is one of the diagnostic factors for ASD (Hodges et al., 2020) and is diagnosed when an individual struggles to process sensory information, often resulting in socially awkward behaviors. It generally results from an over- or under-abundance of stimulation because of the way in which the biological system takes in sensory information. Children with sensory processing disorder do not demonstrate the same maturation in neural processing of sensory information as those without SPD (Davies & Gavin, 2007). They can be less sensitive than their non-SPD peers to sensory input and less discriminant in filtering out redundant or unnecessary information (Davies & Gavin, 2007). Altogether, this suggests that children with SPD thus may become easily overwhelmed by the amount of information taken in, which may naturally result in behaviors that appear to be defiant, inattentive, or hyperactive, and these individuals may *appear* to struggle with EF when in fact their challenge results from the way that they are integrating sensory input.

On the other hand, children with ADHD may seem to have SPD and yet the root of the challenge for these children is not over- or under-active sensory receptors, but an underactive executive control system. ADHD is characterized by inattention and impulsivity (Barkley, 2006), and one of the prominent models of ADHD suggests that specific executive functions such as interference control and working memory are less active in individuals with ADHD (Barkley, 1997). Recall that EF relies on the prefrontal cortex, and ADHD has consistently been linked to an underactive prefrontal cortex (e.g., Tamm et al., 2004). Thus, although sensory systems in children with ADHD generally function similarly to children without ADHD, the effortful control, working memory, and task shifting that requires the prefrontal cortex is less available to individuals with ADHD, affecting a variety of perceptual, behavioral, and cognitive outcomes (Barkley, 2006). The following Case Study illustrates this.

Box 2.1 EF, Perception, and Behavior in the Home

Source: Photograph by author KWA.

Setting the Stage

Joe is a 6-year-old boy sitting at the breakfast table with the family. He is singing, humming, and then gets up and starts jumping up and down. This happens all of the time, and his mother asks him to stop, as usual. He sits down. Within seconds after sitting back down, Joe starts humming again and rocking in his chair. His mother just asked him to stop. Why is he being so defiant?

Application: Individual Differences

With knowledge of executive function, perception, and development, we can try to understand Joe as a whole human and recognize that his behaviors may stem from something other than defiance. Specifically, he may be experiencing sensory overload because of noises that many of us don't even notice, such as the buzz of fluorescent kitchen lights and scraping of forks on ceramic plates, or that rough feeling we often get used to from the tags on a new shirt and the seams at the toes of our socks. Most of us do not notice these sensory experiences, but someone with SPD may be overwhelmed and need to stimulate themselves to drown out the "noise." Alternatively, Joe may have an underactive frontal lobe, making it more difficult or even impossible for him to inhibit thoughts and actions and feel stimulated enough by the silent family mealtime to sit quietly. His attention might be darting around the room, taking in bits of everything in ways that are difficult for him to process. He may feel unable to inhibit his desire to make noise or move his body and unable to see how these behaviors might bother the others.

Application: Strengths

For one of these reasons, or both, Joe may be a very respectful child and yet, he may be misunderstood if not evaluated by those familiar with child and adolescent development. Imagine the potentially long-term consequences of this misunderstanding for his self-esteem, relationships, and academics. Taking a whole-child approach, his caregivers might attend to Joe's needs by first working to understand his intentions and feelings and engaging a professional for help with understanding if Joe is unable to articulate his feelings or needs. He may be just as frustrated as his caregiver about the way he feels, and collaborating with a child can do much to meet their needs while also bolstering their self-esteem.

Reflection

1   Reflect on Joe's age and what you know about EF. How might his caregiver support his inhibitory skills? Working memory? Flexible thinking?
2   Share strategies or advice might you give to help the caregiver to avoid feeling overwhelmed as a parent.

Representation

Cognitive development relies on representation within the cognitive system, which is creating a mental image or symbol. That is, once an object is perceived, in order for further processing to occur, it must be portrayed in the mind somehow. This is true even if the object is still present, but can be even more taxing on the cognitive system when the object is no longer present. Further, when representation requires holding a mental image when the physical object is absent, it must involve some form of memory. Memory takes on different forms and can be demonstrated as motor behaviors, clear explanations of prior experiences, and factual knowledge, to give a few examples. These next sections provide some background on the development of representation and memory, how they are critically linked to EF, and how this knowledge is important to understanding real children and families.

Representation Can Take Many Different Forms

Mental representation involves creating the representation of some perceptual display within the mind as a motor action, image, or sound. Some of these representations are *explicit*, or available to awareness or consciousness, in that you might be able to describe the representation (Callaghan & Corbit, 2015). **Explicit representations** might include spatial locations (i.e., identifying where an object is situated), problems actively being solved (e.g., the numbers and symbols being manipulated within a math problem), or what you ate for breakfast this morning. Some theorists thought infants did not have this explicit ability to represent concepts, ideas, or experiences, but more recent evidence suggests even young infants are able to analyze this perceptual information in a way that provides meaning and thus the basis for thought (e.g., Mandler, 1998).

More apparent in infant behavior, especially in the early months of life, is infants' reliance on physiological and sensory experiences to interact with the world. These earlier experiences may result primarily in **implicit representations**, as infants learn motor patterns, control over their muscles, and refine their neural connections in response to experience (Callaghan & Corbit, 2015). *Implicit* representations can be procedural in nature and are not overtly available to consciousness (Mandler, 1998). They include actions you engage in without being able to articulate how to engage in that action. Some examples might include how to tie your shoe or use a pencil, as well as how you relate to your primary caregiver (e.g., attachment, internal working models, see Chapter 3) or why a certain song makes you feel happy (e.g., emotion). In these examples, you might be able to do or react to something without being able to explain how or why. Few would disagree that the implicit representational system is functioning early, and some researchers have shown evidence for implicit representations, preceding explicit representations, such that they show evidence of the representation before they can explicitly describe their understanding (see review by Callaghan & Corbit, 2015). The remainder of this section will focus on explicit representation, as it shows the greatest developmental shift, with a return to implicit representations in the section on memory.

"TRY THIS!" If you want to have some fun, pair up with a friend and write instructions for how to write with a pencil ... which hand and fingers and muscles should they use to pick up the pencil? How can they move it to hold it correctly? The list of difficult questions goes on.... Now trade instructions and follow them precisely. How well did it work? This representation is implicit for most of us, and communicating the instructions, or making the representation explicit, may not be possible because of how it is represented in our minds.

Although infants rely on exploring the world using sensory and motor skills during the first two years, they develop a greater ability for explicit mental representation after this (Piaget, 1954). Mental representation can vary from simple, such as making available the perceptual display in the mind for further analysis and remembering something is there after it is no longer visible, to complex, such as using one mental representation to stand for another in symbolic representation, and later, holding competing representations in mind. In fact, these modes of representation may appear so different, you see qualitative or discontinuous change as children advance from implicit to explicit or symbolic to dual representational systems. Mental representation could be argued to be the foundation to many other cognitive

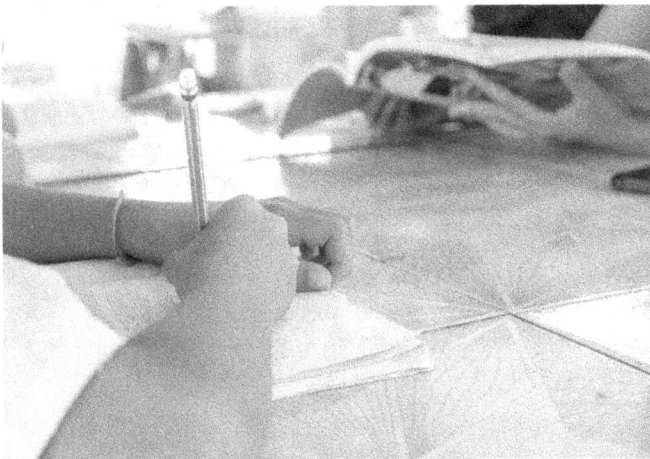

Source: Shutterstock.

and social skills, such as language, pretend play, and using cultural tools (Callaghan & Corbit, 2015). The developmental pattern of these different types of representations, their reliance on the brain, and how EF regulates representation will be examined next.

SIMPLE REPRESENTATION

Cognitive developmental theories point out the nature of young children's thinking is largely rooted in sensorimotor functioning, or based solely on their physical interaction with the world and not engaging in reflection about it (Carlson & Zelazo, 2008). Between six to twelve months, infants begin to represent objects that are not present, and although they still don't reflect on those representations, they are able to act on them. **Object permanence** is one of the first ways infants demonstrate their ability to engage in explicit mental representation, and displays this knowledge that an object exists even when out of sight. Although early researchers thought this skill arose around 9 months of age (Piaget, 1954), novel research methods have helped us to learn that even younger children (3.5 months) begin to represent objects in this way (Baillargeon & DeVos, 1991).

REPRESENTATIONAL INSIGHT

Despite such an early availability of representation, we see marked developmental improvement in how long children can hold information in mind, the complexity of the representation, and the number of representations that can co-exist. As this ability develops during the second year, mental representation allows for the use of symbols in the absence of an artifact or idea. **Symbolic representation** is thought to be uniquely human and allows us to communicate with others using shared meaning through such cultural tools as language (Callaghan & Corbit, 2015).

> For example, we hear a word and our sensory systems take it in to be perceptually processed as a series of sound waves, but that is not what our mind displays—our mind displays the concept it represents. When you read the word, APPLE, what mental representation do you have? It is likely an image or taste or sound of the crunchy red fruit growing on the tree outside. The letters used to write APPLE are symbolic, because they are arbitrary symbols that, outside of learning this shared meaning system, would not convey meaning. Communication and language will be further discussed later in this chapter.

One method commonly used to study preschoolers' representational abilities is called the scale-model task. From this work, we have learned about **representational insight,** which involves an awareness of the symbolic nature of the referent (e.g., object; DeLoache, 2004). To gain this insight about representation, children seem to first need to be able to use **dual representation**; that is, to hold in mind two representations of the same item at the same time—both the concrete representation and the symbolic representation, only then can they use the insight that the symbol stands for something. Between the ages of 2 and 6 years, children gradually become better able to spontaneously generate representational insight (DeLoache, 2004). Think about how this must involve EF skills of working memory and inhibition and how those EF skills develop right around this same age! In fact, decades of research show not only that representational skills become more complex while EFs improve, but also that improvement in representational abilities such as dual representation may *depend* on EF development (e.g., Carlson et al., 1998).

Box 2.2 Can Children Differentiate Appearance from Reality?

Setting the Stage

Brooke sees a photo of her mother. Where is her mother and how can that representation of her mother be accurately understood as an image of someone who may or may not be present? Is it confusing if mom is the one showing Brooke the photo? That is, are there two moms now?! Dual representation plays a role in how we understand the answers to these questions. Let's learn more about how researchers worked to scientifically and systematically identify when children begin to understand symbols in both their concrete and abstract forms together (the concrete photo and the abstract idea of what "mom" means).

Pictured in Figure 2.3, this experimental task involves showing the child a model room, kind of like a dollhouse room, that exactly matches a life-sized

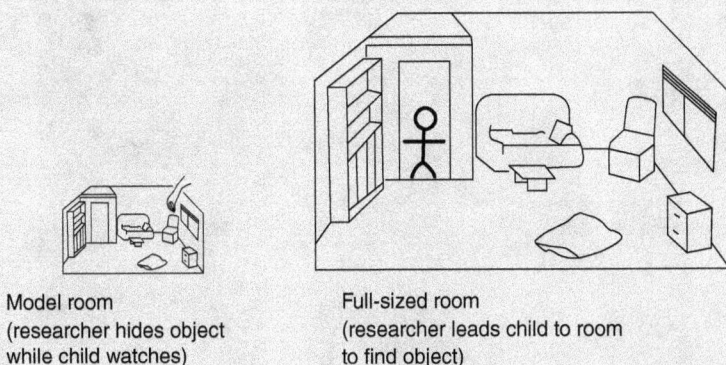

Model room
(researcher hides object
while child watches)

Full-sized room
(researcher leads child to room
to find object)

Figure 2.3 Research on children's dual representation.
Source: Adapted from DeLoache, 1991.

room in the laboratory. The experimenter hides a toy in the model room, then asks the child to go into the life-sized experimental room and find the toy in that same spot. The experimenter counts how many tries it takes before the child successfully finds the toy. To successfully complete the task, children must use the model room as a symbol for the larger room (and hold in mind the representation of the model room while searching in the life-sized room). But it is more complex than this because it involves dual representation—simultaneously holding in mind two different representations of the same artifact. In this task, dual representation involves mental representation of the model room as a concrete object while also representing that model as a symbol of the larger room (DeLoache, 2004).

Once dual representation is achieved *and* when instructions include very detailed and specific mapping of the model room to the full-sized room, 2.5- to 3-year-old children can use that model room symbol to quickly identify the corresponding location in the full-sized room. When instructions are not as detailed and guiding, children do not naturally demonstrate representational insight until around ages 5 or 6 years. Not surprisingly, being more accurate on this task is linked to specific measures of EF: working memory, inhibition, and task shifting (Walker & Murachver, 2012).

What does this all mean in the real world, when we aren't bringing children into a laboratory to find a hidden toy? One application of this work comes from **appearance-reality distinction** (Flavell et al., 1983): representing what is seen while also using inhibition and working memory to hold other thoughts and recognize the seen may not be real. In fact, younger preschoolers are more likely

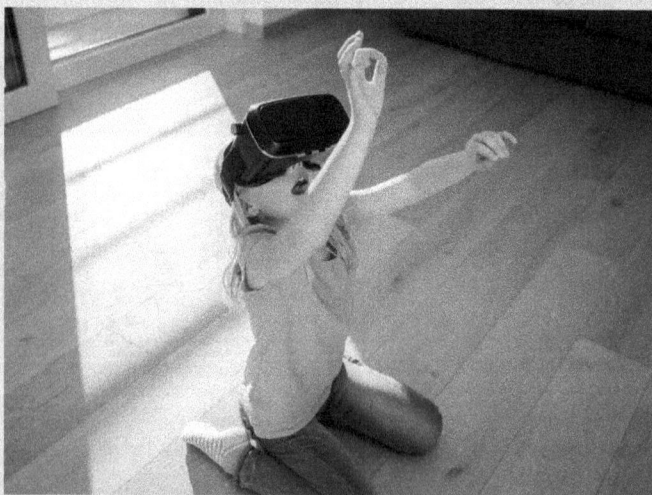

Source: Shutterstock.

to believe television is real rather than pretend (Bailey & Bailenson, 2017). Similarly, 3-year-olds are more likely than 5-year-olds to believe that a human wearing a superhero costume is a real superhero (Flavell et al., 1983). In a final interesting example, virtual reality (VR) allows for a three-dimensional immersive video experience, and so requires sophisticated dual representational skills to make the appearance-reality distinction. In fact, because the pretend world is very "real," even older children and adults may experience VR as real (Bailey & Bailenson, 2017). Understanding how children use representation in context can inform parents and professionals about the value of these tools in development, therapeutic contexts, and educational contexts.

Application and Reflection

I   How would working memory play a role in advances in dual representation in the preschool years? Use the scale model, photograph, and VR as examples to discuss.

2   Given this research, would you recommend VR for recreation? Can you think of ways to use VR as a tool in working with children?

As children become better at holding and manipulating information, inhibiting impulsive reactions, and being flexible in thinking, they more effectively use mental representations to help them understand the way the world works and the actions necessary to engage with that world. But, do these results apply only to children from Western educated communities, who have provided the samples for many of our scientific studies about these phenomena, or can we generalize these across different cultures and contexts? Evidence suggests these findings stand across cultures, although there are interesting variations based on experience, which varies by culture, education, and resources.

Cross-Cultural Understandings of Representation

As a reminder, cognitive development depends on the transaction between the environment and genes, which ultimately affects how the genetic blueprint is expressed over time. This also applies to links between culturally supported representation and EF development. Research including samples in English-speaking communities (e.g., US, UK, Canada) and non-English speaking communities (e.g., China, Japan, Korea, South Africa), find some differences in performance on specific EF tasks that seem to be tied to cultural values. For example, Chinese children outperform US children on EF skills, perhaps because of the early Chinese cultural values and internalized representations that place an emphasis on regulation and limiting impulsivity in both the home and preschool setting (Shabbagh et al., 2006). In a different study, it was found that a group of

Tswana-speaking South African children performed similarly to their US counterparts on some tasks involving cognitive flexibility but not others, suggesting the
culturally influenced representations of learning influence EF skills (Legare et al.,
2018). Despite such cultural and environmental variation, evidence suggests that
the relation remains strong between EF and representational skills across cultures,
when assessed in a culturally relevant way (Sabbagh et al., 2006).

Memory

"Memory draws on the past to inform the present, preserves elements of present experience for future reference, and allows us to revisit the past at will"
(Schacter, 2001, p. 206). Memory goes beyond perception and representation
to facilitate the cognitive processes of maintenance and retrieval, with some
forms of memory relying more heavily on EF than others. This section provides an overview of how memories are processed and develop in conjunction
with EFs, along with brain development and applications of this knowledge.

Let's discuss how information goes from the concrete and objective reality
to a mental representation that may endure forever. We generally consider this
occurring through three processes (Melton, 1963), as illustrated in Figure 2.4.
Information is initially represented through a process called **encoding**. This is
just like typing a letter on your computer keyboard. The system recognizes
there is something there through sensation and perception and takes it in to
form the initial mental representation. From this initial form, representations
that are not lost almost immediately can be maintained for several seconds and
remain somewhat temporarily. Those that are maintained for longer periods of
days, months, and years, are encoded in a more stable manner. This **storage**
process is largely independent of EFs, and memory can be stored in different
formats. Finally, pulling information out of this long-term storage constitutes
retrieval, much like you can open a saved file on your computer. The method
of retrieval is dependent upon the form in which the memory is accessed,
which will be detailed next.

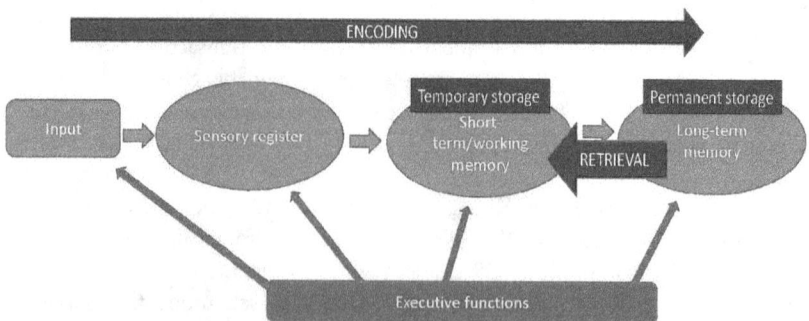

Figure 2.4 Memory and information processing.

Information that is funneled to **long-term memory (LTM)** has entered permanent storage and maintenance, and it is thought that an unlimited amount of information can be stored. In the past few decades, it has been discovered that long-term memory is not a unitary phenomenon, but that memories can be stored and retrieved in different forms. For example, when retrieving a memory, it may be intentional, like when you are taking a test and trying your best to recall a fact. At other times, memories simply come to mind, like when you feel your stomach grumble and remember that you didn't eat breakfast today. Other memories don't really feel like memories at all, because they show up more as a feeling or behavior, like the way a certain song makes you feel or you pick up a pen to write and don't have to think about how to hold the pen or make the letter shapes. Those different forms of LTM are important to understanding EF (e.g., Squire et al., 1993) and how its development plays a role in memory.

Explicit Memory

Representations that require consciously thinking about prior sensory, behavioral, or cognitive events or knowledge are termed **explicit memories**. In other words, it is information that is "on your mind." Explicit memories can be represented in two primary ways: as bits of knowledge or as specific events in your life. Facts and knowledge that are retrieved *without contextual information* are called **semantic memory**. You recall that wood is typically brown in color, but you don't need to remember where you learned that or who was there when you learned that fact in order to have a complete memory for the color of wood. Semantic memory is explicit because of the conscious awareness we have of that information when it is recalled, and semantic because it contains knowledge without context (Squire et al., 1993; Tulving, 1972).

Recalling your first day of school likely produces an identifiable mental representation of the event and its context, such as a mental picture or video; perhaps the way the room looked, smelled, or sounded, the people who were there, what you were wearing, or friends you met. It is this conscious retrieval that makes this memory explicit, and it is the "mental time travel" bound to the context of the experience that makes it **episodic** (Tulving, 1993).

To access explicit memories, experiences and knowledge must not only be encoded and stored effectively, but they must also be connected in such a way that they can be *consciously* accessed. Explicit memories provide long-term maintenance and generally rely on experience *dependent* synaptogenesis, with connections being made between neurons only in response to the unique experiences of an individual. In this way, we play an active role in encoding, storing, and retrieving our explicit memories.

Explicit memories, whether semantic or episodic, increase with development although episodic memories become more coherent and accurate over a longer period of development. But how and why is explicit memory related to EF development? Next is a discussion of the assembly of a memory as a permanent mental representation and how the biological and EF systems support this assembly throughout development. This discussion will clarify the changes we see in developmental patterns of different types of explicit memory.

SENSORY AND WORKING MEMORY

Figure 2.4 illustrates the memory assemblies described next. For something in the environment to be represented in long-term memory, information first enters sensory and perceptual systems, and each sensory system serves as the initial assembly of information (Atkinson & Schiffrin, 1968). **Sensory memory** (or sensory store) is distributed throughout the brain as it reaches the appropriate processing area in the cortex (e.g., visual information goes from the eyes, through the optic nerve, to the occipital lobe or visual cortex in the back of the brain for processing). Perceptual information that does not continue being processed after this brief sensation will be lost quite rapidly (half a second; Sperling, 1960). A small portion of sensory memory may be maintained for a longer period, albeit still temporary, by moving to the next assembly.

That next assembly contains a buffering space called **short-term memory,** where input can be temporarily maintained and stabilized for further storage. This temporary storage buffer can hold about seven bits of information (somewhere between 5 to 9; Miller, 1956). *For example, maybe you need to buy four things at the grocery store: eggs, fruit, milk, and candy. You can repeat "eggs, fruit, milk, candy … eggs, fruit, milk, candy …".* You can continue rehearsing this list to keep that temporary storage buffer active until you get to the store to purchase the items, and if you stop repeating the list you are at risk for forgetting something (or everything!) at the store.

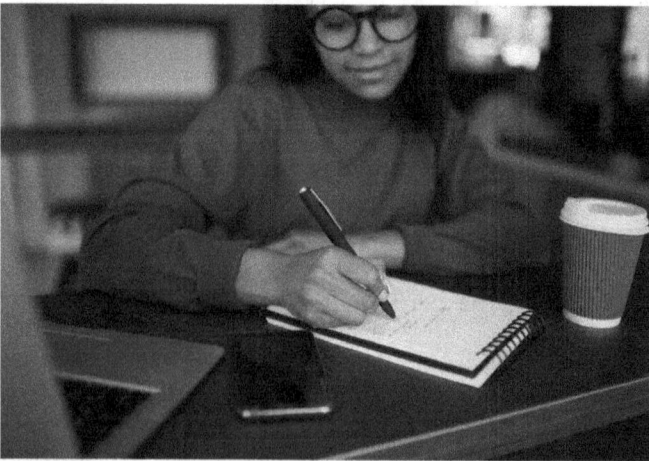

Source: Shutterstock.

And yet, this assembly of information can do more than simply hold items in memory for a short time; representations can also be manipulated or integrated with existing ideas. *Maybe you realize that the eggs and milk are in the same area of the store and so you re-organize the four items you are holding in mind: "eggs, fruit, milk, candy" becomes "eggs, milk, fruit, candy ..." so you can find like items together.* It is the same information, but you manipulated it to help you remember. We also manipulate briefly stored information when we are doing mental math problems. When asked, "What is 8+13?" we represent 8 and 13 and plus but that does not give us the answer. We must operate on those numbers to calculate the answer, which requires **working memory**, and working memory improves with age from preschool through young adulthood (e.g., Luciana & Nelson, 1998).

But wait ... we have been referring to working memory as an EF and now we are saying it is an assembly for memory; a processing buffer? Yes, this is true— working memory serves both functions! Note that working memory as an assembly system is the place where we hold the information we are currently thinking about—both from the past and the new information. Some of what you are thinking about right now may be from your past (i.e., maybe an idea reminds you of something you learned in another class) and some is new (i.e., the words you are reading), and working memory is the place where all of that can come together to be represented and transformed. Although the overarching concept is similar in terms of the functions working memory serves as an EF to the idea of working memory as an assembly system, theories of working memory as an assembly work to define in greater detail its storage and processing capabilities in addition to its role in control of information flow (e.g., Baddeley, 2002).

You may recognize that there are a few different ways we can hold information in mind—for instance, we can have mental images, symbols, and linguistic formats (language-based). In other words, we can represent information according to the sensory system it was processed through, and theories of working memory argue that these are separate processing modules (Baddeley, 2012). Because it has critical implications for how we apply our knowledge of EF to real children and families, let's spend a bit more time differentiating some of the most-studied modules within working memory (see Figure 2.5): the central executive, phonological loop, visuo-spatial sketchpad, and episodic buffer (Baddeley, 2012).

CENTRAL EXECUTIVE OF WORKING MEMORY

The central executive could be likened to those aspects of EF not specifically required to actively maintain and manipulate information, although evidence ties it most directly to inhibition and direction of attention (Baddeley et al., 2021). This aspect of this working memory model is quite similar to many of the developmental processes relevant to EF that we have discussed in other sections of this book. Because of that, it will not be elaborated on much here except for two important ideas:

1   Working memory is limited in its capacity, and so controlling attention, inhibition, and transformation of information by the central executive is critical to making space in working memory; and

2   There are multiple formats to hold and transform information in working memory, and the central executive controls input and output from all of these.

Consider, for example, you are playing four-square for the first time with your best friend, using a big red ball. You have visual input, auditory input, proprioceptive input (balance/spatial), and emotional input to represent and process as it comes in (e.g., the ball's texture, shape, size, and color; the sound of the ball, other children speaking, and general playground noise; your balance, hand-eye coordination, and location of the ball and other players; how good you feel about your game, how you feel about your best friend). Your central executive needs to manage all of this new sensory information as well as any memories retrieved from long-term memory at the time, such as interfering thoughts about your homework for your next class and what your friend said earlier today. If you try to hold all of this actively in mind, suddenly, you may no longer attend to where the ball is in space and get hit in the face or you may say something without regulating your reaction because you had no more space to think about it first. This example underscores the importance of the central executive's job in working memory.

Source: Photograph by author KWA.

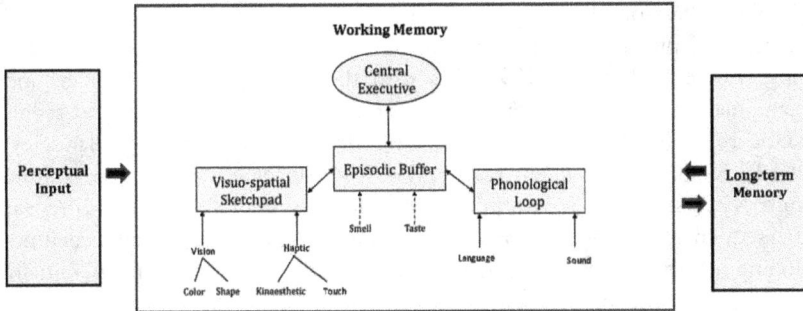

Figure 2.5 Current model of working memory systems.
Source: Adapted from Baddeley et al., 2012.

SUPPORT SYSTEMS OF WORKING MEMORY

For the central executive to operate on information, it must be stored for this temporary period of time. The **phonological loop** contains mechanisms for both storage (phonological store) and rehearsal (articulatory loop). It is where representation of signed and spoken languages occurs temporarily for current processing (e.g., sign or sound features; Baddeley, 2012). The phonological loop is linked to language development and learning new words (Baddeley et al., 2021). It holds a limited amount of linguistic information for a few seconds, and it allows you to mentally transform or rehearse that information. As a fluent reader, you are likely using the phonological loop while you are reading right now, as you decode words that you haven't memorized and articulate each word in your head, as maintaining these representations allows you to connect the letters and words to comprehend their meaning. If you were not able to maintain all of this in mind, you might get to the end of a sentence and not understand the purpose of the sentence. This can happen in people with learning disabilities, and it can happen in people without learning disabilities but with limitations to EF or the central executive aspect of working memory that maintains focus and inhibits distractions. It is thought that EF operates outside of the phonological loop support system to control and allocate resources to or away from this system (Baddeley, 2012).

The **visuospatial sketchpad** is the sister to the phonological loop, temporarily holding visual and spatial information for current processing. As is illustrated in Figure 2.5, this system includes information from the sense of touch (i.e., haptic), as this provides information about how things are organized in space and input about spatial organization (Baddeley et al., 2021). Representations in this system may be maintained visually (in a **visual cache**) or using a spatially-oriented representation, sometimes called the **inner scribe**

(Logie & Pearson, 1997). This system is active when engaging with visiual perception, but also when engaging in movement sequences such as dancing (Logie & Pearson, 1997). As with the other perceptual storage and manipulation systems in working memory, the visuospatial sketchpad seems to be regulated by EFs to control attention and task shifting (Baddeley, 2012). Similar to the fluent reader, the fluid dancer learning a new routine must rehearse several moves in sequence and maintain all of them to repeat the sequence. Distractions or lack of attention, indicative of reduced functioning of the central executive, would hinder the dancer from initially learning the sequence.

A third temporary processing space in working memory is the episodic buffer. The **episodic buffer** could be likened to the temporary storage area for the separate pieces of experiences that need to be bound together. The storage and processing systems in working memory that were described thus far do not allow for encoding of entire experiences into long-term memory; that is, putting the sights, sounds, touch, and smell together as we do when we remember an experience like our first day of school. The episodic buffer plays this role by binding various perceptual features together to prevent these fragments from remaining separate pieces in your mind (Baddeley et al., 2021). In other words, when playing four square and you see a red ball, you have the perceptual information about both color and shape in your visuospatial sketchpad. But the rules and what your best friend is saying to you might be represented in your articulatory loop. **Binding** different parts of the event together then allows you to maintain or permanently encode the visual input beyond the current moment, if the central executive directs your EFs accordingly (Baddeley et al., 2012).

BRAIN DEVELOPMENT IN WORKING MEMORY

Development of the brain plays a large role in the increased efficiency with which information is processed in working memory. In fact, prefrontal structures play a role in the initial *encoding* process (Cabeza et al., 1997; Nelson et al., 2006) as well as *maintaining* information in working memory (Bauer & Dugan, 2020). In children and adults, the same areas of the prefrontal cortex appear to be activated when holding and manipulating information; however, adults' activation is more intense and focal than in children (Casey et al., 1995). And when working memory is increasingly overloaded, younger children's brains do not increase activation like those of adults, as may be needed to process this larger amount of information (Thomason et al., 2009).

This is consistent with other evidence of changes in the structures of the prefrontal cortex during this time, such as pruning away of excess synapses and formation of myelination to speed up processing. Having more synapses or connections in younger children spreads activation out more, and pruning those connections serves to concentrate the signal, as occurs from about age one through late adolescence (Nelson et al., 2006). Similarly, the insulation that myelin provides on the axons of the neurons creates a more intense signal, and myelination of the prefrontal cortex increases through early adulthood (Klingberg, 2008). Once input is represented and maintained briefly in working memory, it can either be lost or be stored for later access.

Critical to this process of **consolidation of memories**, which is the term used for how the brain saves information to long-term memory, is a subcortical structure known as the **hippocampus**. This is a structure within the **limbic system** that is embedded within the medial temporal lobe of the cortex, which is about as far back as your ears (McGaugh, 2000). It works with the sensory association areas to take new information and helps with integrating new and old information over time (Bauer & Dugan, 2020). Once the input is stabilized, it is integrated in various areas of the cortex for long-term storage. Most of the structure of the hippocampus is formed prenatally; however, new neurons appear in this area and connectivity and pruning is not complete until about age 5 years. Changes in the hippocampus have been linked to improvements in episodic memory that occur in childhood (Nelson et al., 2006) as well as declines seen with typical aging, dementia, or some forms of brain damage (Driscoll et al., 2003).

Once memories are stored, the prefrontal cortex again takes the stage. Although there are shifts in how children, young adults, and older adults *use* the prefrontal cortex during retrieval, it is one of the major areas activated during that part of the memory process (Cabeza et al., 1997; Nelson et al., 2006). Importantly, working memory often accesses other EFs and cognitive functions, thus requiring an increasingly complex and adapted set of connections within and among brain regions (Müller & Kerns, 2015). Because the development of the prefrontal cortex, gray and white matter, synaptogenesis and connectivity, and neurochemical changes was described earlier, we will refer you back for a reminder of these changes.

PUTTING IT ALL TOGETHER: DEVELOPMENT OF EPISODIC MEMORY

The accuracy of children's episodic memory increases with age, as does their ability to provide more complete accounts of their experiences (Schaaf et al., 2008). The ability to bind numerous details together for retrieval over longer periods of time increases with age (Lloyd et al., 2009). Moreover, the ability to resist suggestion and reject false memories increases with age (e.g., Alexander et al., 2002). What causes this improvement in episodic memory?

Numerous factors contribute to age-related improvements in episodic memory, but research increasingly supports the critical role of EFs in this development. More generally speaking, multiple measures of EF are related to children's ability to provide accurate information, and EF is most strongly implicated in the face of suggestion and overt pressure (Karpinski & Scullin,

2009), arguably when presented with the greatest needs for working memory capacity (maintaining event information along with current feelings and coping strategies), inhibition of irrelevant information, and flexibility and planning.

Working memory and inhibitory skill work together to retrieve accurate representations. Recall that working memory increases in efficiency with age, and this includes the episodic buffer thought to be critical for initial binding of episodic memories (Baddeley, 2012). Further, we know cognitive resources are limited and so inhibition of irrelevant information becomes critical to allow those resources to be allocated to the experience itself. For example, in one study, the EF of effortful inhibition was associated with increased activation in the prefrontal cortex (Depue et al., 2010). In fact, inhibition is related directly to resisting suggestion and rejecting false memories across childhood (Alexander et al., 2002; Schaaf et al., 2008), so as inhibitory abilities increase across development, the associated ability to provide increasingly accurate memory reports logically follows.

Cognitive flexibility allows for less interference from pre-existing ideas about how things *should* go and may allow for a more accurate representation without biases from expectations. For example, some research shows that expectations can actually interfere with adults' accuracy in some situations (a kind of indicator of *lack of* cognitive flexibility), causing them to be less accurate than their younger counterparts (Otgaar et al., 2018). Yet when expectations are not being violated, as in when listening to an unfamiliar story, adults outperform children in memory, and this skill is specifically linked to cognitive flexibility and shifting EF (Arterberry & Albright, 2020).

Higher-order EFs, such as metamemory, also increase dramatically with age. **Metamemory** is the ability to think about and monitor your own memory function. It operates by using what you know about how your memory works to help you decide what is true and what is not, consider strategies to use to better remember something, and even actively try to avoid remembering something. Metamemory is what helps you decide to write down a grocery list rather than trying to remember it as you shop, because you recognize the limitation in your memory and engage a strategy to overcome it. Increasing metamneumonic skill with age is associated with improvements in episodic memory generally (Ghetti et al., 2008) as well as accurately denying that an event occurred even when the interviewer insists that it did (Ghetti & Alexander, 2004).

Implicit Memory

Implicit memory (i.e., nondeclarative) involves representations maintained over time that can affect behaviors but are not consciously accessible. Implicit memories are lasting and can be impactful across contexts; that is, they are not tied to discrete objects or events. Here we provide some basic information about how information is stored and retrieved in implicit forms; however, because it is generally independent of EFs, we keep this section brief.

Similar to different types of explicit memory, implicit memories come in various forms (Squire et al., 1993). They can be **procedural memories** that hold long-term skills and habits, such as riding a bike or driving home. They do not require conscious access to perform, and in fact, we struggle to declare exactly how to do things that use procedural memory because our bodies simply know how. A second form of implicit memory involves **priming**, when prior memories affect our choices or behaviors without us realizing it. You may be more likely to cry when you hear a particular song, without understanding why. In fact, maybe you listened to that song on the last night of summer camp when you tearfully said goodbye to new and old friends and you don't "remember" that song, but your implicit memory system has stored it in such a way that the song primes you to cry (kind of like an increased readiness to cry), seemingly without explanation. Alternatively, **conditioning** is another form of implicit memory, wherein our long-term memory has strengthened a connection between a sense and an action, such as the physically abused child who has developed a heightened fear reaction to hearing the front door open. This can continue to happen even when the child finds a safe home, because that connection has been made in long-term memory, so the sound of the door elicits a fear response even in the absence of explicit recollection.

ENTERING IMPLICIT MEMORY

All forms of implicit memory require information to be sensed, but the manner in which they are encoded from there to create stable representations can vary. Some researchers argue the form of the input is critical for implicit memories to be encoded in a way they can be retrieved and used to affect behavior; that is, whether processing is perceptual in nature (relatively lacking use of EFs) versus strategic and relying more on EFs (Roediger, 1990); however, most research has focused on how the memory is accessed at retrieval (Squire, 2004). Most of what we currently know about implicit memory is that it can follow various pathways to enter long-term representation, and the critical part is whether the prior experiences or knowledge are accessible in working memory. For example, a child who is attacked by a big dog likely has an explicit memory of the episode but may also show implicit memory by developing a fear response that is activated when faced with large animals, even when not thinking about the experience—the event does not need to be active in working memory to affect behavior or a fear response. Moreover, implicit memories sometimes give rise to more explicit memories with the use of EFs; that fear response to seeing a big dog as an adult might also cause me to ask myself why I have that response and with effort, I may recall that dog attack as an explicit memory as well.

Consider another example of two adult swimmers who enter the pool to do laps for exercise. The first, Ireland, learned the freestyle stroke as an adult and although she is quite athletic, she is still working on her technique after one year of regular practice. She can hear the coach's voice in her head telling her where and how to place and move her hands, rotate her body, and kick her feet. The swimmer in the lane next to her, Sydney, used to swim freestyle competitively as a child, although she hasn't done laps for years. Which swimmer is probably going to swim faster?

Because swimming is such a complex muscular task relying on implicit procedural memory, Sydney likely has an advantage. Sydney might use her working memory to think about her day and plan her upcoming trip, because she does not need to think about how to swim. Though Ireland is more fit, she is likely using much of her working memory space on sustaining attention to use explicit memory of how to swim to support her exercise. Consider how Ireland is using EF to control her swimming and why that effort, in this case, does not give her a benefit. Also think about how Ireland and Sydney might be differentially affected by fatigue, age, or pressure from themselves, coaches, or fans.

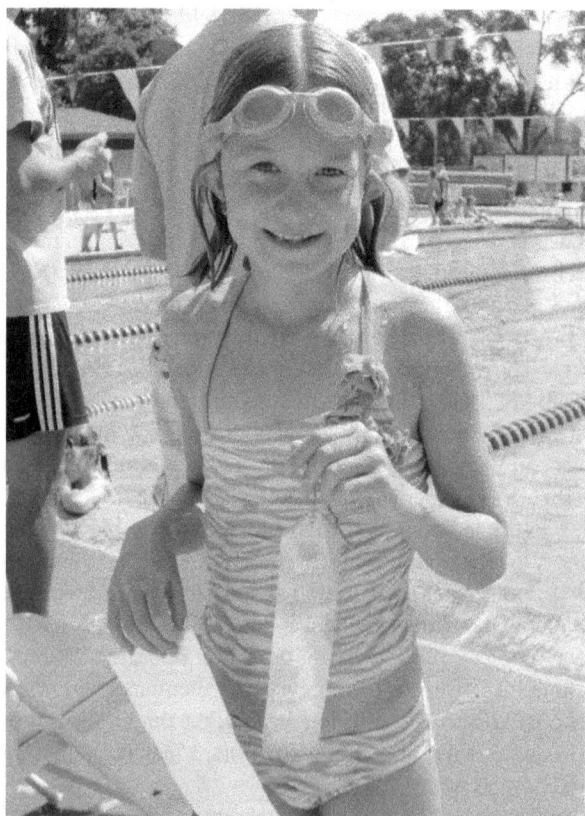

Source: Photograph by author KWA.

BRAIN DEVELOPMENT

Implicit memories are not expected to be regulated by EFs and are largely independent of the prefrontal cortex because of their automatic nature (Bauer & Dugan, 2020). In fact, implicit memories rely on a more varied set of brain processes than explicit memories, depending on the nature of the implicit response (Schacter, 1992). That is, procedural memory and conditioning rely more heavily on the subcortical structures of the basal ganglia, striatum, and cerebellum, which are responsible for motor control and are relatively well developed at birth. Priming can depend more on the sensory source of the information, and repeated signals reinforce synapses in relevant areas. Further, implicit memories that include emotional information are also generally linked to yet another area of the brain: the amygdala. As brain development occurs, although these areas involved with implicit memory are well-developed at birth, connectivity with the prefrontal cortex and with each other increase over time, resulting in more rapid or flexible responses (Schacter, 1992).

Language

Language plays a huge role in our lives as humans; it provides an organized system that allows us to engage in shared communication through use of symbols about the past, present, and future, as well as our thoughts and feelings (Bjorklund & Causey, 2017). Language also serves as a tool for thought, as we regulate, represent, and transform our own experiences (Vygotsky, 1987). As such, EFs and language mutually support one another across development, from the earliest ages through adulthood. As we continue this discussion, it is important to note the principles of language discussed here apply to all studied languages, including spoken and signed languages. Although most studies of EF and language have been conducted in hearing individuals using spoken languages, sign language research will be included when available. Sign languages are similar in acquisition phases, development, and broad relation to EF in most ways, particularly for infants who are Deaf or hard of hearing from birth and are exposed to an accessible language from birth (Petitto, 1997).

Language Learning and Executive Functions

Although multiple theories of language acquisition exist, most focus on the exceptionally rapid growth and somewhat universal milestones young children go though in language learning. Already when they are born, hearing infants have preferences for familiar voices and rhythmic sounds (e.g., DeCasper & Spence, 1986), and as they grow, they rapidly learn to mimic portions of the language they are exposed to. Through a rapid process of language acquisition, infants move quickly from cooing to babbling and producing their first word to having a vocabulary of over 14,000 words by age 6 (MacWhinney, 2015).

In fact, many of the building blocks for language acquisition are bottom-up processes that use experience-expectant synaptogenesis. Recall that this means that relevant areas of the brain over-produce connections in anticipation of a common experience (in this case, language exposure) for humans during the early years. This makes the first few years of life a **sensitive period** of human development during which infants and toddlers have resources to learn language in a way they will not have again in their life.

Language learning, like all other areas of human development is a process occurring within a social context with an active human using their EFs for cognitive control (Baldwin, 1995). Insofar as EFs are involved in perception and implicit memory, they are also related to language by supporting attention and being guided by motivation from the human, both internal (such as hunger) and external (such as seeking proximity). As future practitioners in the field of child or adolescent development, understanding such links will be critical to leveraging strengths of infants in engaging their EFs and recognizing those infants, preschoolers, and caregivers who might benefit from additional support.

Another body of research examines how EF and language develop in parallel during infancy and early to middle childhood and how they support one another during this developmental period. As the brain develops, children gain increasing control over their thinking and behaviors via developmental improvements in inhibitory control, working memory, and flexible thinking, which pave the way for higher order EFs, such as planning and reasoning (Diamond, 2013). In parallel, and as we have just described, children also gain increasing mastery over the language to which they are exposed (MacWhinney, 2015). These two major developments certainly support one another in many ways relevant for parents and professionals supporting growth.

This active bi-directional EF-language relation becomes more sophisticated during the later preschool years. EFs like working memory, and particularly the phonological loop, are linked to word learning and narrative coherence (i.e., story-telling; Adams & Gathercole, 2000). Further, greater cognitive flexibility is associated with preschoolers' improved ability to comprehend and correct understanding of ambiguous or previously misunderstood phrases (Woodard et al., 2016). In essence, as children are able to hold more in mind and control the focus of their thoughts, they can engage in more adult-like language processes. Understanding humans' developmentally appropriate differences in control and flexibility has applications across multiple contexts for serving children and families to regulate expectations and to understand the contexts that support these developing humans and their families.

Executive Functions and Interrelationship between Language and Thought

A well-known theorist in the area of language and cognition is Lev Vygotsky, who argued that the way we think is shaped by our social interactions and is deeply dependent upon language. In his **genetic law of cultural development**, which is not at all related to the genes that carry our DNA, Vygotsky uses the term *genetic* to refer to the origin (of culture). He argues that first, cognitive processes occur outside the individual in a social and interactive setting. Ultimately, this ***inter-mental*** functioning gives rise to ***intra*mental** functioning as the cultural world is internalized to allow for independent thought (Vygotsky, 1981). This idea suggests that for us to pay attention, remember, and fulfill our goals (in other words, to use our EFs), we must internalize these cognitive processes based on foundational social interactions.

An example of these ideas in action comes from Vygotsky's ideas about language and thought. Children develop language though social interaction, as more advanced humans around them use language to communicate. This is an intermental process that occurs external to the individual and between multiple people. Language is then internalized to allow for intramental processing, which is internal for the individual. After the first few years of exposure to language and language learning, **private speech** emerges around the age of three years as preschoolers use language as a tool to help them regulate behavior, control attention, inhibit distraction, and think about alternatives (Vygotsky, 1987). This use of language as a tool for the self expands the purpose of language acquisition that we discussed earlier. Throughout early childhood, private speech is used to help children regulate thoughts and behaviors by using language to give themselves instructions, and its usage starts

Source: Shutterstock.

to decline around age seven (Alderson-Day & Fernyhough, 2015). This self-talk does not disappear, but instead it becomes internalized into what Vygotsky called **inner speech**, which contributes greatly to EFs. Adults continue to use inner speech as a tool to control thoughts and behaviors (Luria, 1961), and when task demands increase, adults and children or all ages revert back to using private speech (Alderson-Day & Fernyhough, 2015). (As an example, if you have a lot on your mind, you might repeat out loud why you are going to the other room—using your private speech to support your memory and behavior.)

There are many studies that show evidence for the support language provides to EF. One EF we have discussed is inhibitory control, which requires the attention and self-control to stop yourself from an automatic behavior or thought. Evidence shows that as children's ability to express language about negative emotions grows, they tend to become better at regulating emotion (Cole et al., 2010), perhaps because of self-talk and being socialized by parents who modeled how to talk through negative feelings. Even prelinguistic infants and toddlers who may not have the language to express their private speech can use manual gestures to convey emotion messages that can be used to self-regulate (Vallotton, 2008).

A second aspect of EF is working memory, which plays a role in inner speech itself as conscious thoughts are maintained and transformed. Around age seven, short-term memory can hold verbal information to mediate thought (Gathercole, 1998). Working memory also supports other EFs through inner speech by self-cuing, and this link is supported by research on those with developmental language disorders who use inner speech less effectively (Baron & Arbel, 2022). A third aspect of EF we have re-visited often is flexible thinking, which allows children and adults to switch rules and tasks and think about alternative perspectives. Inner speech is not necessary for this EF, but it is frequently used as a tool to support flexible thinking (Cragg & Nation, 2010). Inner speech continues to be used in higher order EFs, as individuals work through problems, choose strategies, and plan multi-step methods to reach goals.

Executive Functions and Literacy Development

Creating and understanding written language has long been used across cultures to pass on information, promote academic advancement and learning, tell stories, and record historical events, playing a large role how we use language to shape culture (Kramsch, 2014). Written records of language involve an additional symbol system to be learned, heavily reliant on EFs.

READING

Initially, EFs support **emergent literacy** skills such as directing and sustaining attention, monitoring behavior, and regulating the flow of information into long-term memory for representation. As learners become more familiar with the written system (e.g., which direction words go; which way to turn pages), they become more equipped to tackle the difficult task of decoding this new symbol system. Different languages are represented in different ways depending on the types of symbols used, but all involve the learner using these written symbols to understand an object or idea. In English, words are formed using letters that each carry a "sound" and when combined, they make up the word that one can use in the spoken language. This decoding process is improved with greater EF skills, and improved decoding predicts better reading comprehension (Haft et al., 2019).

Working memory is critical for deciphering words as well as putting them together to understand meaning. When children are learning to read English, they will first "sound out" the letters in a word and work to blend those letters into a word that is familiar in their language. Holding each sound in mind, then transforming those individual sounds into a word, requires several aspects of working memory (Kibby et al., 2014). As we become more fluent in reading, each individual word is less taxing on working memory (less effortful, more automatic) and we are able to combine the words together into sentences and ideas. Improved working memory is related to better reading comprehension (Cain et al., 2004). Take a moment to think about how you are reading this text. To learn from the words, you have to keep in mind several words back to understand the context of the next word. Working memory has limited capacity, so if we come to a difficult word or we have intrusive thoughts, fewer resources are available to put the words together and comprehend what we are reading.

This leads to the importance of inhibitory control in learning how to read and using that knowledge to comprehend what is being read. Regulating

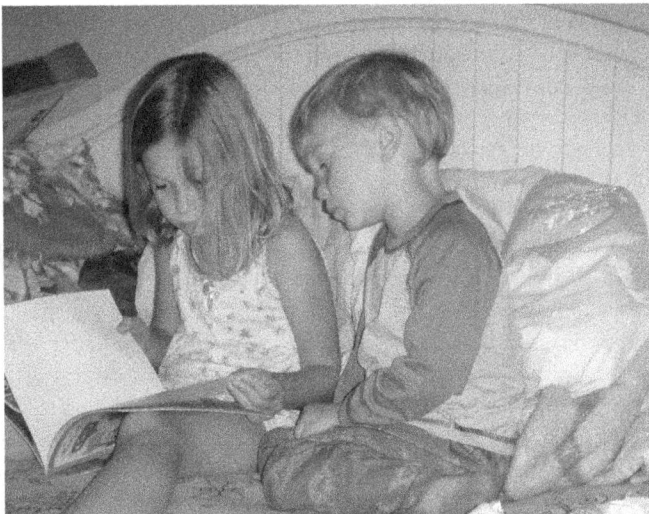

Source: Photograph by author KWA.

behaviors (e.g., not running across the room) as well as cognitive control (e.g., not letting your mind wander) are necessary for reading comprehension. Using the limited capacity of working memory to store information about the words and symbols while inhibiting distractions from the environment or intrusive thoughts is an ability we continue to improve upon in adulthood (Chiappe et al., 2000). Take a moment to think of a time you read a set of sentences, got to the end of a paragraph, and recalled nothing about what you read. This means you are a fluent reader—you automatically read the words and it did not take cognitive control to do so—but your EFs did not inhibit distracting thoughts and focus your attention on the meaning of words and so you did not encode that information for long-term storage.

Finally, flexible thinking is critical to reading for various reasons. Cognitive flexibility plays a role in making decisions about which features of words to attend to, choosing amongst multiple meanings of a single word, and making assumptions about what will come next in a sentence (Cartwright, 2008). It also allows us to switch between the processes we are using; that is, if we come to a word we do not know, we might slow down, sound it out, and even pause to look up its meaning. Another important support cognitive flexibility provides in reading is comprehension of words with multiple meanings. For example, the word "automatic" can refer to the transmission of a car or ease of processing, and the way you comprehend it would require flexible thinking and consideration of context.

WRITING

Learning to write involves the mechanics and motor skills to form characters and symbols. We will focus here, though, on the cognitive aspects of learning to write, such as organization, speed, and fluency. Writing involves many of the same EFs as reading, with the added task of sharing ideas that are purely symbolic representations in a way that others can understand. Cognitive measures of flexibility, inhibitory control, and working memory predict more fluid writing (Berninger et al., 2017).

Let's consider some explanations for this link based on what we have discussed so far. Working memory functions to hold ideas in mind, manipulate those ideas, and retrieve knowledge from long-term memory for integration of ideas (Ruffini et al., 2023). It has been linked directly to a variety of specific writing skills, such as writing fluency, spelling, and written expression (Soto et al., 2021). You may have had the writing experience where you have a point you'd like to make, but as you write, you struggle to keep track of all of the ideas and fluently communicate. You need to sustain attention and maintain old ideas to put it all together. (You may also choose to use higher-order EFs and use of strategies such as planning to organize your writing in advance by using an outline or information map, and greater EF skill is linked to stronger organization in writing (Harris et al., 2018).)

Inhibitory function controls irrelevant information from intruding. It has been linked specifically to spelling (Soto et al., 2021) as well as selecting relevant resources to support ideas, across a variety of samples including those with ADHD and writing disabilities (Ruffini et al., 2023). Additionally, cognitive flexibility has been less studied, but has also been linked in some studies to writing, both mechanically (e.g., writing words as combinations of letters or symbols) and in taking multiple perspectives and considering different ways to convey information. For example, the authors of this chapter are using cognitive flexibility as we write examples for you as readers, in hopes of finding a concrete example to make the ideas more understandable to readers from a variety of backgrounds.

Considering the process of writing within the context of human development provides a clearer picture of some writing behaviors. Young children may have learned how to write elementary sentences in their early school years, but organizing complex thoughts and considering how a reader might interpret those ideas is a task that would not be developmentally appropriate until adolescence and emerging adulthood. In fact, it is likely a complex interplay of EFs that support the learning and fluency of writing skills (Ruffini et al., 2023). Knowing how to think about the role of EF in writing can help professionals and parents better support the process of developing as a writer.

Language and Executive Function in Action: Bilingualism

One important environmental factor that has been linked with increased EF is the ability to speak and understand two or more languages, or being bilingual (or multilingual). Historically, theories have been mixed regarding whether there are cognitive benefits to bilingualism. Does being bilingual delay language acquisition and therefore its benefits for EF in development? In other words, does learning multiple languages make it more difficult for children to develop inhibitory skills, working memory, and cognitive flexibility, and consequently be impaired in planning and reasoning? The answer is a resounding no, and research shows that learning multiple languages has an advantage for the development of EFs. But, why?

Perhaps when one has two languages in mind simultaneously, there is continual practice at switching flexibly between languages and controlling attention to one language while suppressing the other in order to speak or listen. In fact, upon careful review of research examining cognitive performance of bilingual children and adults, Bialystok (2001) argued that many EF-related tasks showed similar findings across language groups, but when the task required specific types of cognitive control, those who were bilingual did better. Similar results even show that as toddlers, bilingual children have greater inhibitory control than their monolingual peers (Crivello et al., 2016), and that such benefits are evident across languages (Barac & Bialystok, 2012). The advantages in attention are specifically evident in native bilingual speakers,

Source: Shutterstock.

or those who have learned two languages from a very early age (Carlson & Meltzoff, 2008). Moreover, not only are EFs advantaged, these positive effects extend to other areas such as visual processing (Morales et al., 2013). Interestingly, positive effects of bilingualism continue to be evident in late adulthood, when typical declines in cognition that are associated with aging are buffered by bilingualism (Bialystok et al., 2012).

Linking to Theories and Concepts

We have just provided a lot of information on how EFs are integral to, and part of, cognitive development. Here, we would like to pause and relate some of these examples back to theories we have threaded throughout the book. One recurring theme is information processing and how we take information in. Perceptual development provides the entry point for information, memory allows us to maintain this information for short or long periods of time, and language is an important example of this long-term learning as well as a support for the EFs that play a role in the earlier phases of processing. As processes become more automatic (such as swimming technique as discussed in the example of implicit memory, or learning to read as discussed in the section on language), they require less effortful working memory, thus allowing for increased processing space and higher-level thinking (Case et al., 1996). Additionally, prior knowledge and faster processing are thought to support a greater space in working memory for manipulating and integrating information (Chi, 1978). In fact, some studies of preschoolers have found that they can engage in what appears to be more complex processing when the resource demands (such as the need to inhibit) are reduced (Setoh et al., 2016).

Another theoretical approach that can be used to frame the role of EFs in cognition is Systems theory, which suggests a change in one part of the system leads to a re-organization in the entire set of systems (Fischer & Bidell, 2006). One such theory shows how developmental shifts occur because of a change in one system, such as a period of rapid synaptogenesis in the prefrontal cortex setting off a cascade of changes in other systems that then comes together as a new skill (Thelen & Smith, 2006). As these top-down processes direct changes amongst themselves, each changing part initiates re-organization. For instance, as representational abilities become more complex, our interpretation of perceptual information can change (Crick & Dodge, 1996). Perception and representation alter growth in language ability, which affects memory within the context of social interaction and culture (Fivush & Nelson, 2004).

Variations in Cognition and Executive Function

Not all children develop along the same pathway. In fact, every human has a unique pathway resulting from the interplay between their biology and experiences throughout life. This next section reviews some evidence for how this variation applies specifically to EFs and cognitive development.

Individual Differences

Across development, each human has a unique set of characteristics to support cognitive development with a basis in genes, psychophysiology, and resultant behaviors. Children with ADHD have an underactive prefrontal cortex, and they struggle with aspects of cognition because of cognitive overload (Barkley, 2006). Further, children with autism spectrum disorder (ASD) show some very specific memory challenges, with working memory and task shifting predicting how detailed their memories for experiences are (Maister et al., 2013). Such individual differences can also have positive effects. In fact, some studies show children with ASD have semantic memory that matches their typically developing peers (Gaigg et al., 2014).

Box 2.3 Case Study: ADHD in the Classroom

Setting the Stage

Joe is struggling in third grade and is at risk for falling behind. One of Joe's biggest challenges is sustaining attention on an independent classroom task. When it is time for independent work, he is easily distracted and is quickly found wandering around the classroom or standing at his desk staring into space. Joe enjoys drawing and coloring, but struggles to keep his space organized. He often misplaces assignments in his desk or backpack and cannot find them because they are messy. He has a classroom mailbox, along with the other students, and yet he forgets to take things out of the mailbox to take home and when he is reminded, he often forgets to put them from the mailbox into his backpack. Planning ahead is also difficult, as Joe often asks to use the restroom right after recess, even after being reminded to use the restroom during that time. Joe's biggest academic difficulty is in reading and comprehension, as he forgets what he has read and is not able to answer questions about it. If asked to re-read the assignment, he still struggles to focus and may end up talking about something else entirely.

Application: Context

Joe is a 9-year-old boy currently living in a foster home awaiting adoption by his two current foster dads, along with his older biological brother. He has three foster siblings. He was initially diagnosed with ASD and ADHD when he was a 4-year old and has since entered a loving and stable family. Joe has been supported by an occupational therapist, which is a health care specialist trained primarily to assist individuals in need of sensory or motor support to learn or regain the ability to complete functional daily activities. He also receives specialized academic instruction in reading each day from an Educational Specialist (i.e., a teacher certified in special education) and is otherwise in an *inclusive classroom*, where students with and without learning differences are served together in a general education classroom.

Application: Executive Function

Knowing Joe's ADHD diagnosis gives us an idea that he may struggle with an underactive prefrontal cortex, and thus he may struggle with EF. His underactive prefrontal lobe may result from impoverished early experiences, trauma, or a genetic predisposition to ADHD. He is not able to inhibit distractions, both from the environment in the classroom and from his own thoughts. Because this is not a new behavior, he has likely been struggling in reading and as he moves into higher grades that rely more on his reading to learn material, Joe is likely to fall further behind without intervention. His struggle with reading may also reflect difficulties with working memory; either that the limited capacity of working memory is overloaded by interfering thoughts or that his working memory or processing speed do not allow him to maintain as much information in mind. This is particularly important during reading, as the individual needs to hold the previous few words in mind while integrating them with the incoming words and then putting them together into a complete thought that merges with prior knowledge and new ideas. Joe's struggles with EF have also contributed to his disruptive classroom behavior, which can have further consequences for his own identity, relationships, and motivation to learn. Thus, although his learning difficulties are manifest in the academic setting, the support Joe needs to succeed extends to other contexts and skills.

Application: Individual Differences

Joe's perceptual abilities are strong—he can see and hear well, although he does lack motor coordination, as is typical of some kids with ADHD. He struggles to hold multiple items in mind at once, limiting some complex representational tasks, although when he is focused, his ability seems intact. When he is paying attention to things, he remembers them quite well—for example, he can tell you about his video games and complex characters and scenes, but he struggles with listening to long instructions or carrying out tasks that require several steps if it is not written down. His language ability is strong, although because of limitations to his reading comprehension and lack of interest in reading, his vocabulary is limited.

Application: Strengths

Joe seems to easily adapt and switch tasks when asked, and he does fine with last-minute changes to the schedule, such as when there is a surprise fire alarm at school. Being able to switch tasks also relies on EF, showing that he is able to use EF and may be showing improvement as he gets older. He is also very energetic and has channeled this to become quite skilled at soccer and baseball. Joe is an enthusiastic and kind teammate and friend.

Reflection

1   Consider a context other than school. Given what you know about Joe, in what context might he excel? Why? Which individual differences, EFs, and strengths could support him in that context?
2   If you were a professional working with Joe, how could you leverage his strengths to support his learning and investment in school work?

Environment

Regardless of the tools an individual brings, their context will affect how they use those tools to adapt and grow to best succeed in their environment. Context includes many aspects of the environment outside of the individual, including the family, school, and neighborhood as well as larger culture, society, politics, and even socio-historical time (Bronfenbrenner & Morris, 2015). We will use an example of the home here to make concrete the importance of experiences on the cognition and EF of developing humans.

Household Chaos

Within the home, many contextual factors can be considered, such as parenting style, relative stability within the home, and elements of safety and trust. Some studies link poverty with reduced EF skill (Raver et al., 2013); however, as discussed elsewhere in this book, the *elements* associated with poverty are critical to identify because poverty in and of itself does not challenge EF development. Households in chaos (Andrews et al., 2021) may be characterized by both instability (high degree of change, unpredictable) and disorganization (clutter, lack of structure). In fact, Andrews and others (2021) found that chaos is related to children having lower EFs. Further, chaos was associated with having parents who were less sensitive and emotionally available, and parents higher in these characteristics had children lower in EF as well. EFs provide a structure for controlling input and thinking about the world, and if that structure and predictability is lacking in the environment, it appears more difficult for children to internalize a structure to support higher cognition.

Stress and Trauma

Some children experience chronic stress or trauma, which can have drastic effects on EFs and cognitive development, depending on the duration and timing of the experiences. Child maltreatment, experienced as physical, sexual, or emotional abuse, has been studied as one of these stressors that can change the way an individual perceives their world, structures their memories and narrative of their life story, and learns how to communicate with those around them. The effect of trauma on memory is based on the processing of one's experiences.

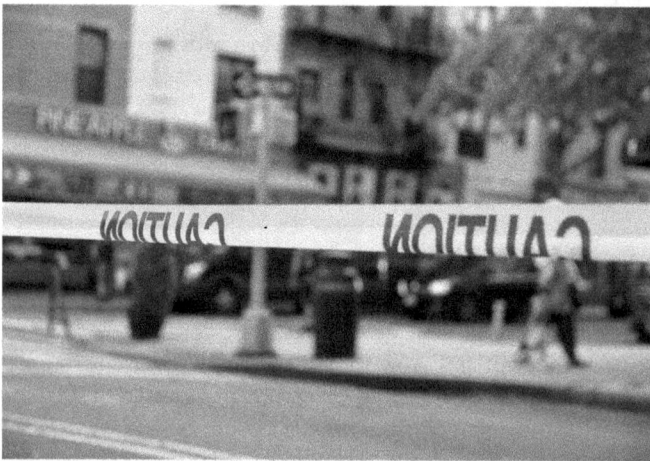

Source: Shutterstock.

As we will present in more detail in the next chapter, experiences of abuse can heighten senses and strengthen neural pathways from environmental triggers to the stress response. As such, children with this trauma experience may be more or less sensitive to specific sensory experiences than their non-abused peers because they become accustomed to some experiences. If a child is coping with trauma, they may spend more EF on regulating emotion during or after their traumatic experience and have fewer limited cognitive resources for processing additional details of the environment (Crick & Dodge, 1996). This can apply to memory, but also to larger cognitive outcomes such as academics (e.g., can a child engage their inhibitory system and advantage working memory in the classroom when they are thinking about their fear and coping?).

Careers and Executive Function

Understanding the interplay between EFs and individual differences, context, and cognitive development, such as knowing developmental strengths and age-appropriate limitations in thought and language, is useful for many careers working with infants, children, adolescents, and families. Within hospital settings, legal arenas, educational contexts, and therapeutic spaces, professionals with this knowledge can better identify strengths in their students and clients to then create ways to support their unique needs. Further, policy makers can use this knowledge to increase equity in resources in ways that are appropriate and lasting.

Children and adolescents exposed to poverty, early maltreatment, or long-term medical treatment, in addition to those experiencing learning, social, or psychological difficulties (e.g., ADHD, autism, dyslexia, sensory processing disorder, anxiety or depression) may need more support than their peers in order to use EF effectively to promote cognitive development. For example, to facilitate learning and strengthen semantic connections, professionals such as teachers can support effective use of strategies and provide environments that support active learning and engagement (Whitehurst & Lonigan, 2008). To promote accurate and strong episodic connections, professionals such as law enforcement officers, social workers, and counselors can acknowledge the memory information provided by the client and avoid introducing potentially erroneous information that may interfere with accurate retrieval (e.g., Alexander et al., 2002). All of these professional provisions require understanding of EF, its development, and how to encourage access and use at various ages and in different contexts.

Summary

Cognitive development and EF skills are entangled throughout development as they mutually support one another. Both become more complex across infancy, childhood, and adolescence. Information first enters the mind through sensation and perception, which is largely a bottom-up process. Mental representation occurs, such that the pattern of neural firing creates a symbol in working memory. Our ability to hold multiple representations in mind and choose amongst conflicting representations improves throughout the preschool and early childhood years. Some representations become stabilized for permanent storage in long-term memory, allowing us the ability to retrieve memories in the form of knowledge and personal events. Some forms of memory permit learning language, a process that begins in the earliest days of infancy, undergoes a period of rapid growth in the first few years of life, and provides a structure for thought and memory. All of these cognitive functions require focused attention, inhibitory control both cognitively and behaviorally, maintaining and manipulating increasingly complex mental representations, and being able to shift between and among different tasks and strategies. Further, EF and aspects of cognitive development are heavily reliant on the prefrontal cortex and critically dependent upon environmental factors, such as socio-cultural tools, resource availability, and traumatic stress.

Further Resources

Bjorklund, D.F. (2017). *Children's thinking: Cognitive development and individual differences* (7th ed.). Sage.

Gathercole, S., & Alloway, T.P. (2008). *Working memory and learning: A practical guide for teachers.* Sage.

Gopnik, A., Meltzoff, A.N., & Kuhl, P.K. (2001). *The scientist in the crib: What early learning tells us about the mind.* Harper Perennial.

Noble, K. (2019, January). How does income affect childhood brain development. [Video]. Ted Talks. www.ted.com/talks/sabine_doebel_how_your_brain_s_executive_function_works_and_how_to_improve_it

Chapter 3

Foundations for Emotional Development and Regulation

Newborns come into the world with an exquisite set of skills and responses that make them perfectly prepared to attune to their environment. This synchronizing of oneself with others in context helps form foundations for emotional development. In fact, minutes to days after birth, infants recognize the sound of their parents' voices, prefer their mother's voice over other voices (DeCasper & Fifer, 1980), and imitate certain facial expressions of adult humans (Meltzoff & Moore, 1983). In this chapter we will explore the foundations for emotional development with a focus on internal aspects of emotional development, including early regulation and adaptation to the environment as inextricably linked to EF throughout life. We will also examine the ways that individual differences in emotional development, culture and context, and burgeoning EF abilities impact the ways that professionals can support positive development in various contexts.

What is Emotional Development and Regulation?

Early interactive experiences lay the foundation for developing social and emotional skills, and as such impact brain development and form patterns of attunement and attachment beginning from the day an infant is born. Building on initial biological and contextual tendencies and the developing internal regulation of biological stress-response systems, early relationship bonds are particularly important. Emotions, including the biological, cognitive, and behavioral experiences that come with them, have a bidirectional relationship with EF throughout development. Brain and body patterns, control of emotional impulses (e.g., anger, aggression), attunement, and attachment security in interactions form some of the earliest foundations for further social and emotional development that persist throughout life.

Although many of these early processes are rooted in biology and occur somewhat automatically, EF both contributes to and is dependent upon some of these early processes. Thus, a primary focus of this chapter is the role of early physiological, biological, and cultural experiences surrounding self-regulation and emotion in the development of EF. We further explore how

DOI: 10.4324/9781003131052-3

professionals and communities can leverage the developmental assets resulting from earliest relationships and experiences as well as those that occur later in life to optimize EF development.

Universality in Basic Human Emotions

Regardless of which society or culture you identify or interact with, when people feel basic emotions such as happiness, sadness, fear, or anger, the accompanying facial expressions and biological responses tend to be consistent and predictable. This subset of basic emotions has thus been considered **universal**, in that they are innate (i.e., we are born with them), facial muscles in humans around the world are wired to form similar facial expressions, and humans in different cultures reliably recognize the facial expressions within the intended category (Darwin, 1872; Ekman, 1992). In fact, having these basic emotions across contexts and cultures is considered to be adaptive and promote survival (Izard, 1994). When a baby sees a happy face, there is universal communication about happiness; furthermore, when the baby smiles, important physiological feedback helps to organize the baby's emotional development.

As individuals organize those basic emotions into more complex and interactive emotional systems, and in coordination with biological development and the social world, more sophisticated secondary emotions emerge, such as guilt, pride, and shame (Damasio, 1994). Although secondary emotions may be experienced and expressed in less universal manners due to their reliance on experiences for interpretation, development of EF, and social rules about displaying emotion, the emergence of emotion tends to follow fairly predictable

Source: Shutterstock.

patterns in humans (Russell, 1980), which help us to uncover generalizable principles and mechanisms of emotional development.

Biologically Based Individual Differences in Emotion Expression and Processing

Note that although emotion expression and interpretation of basic emotions is relatively universal, there is individual variation in the internal/biological *experience* of emotion. Several theories exist to explain how and why different humans interpret and respond to emotional experiences in various ways, with some focused on individual differences in how the body and brain process emotions (e.g., Engel & Gunnar, 2019). The basis of these individual differences will be explored later in this chapter, detailing specific biological factors relevant to emotion and how experience of internal states can impact ongoing social-emotional and EF development. Some of these differences can also be due to dramatic developmental differences in perception and in fundamental differences in certain brain structures devoted to emotions, such as in Autism Spectrum Disorder (ASD). We are all born with different tendencies to process and react to different types of emotions, but these differences utilize the same universal emotional brain regions.

Adaptation to a Context by a Biological Being

Although universal and internal influences on emotion are critical, external influences also envelop the developing human. This includes social experiences as members of communities as well as elements of time that shape further development (Bronfenbrenner & Morris, 2006). Notably, it is not one or the other, but the intertwining of the internal and external factors throughout development that creates emotional expression, understanding, and regulation and helps individuals relate to others and adapt to their surroundings. For example, some cultures consider it an asset to freely express emotion whereas others find this free expression distasteful, resulting in cultural variation in expression of emotion in private and public (Ekman et al., 1969). Individual differences in predisposed biological patterns interact with such contextual diversity to promote different patterns of emotional development that are tailored to adapt to the context in which the human lives.

As presented in previous chapters, Systems theories of development view the human as a self-organizing organism, with biological predispositions transacting with, and adapting to, environmental and cultural pressures. One such theory provides insight into potential mechanisms underlying the critical and bidirectional contributions of biology and environment. Scarr and McCartney (1983) proposed three primary mechanisms through which genes affect context to shape a human:

1   **passive effects** come from biological parents making choices for their biological children, thus indirectly influencing gene expression (e.g., parents guide children according to their own gene path, such as parents who played college-level soccer and enroll their children in soccer because of their own soccer interest);

2   **evocative effects** occur when personal characteristics of the individual evoke a specific reaction from the environment (e.g., a smiling, quiet preschooler who receives consistent positive feedback from adults); and

3   **active effects** arise when humans seek out people and places they find comfortable and satisfying (e.g., the musically-talented teen joins the high school band).

Active effects occur through **niche-picking**; that is, based on predispositions, humans choose environments compatible with their needs. Although many researchers focus on niche-picking in older children, even infants make choices about the most compatible environments, by turning their head, closing their eyes, and, once mobile, gravitating toward or away from certain people or things. Such an expression of control is an example of how EF might begin to interact with emotional development in the early years.

Throughout this book, we may separately discuss and examine contributions of genes, physiology, brain, and context, Systems theory highlights that we cannot truly separate the contributions of each. Biological predispositions toward sights and sounds, internal feelings of discomfort or connection, and tendency toward impulsivity or control interact with the tools and resources in the environment to shape emotional development over time. Another critical point of Systems theory is that nothing is unchangeable—the system is open and acute changes in environment or biology can have drastic effects on further developmental outcomes (Snell-Rood, 2013). Such changes can come in the form of support from families, communities, and professionals interested in promoting well-being.

Emotional Processing is Intertwined with Cognitive Development

In the previous chapter, we discussed cognition and thinking as largely related to what is referred to as "cold" cognition – meaning without emotional content. **Hot cognition** involves processing information that is emotional, relevant to survival, or social in nature, whereas **cool cognition** processes sensory information that is not related to emotion and might be considered more independent of the context (Abelson, 1963). Consider the difference between memorizing a list of words related to geology—such as metamorphic and igneous. For most of us, these concepts do not engage an emotional or a stress response—so thinking about these terms is primarily considered cool. However, consider memorizing your wedding vows or practicing testimony for a criminal trial. For most of us, these memory processes would have a strong emotional undercurrent, or hot cognition.

Source: Shutterstock.

Although much developmental research on EF has focused on cool cognitive processes, more recently developmentalists have urged us to differentiate between these two types of thinking and to consider the *ecological validity* of our understanding (e.g., Ristic & Enns, 2015). (Ecological validity refers to whether the knowledge we learn from science applies to the real world instead of only applying to contrived situations in a laboratory.) The applicability of this new knowledge is still being explored by developmental scientists, and how to use this knowledge to help children with learning difficulties such as ADHD is yet unclear.

Importantly, all cognitive processes can be hot or cool, including EF, attention, perception, representation, and memory. **Cool EFs** are used in emotionally neutral contexts in which an individual needs to inhibit, attend, and control their thinking. **Hot EFs** become necessary when intentional inhibition, attention, or control are necessary under emotionally-charged or motivationally important conditions. In fact, because EF development occurs well into adolescence, and because adolescence can be a time of heightened emotion given biological and hormonal changes, this may be a renewed period of plasticity or adaptability of EF during which support and intervention have great potential (Zelazo & Carlson, 2012).

Examination of the neurological processes underlying hot versus cool cognition helps us to better understand the mechanisms and development of EF in greater detail and their relation to motivational systems. For example, Chapter 2 detailed the mechanisms of inhibitory control, working memory, and cognitive flexibility in situations that are without emotional or stressful content. Later in this chapter, we will examine the additional resources required for EF when one's survival or sense of well-being is involved. These same components of EF, particularly within the prefrontal cortex, are taxed to a much greater extent when emotional reactions, specifically involving the **limbic system** (critical for the processing of emotion) are also activated in a "bottom-up" fashion and pull energy away from the limited resources available for EF.

> *Charlie is studying for a math test. He organizes his space and has all his materials out and ready for the study session. He is a neurotypical 15-year-old, and generally does not have difficulty focusing his attention, and he actually enjoys math. Ten minutes into his study session he begins to worry about his mother. She is usually home from work by this time and he has not heard from her. He decides to send her a text, but it comes back as "undeliverable." He tries to return to his studies but now he is having great difficulty focusing and he keeps having to re-read the problems many times. He feels his hands getting sweaty and he cannot stop looking at the clock. His mother finally arrives home, but it takes him an hour to get back to being able to focus on his studies.*

Think about how Charlie's worry and stress impacted his EF, specifically his inhibitory control and working memory, and how he might have more effortfully engaged his EF. Similar impacts might occur in situations of poverty, maltreatment, or even when feeling positive emotions like getting ready for a vacation.

Cool EFs tend to develop earlier than hot EFs, perhaps because of the additional mental resources needed. Some evidence suggests cool EFs improve in early to middle childhood because of more efficient neural pathways in the prefrontal cortex, whereas hot EFs may depend more on the integration of these areas with the limbic system (Fernandez Garcia et al., 2021). In contrast, for some simple measures specifically of effortful attention, Ristic and Enns (2015) argued that cool attention increases with age, whereas hot attention seems to be mature in infancy. This means that things like attention to faces, emotion cues, and the context from which the information comes seem to engage attention early and at adult-like levels, thus potentially not contributing as strongly to the effortful processing required for EF in cool cognitive situations.

The Physiology of Emotion

Understanding the underlying physiological processes associated with emotions and emotional development gives us greater insight into the way emotions and EF are interconnected. We have all experienced emotions. We know what it's like when we feel happy, or sad, or scared. We often view these emotions as a reaction to external events or things that are happening outside of our body, but internal biological processes contribute substantially to our individual experience of these external events. If you drop your phone and the screen shatters, what might you feel? Maybe you feel despair and sadness or maybe you will feel enraged. Your face may flush or your body may feel hot or sweaty or numb. Emotions are not simply the labeled feelings, or **subjective experience** that we have, but a complex interplay between aspects of each individual (i.e., their current physical state, individual differences in their biological function, their cultural experiences) and the external event, context, and meaning. Important to note for our discussion of EF is that much of the initial physiological response that happens and is described here is almost instant—we do not have conscious control over the reaction of our body to the stress.

Appraisal

The cycle of emotional response, although different for each individual, follows a universal pathway within the brain, leading to what we think of as an emotional or stress response to a stimulus. The cycle begins first with the individual's unconscious and bottom-up appraisal of the event based on some initial internal processing (Scherer & Moors, 2019). For example, a fireworks show might be appraised as positive by one person because they have generally low arousal (less fearful), have a history of positive experiences with fireworks, and they are in a relaxed of happy state of mind. However, another person may automatically appraise the fireworks as negative because of a prior bad experience with fireworks, a negative mood, or simply having a proclivity for reacting strongly to stress.

Reactivity

Once the individual has appraised the event, the emotional reactivity response begins. Although still largely outside of EF and conscious control, pathways from our senses and from our prefrontal cortex, usually driven by our thoughts and memories, trigger a response within a subcortical structure known as the **amygdala.** This tiny almond-shaped structure is critical for our survival responses, such as a fear response to threat (Lupien et al., 2009). This initial response is often referred to as "fight or flight or freeze" (Sapolsky, 2015). When the amygdala is triggered by the senses and thoughts, it sends signals to several other regions of the brain and the body. One of the critical chains of reactions in this process is the triggering of what is referred to as the **hypothalamic-pituitary-adrenal axis** (HPA axis).

Once the amygdala has sent the signals for initial reaction, the first step in the HPA-axis stress response is the triggering of the **hypothalamus,** a small cluster of cells in the center of the brain that are largely responsible for maintenance of hormonal and bodily responses to the environment. It can initiate changes in heart rate, breathing patterns, and even muscle-tension and thirst. In the case of the HPA-axis, the hypothalamus produces corticotropin-releasing hormone (CTRH) that binds to the pituitary gland, or the "master gland," which responds with the release of adrenocorticotropic hormone (ACTH). This causes the adrenal glands to release a stress-hormone known as **cortisol.** Most people are familiar with the idea of cortisol, or even adrenaline, and when released it causes a cascade of effects throughout the body.

STRESS RESPONSE SYSTEM

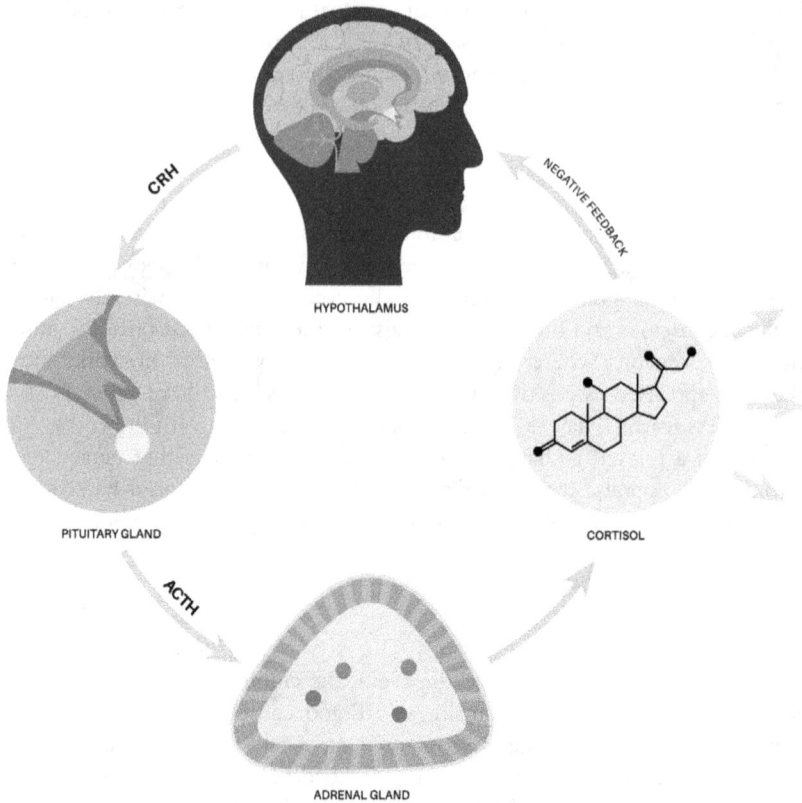

Source: Shutterstock.

The first thing that cortisol does is stimulate the release of glucose within the body. This is why during stress people often feel a rush of energy. This important process prepares the individual to run from the threatening stimulus ("flight"), or to fight it, or at times when these are not possible, to "freeze" (Bracha, 2004). This physiological response activates the **sympathetic nervous system** (SNS), which helps us to maintain a heightened state of arousal and therefore our preparedness to react to changes or threats within the environment, or even opportunities for food or mating. As soon as the sympathetic nervous system is initiated, triggering the cascade of effects of cortisol, the **parasympathetic nervous system** (PNS) is activated to balance the SNS and return the body to equilibrium or **homeostasis.** Once the PNS is activated, it begins the reverse of the HPA-axis, and instead triggers the vagus nerve, which connects to internal organs to begin to lower the heart-rate, and begin the process of returning the body to a resting state in what is termed a **negative feedback loop**.

Chronic Stress

The automatic stress response that was just described is adaptive and has been since the dawn of time—being able to quickly and without conscious control assess and prepare to respond to an environmental threat like a poisonous snake or grizzly bear would help us survive. However, most of us do not need to activate this threat response on a regular basis—instead, we worry and stress over traffic, our "to do" lists, and bills we need to pay. This kind of long-term, uncontrollable stress can lead to dysfunction within our exquisitely designed sympathetic-parasympathetic nervous system balance. For example, if a person is anxious about lack of housing and worried about paying their bills, flight-fight-freeze responses will not help. And yet, another bill arriving or feeling hunger pains and thinking about where the next meal will come from reminds them over and over that, soon, they may not have a place to live. In these cases, the continual release of cortisol within the brain causes structural and functional changes in emotion reactivity and its related systems that can be short-term (e.g., sleep problems) and long-term (e.g., SNS sensitivity), especially when the chronic stress occurs during the early formative years and prior to or during puberty (e.g., structural remodeling of the brain targeted in amygdala, hippocampus, and prefrontal cortex (McEwen, 2007)).

Imagine a child who is continually worried about stresses at home because of parental absence, job-loss, or abuse or neglect. Children may worry about their caregivers' state of mind, the stability of their home situation, and how to stay safe from harm while also receiving the attention and love they need. This chronic and early stress poses a serious risk to healthy development of their EF (in addition to many other deleterious outcomes not covered here (Andrews et al., 2021)).

In cases of chronic stress, the physiological response of releasing cortisol in a continual cycle leads to **long-term depression** (Goosens & Sapolsky, 2007). This is not depression in the sense we tend to think about psychologically, but depression in terms of the down-turn of the initial increase in glucose. The HPA-axis works on a negative feedback loop, which means the activation of the SNS also triggers the PNS to begin to shut down the stress response. However, if the stressors continue, over time this negative feedback loop begins to degrade and hinders the body's ability to both mount a successful stress-response (activation of the SNS) and shut it down (activation of PNS (Sapolsky, 2015)), while also causing high levels of circulating glucose and resultant damage to key areas of the brain, including the prefrontal cortex (Goosens & Sapolsky, 2007).

Recall that EF relies on physiological support for gene expression to create foundational structures and functions of the prefrontal cortex. In fact, chronic stress causes architectural changes in the prefrontal cortex, actually reducing the length and number of dendrites, and thus the connections within and between the prefrontal cortex and other regions of the brain (Arnsten, 2009). Stress disturbs the fine balance of specific neurotransmitters in the prefrontal cortex that focus attention and maintain inhibitory function. Further, it causes long-term changes in gene expression responsible for brain structure and function. Remember that *histones* (i.e., chemicals binding to DNA structures to change gene expression) caused by malnutrition or negative experience prevent or increase particular gene function.

Interestingly, researchers examined histone patterns of 7-year-old children who had experienced negative emotional events ranging from abuse to severe lack of physical resources, and they found that the histone patterns of these children had changed since birth, especially when negative experiences occurred prior to 3 years of age (Dunn et al., 2019), and altered gene expression affects long-term developmental outcomes (Casey et al., 2009). These effects of stress on the prefrontal cortex and EF point to the importance, both physiologically and psychologically, of regulating how we react to and experience stress.

Specific Foundations of Emotional Development

We now turn to describe some foundational concepts in the development of emotion that critically rely on and influence EF. We separately describe temperament, self-regulation, and attachment; however, these concepts are inextricably linked and are tied to the neurological systems of emotion and stress regulation that we have just described. It is thus important to recognize at the outset that many concepts overlap and the ideas flow into one another. To guide our exploration of these foundations, we will begin with a scenario that will be referred to as an example throughout the remainder of this section.

> *You and your child are planning a trip to the zoo. The day of the outing you are not feeling well; or the weather is bad; or the zoo is closed and therefore the outing must be canceled or postponed. Your child is quite disappointed, which can result in numerous feelings and actions. How does the child respond to such disappointment (temperament)? Does the child engage EFs of impulsivity control, working memory, and flexibility in responding (self-regulation)? How do you support them and what do they expect from you as they deal with this disappointment (attachment)?*

Temperament

We discussed earlier how biology, brain, and physiology contribute to emotion and how our bodies react to stress or arousal. One factor thought to be critical to these is temperament, which includes the tendencies of an individual to approach or withdraw, adapt, and persist (Thomas & Chess, 1977). Although specific definitions may vary, **temperament** commonly refers to the individual

Source: Shutterstock.

differences in physiological reactivity and stabilization of that reaction (Rothbart & Derryberry, 1981). Not only does temperament shape our emotional or physiological reaction to a stressor, but temperament also influences our response to that initial physiological reactivity; that is, whether arousal or stress remains high or the biological system is able to regulate and stabilize quickly.

Across theoretical models, temperament is rooted in physiological differences at birth that remain relatively stable throughout development and can be mediated by the environment (Thompson, 2015). In other words, even if you and I share an identical experience, our bodies will respond differently according to individual differences in our temperaments.

> *For example, when our trip to the zoo gets canceled, some children may experience a great deal of arousal over the change—perhaps stemming from feelings of anger, sadness, or fear—whereas others might not have strong feelings about the change in plans.*

Reactivity and Behavioral Inhibition

Our discussion of temperament will begin with reactivity and then move into regulation. **Reactivity** refers to the timing, intensity, and duration of the initial response to an experience (Rothbart & Derryberry, 1981). Reactivity can be defined in a variety of ways, but it is largely accepted that it is biologically based, early developing, and stable over time. One model of temperament relies entirely on the concept of behavioral inhibition to explain reactivity. **Behavioral inhibition** is a continuum of reactivity centered around fearful and anxious responses to unfamiliar or unexpected situations, with high behavioral inhibition (i.e., shy) or low behavioral inhibition (i.e., outgoing or extroverted) predicting stable, long-term physiological and behavioral differences (e.g., Kagan, 2022). For example, infants with behavioral markers of high inhibition have higher levels of cortisol at rest and higher levels of sympathetic nervous system arousal in general (Buss et al., 2003).

These early individual differences in behavioral inhibition appear to be rooted in early biological function and have lasting implications for thoughts and behavior well into adulthood (e.g., Kagan, 2022). Kagan et al. (2007) followed infants who, as 4-month-old babies, were classified as high or low in behavioral inhibition based on their responses to a novel laboratory experience. Infants high in behavioral inhibition displayed high levels of tension and distress to novel stimuli during their laboratory visit, and these same children were identified as being more fearful, shy or inhibited in later childhood. Further, children high in inhibition displayed a *lower* threshold of reactivity within certain regions of the amygdala; this means that it takes less stimulation from the environment to trigger the reaction of the HPA-axis. Even into late adolescence, individual differences in highly inhibited infants and children predict greater inhibited behavior, such as being tense, smiling less frequently, and feeling generally less comfortable in unexpected or new situations (Kagan et al., 2007).

Research has suggested that children high on behavioral inhibition are more prone to anxiety and depression (Kagan, 2022). This may be due to the nature of behavioral inhibition in and of itself. In these cases, there is a continual tension between behavioral inhibition and behavioral activation. Behavioral *inhibition* promotes a strong motivation to avoid punishment or aversive stimuli, or more of a fearful disposition, whereas behavioral *activation* is driven by an underlying motivation toward rewards or things that stimulate our desires, such as food, social interaction, and thrills (Gray, 1990). When individuals are higher in inhibition and physiologically more sensitive to stress or harm, they tend to have stronger negative reactions and lack of movement toward accomplishing goals (Gray, 1990). Frontal lobe activity is related to these temperamental systems in infants, children and adults: Those higher in inhibited behaviors show greater right frontal activation, whereas those higher in behavioral activation show greater left frontal activation (Fox et al., 2005). It is not a coincidence that the frontal lobe is involved here, as inhibition, working memory, and cognitive flexibility play a role in how an individual's response to their environment impacts their future thinking and behavior.

Environmental Context of Temperament

Despite the lasting biological foundation of temperamental behavioral inhibition, this discussion cannot continue without a reminder that context is critical. Recall our discussion early in this chapter about the interactive nature of genetic contributions with the environment and how children act to choose, elicit, or passively experience their surroundings (Scarr & McCartney, 1983). Importantly, environment in the form of family, community, and culture can interact to shape the developmental pathway in positive and negative ways from the earliest to latest days (Kagan, 2022).

To illustrate this point, let's revisit our trip to the zoo and our disappointed child. The behaviorally inhibited child may be sensitive to this disappointment and feel motivated to withdraw, reacting to this unexpected event with greater physiological arousal, muscle tension, and negative emotion than the non-inhibited child. This same child may be generally shy and react very strongly to stress, usually enjoying more quiet and low-arousal types of activities such as reading. Knowing this about your child may allow you to better anticipate their needs when the plans to go to the zoo change and help you to better support their well-being.

Temperament and Behavioral Control

While temperamental reactivity systems are found to be present early in life, the systems that underlie the development of the regulation of that reactivity develops more extensively in the early years. Before turning to detail EF regulatory systems, it is important to mention that some temperament theorists include regulatory control as a component of temperament. For example, **effortful control** is the temperamental dimension involving biological proclivity to inhibit actions, focus attention, engage in alternative and flexible actions, and plan (Posner & Rothbart, 2007). Although reactivity may produce behavioral inhibition very early in life, effortful control develops extensively throughout the early years in concert with executive attention, as children become better able to stop themselves from immediate gratification to engage

Source: Shutterstock.

in a solution deemed more effective (Posner & Rothbart, 2007). Even by the age of 2.5 years, children show stability across different situations and over time in measures of effortful control, and such measures relate to more sophisticated emotions and behaviors over time (Kochanska et al., 2000).

> *These concepts are illustrated as we return to our child disappointed by the change of plans to visit the zoo. The child may exhibit a great deal of behavioral inhibition (and higher reactivity) and also a great deal of effortful control to be able to regulate behaviors and thoughts. Often these abilities are supported by the adults present, who help them to think about the situation, reframe their reactions, distract their attention from the disappointment, and even support their physiological response with physical comfort. This example illustrates how different aspects of temperament work together to shape the individual in interaction with their environment.*

Effortful control may seem quite similar to EF. We have reviewed evidence that temperamental control as well as EFs of inhibition, working memory, and cognitive flexibility are all involved in regulation of that initial reaction and that they develop extensively after birth. Although temperamental effortful control is often studied in the context of emotion, studies show these two concepts are strongly related in a variety of contexts, particularly the EFs of inhibitory control and directed attention (Kim-Spoon et al., 2019). We thus turn to regulation in the broad context to discuss how EF helps us to coordinate emotions, biological reactions, and behaviors.

Self-Regulation

Children's growing EF is closely connected with the development of critical components of emotion regulation, cognitive control, and social behavior. **Self-regulation** is a broad term that encompasses these human regulatory functions as increasingly complex interactions among different internal and external human systems, including but not limited to internal physiological and biological systems and external social and cultural contexts (Gottlieb, 2007; Thompson, 2015). Most simply stated, self-regulation involves behavior directed toward a goal, stemming from the interplay of emotions, thoughts, and attention (McClelland et al., 2015). It is the effortful process we use to maintain a balance of emotional and cognitive arousal that allows us to interact with the environment, adapt to changes, and behave in ways that match our own or others' expectations. Self-regulation thus requires intentional coordination and active balance of different parts of the human system, such as how we feel and how fast our heart races. Self-regulation can adjust internal thoughts, feelings, and perspectives as well as external behaviors, communication, and actions.

Self-regulation develops very gradually over the first years of life. A general trend in development shows that early self-regulation, both of behavior and of physiological functions such as breathing and heart rate, develops from the "outside-in" (Thompson, 2015). In the earliest days, this means that self-regulation begins through interaction with caregivers. Supporting the newborn's regulation helps them to begin to take control over these systems for themselves. For example, infants have difficulty regulating their breathing and heart rates in the first few days of life, as their nervous systems are so fresh and new to the outside world. However, with input from a developmentally supportive environment these systems begin to become functionally integrated and to stabilize (Hofer, 1994). Through features of caregiving such as close physical contact, cuddling, and rocking, the infant becomes more able to adopt these regulatory functions into their own physiological and behavioral systems. This will be further discussed in the next section on attachment and interactions.

Inhibitory Control and Prefrontal Cortex

Self-regulation is often tied to the executive function of inhibiting impulsive thoughts and behaviors. Consider that we often tell children *not* do something—"don't hit," "don't touch," and "stop doing that." Inhibitory control is engaged whenever we exercise the ability to inhibit the initial response to any stimuli, whether it is threatening (a sideways glance or bared teeth), positive (a person or a toy we really like), or neutral and boring (learning to wait, not interrupt). Such inhibitory control is a key part of conforming to social norms and expectations and behavioral self-regulation, or what we think of as healthy social development. Importantly, social norms are decided by the context and so different contexts support self-regulation in different ways, with some relying more heavily on inhibitory control of emotions than others.

Infants exert more control over their physiological regulation as their nervous systems become more fully integrated, and yet this is only the beginning of self-regulation, as executive function takes a much longer time to develop. This developmental timeline correlates strongly with the gradual maturation of the prefrontal cortex. A large body of evidence has shown that this area of the brain is largely responsible for what we referred to in Chapter 1 as top-down processing—suppressing stimuli from lower regions of the brain's more automatic bottom-up processes. As the prefrontal cortex develops, children's physiological regulation improves, and the cognitive and emotional capacities underlying executive functions become more sophisticated and differentiated. Because the prefrontal cortex is impacted by the environment, such as nutrition, parenting, and home environment, we can support children's developing EF best when we know about the conditions that support healthy regulatory and brain development.

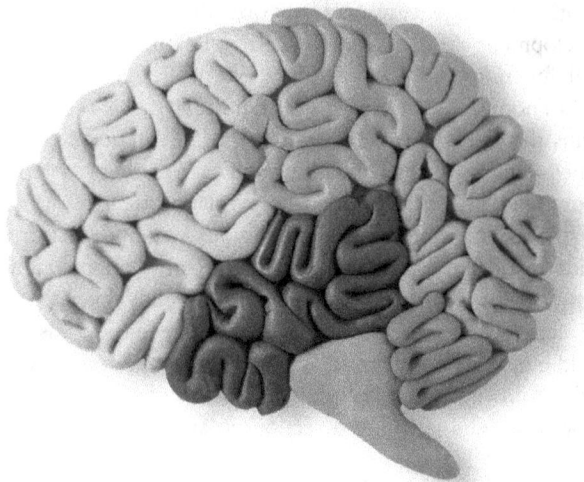

Source: Shutterstock.

An illustration of the interactive effects of development of the prefrontal cortex, physiology, EF, and self-regulation comes from the development of individuals diagnosed with Attention Deficit Hyperactivity Disorder (ADHD). A hallmark of ADHD includes a lack of inhibition (Barkley, 1997), and research on the neuroanatomical differences in children and adults with ADHD show slower development of areas of the prefrontal cortex, especially those believed to underly inhibitory and behavioral control (Friedman & Rapoport, 2015). Although this discussion aptly fits within most chapters of this book, we include it here because of its relevance to behavioral control and inhibition of action. An interesting aside is the neuroplasticity in EF that is displayed by some individuals in this study. Specifically, people with ADHD in early childhood who were no longer symptomatic in late adolescence showed cortical thickness similar to their typically developing peers (Friedman & Rapoport, 2015). However, those who remained symptomatic for ADHD into adulthood showed even greater thinning of these cortical areas. We will refer back to ADHD elsewhere to highlight additional applications.

Anger and Aggression

Many people tend to think of anger as a negative emotion, and of course if not modulated it can lead to aggression, anti-social behavior, and even violence. However, anger also conveys very important information to the person feeling it as well as to those around them, and it can be highly motivating.

We will use these emotions as an example for how emotional processing occurs. If someone takes something that belongs to you or breaks a promise, anger can motivate you to act in a goal-oriented manner. Automatic appraisal may initiate a physiological reaction that affects the brain, body, and emotion, and this depends on a number of factors such as temperamental reactivity, appraisal of the event, and situational context. Therefore, depending on the level and quality of reactivity, regulatory systems may have some work to do in order to diminish the stress response. This regulation may, in the moments before a behavior is initiated, involve inhibitory control of one's first tendency to respond, holding various ideas in mind about how to respond, and/or brainstorming new solutions and their effectiveness. Sometimes these regulatory behaviors diffuse the anger and things move on as before. Yet, as you may have experienced, this is not always the case and sometimes these reactions intensify the situation for one or both of the people involved.

Children have limited EF and thus, limited regulation of their emotion-related behaviors. When children cannot manage their emotions of anger or disapproval, situations can arise in which they express their feelings using aggression or social rejection, and perhaps heightened stress. Many times, especially in early childhood, such aggression is simply a means for expression of current emotional state, albeit in a manner that is less regulated than we might expect from older children.

You may be familiar with this process of working to help children manage overwhelming feelings and reactive behaviors. We may ask them to take a deep breath (physiological regulation). Or we may ask them to think about their actions, supporting behavioral self-control. Or we may even ask them to consider what the other person, the perpetrator, might have intended (re-attribution or re-appraisal). In all these situations, we are engaging the child's top-down, effortful EF skills to help them to modulate this aggressive behavior.

Box 3.1 EF and classroom behavior

Setting the Stage

This in an interview of V.T., a preschool teacher in an urban community in the United States. She has been teaching preschool for over 10 years and believes in a play-based preschool education. As you read this interview, consider how understanding individual differences in temperamental reactivity and self-regulation are important to supporting children's EF in the classroom context. Also, think about how relationships with caregivers in the family and school context may be important for emotional development and EF across contexts.

Source: Shutterstock.

Interview

DR O'HARA: What are some things you notice about children who over time have trouble with social-interaction or peer relationships? What are some tell-tale signs that you think signal they are going to struggle?

V.T.: Some things I have noticed about children who have trouble with social-interaction or peer relationships is that they tend to be more reactive and have a harder time controlling their strong emotions. These children react physically when they are frustrated or upset and have a hard time stopping their impulses to express their emotions with words instead. Other children tend not to want to play with these children because they do not want to get hurt.

Some other tell-tale signs that signal when children have a hard time with social interaction or peer relationships is also when children are introverted and withdrawn. They have a hard time initiating play with others and often need a teacher or adult support to help them engage in play until they are comfortable.

DR O'HARA: What are some strategies that you've seen children just adopt spontaneously that help them to interact socially?

V.T.: One strategy that I have seen children adopt that helps them interact socially are acts of empathy and kindness towards other children. This happens when another child is upset and children often display one of these acts: comes over to check on the hurt child, ask if they are okay, give the hurt child a toy, get a teacher for help or tap/rub their back to help the hurt child feel better. Teachers always acknowledge and praise acts of kindness (which is essential in building peer relationships) and reaffirm what it means to be a kind friend (checking on them, asking if they need any help, making friends feel better when they are sad, etc.) and how those acts contribute to a child feeling better.

Another strategy that we have seen children adopt is actively joining in other children's play with a purpose. There are some children who wait to be asked to join into play, others watch from afar, and others ask for a teacher's help to join into other children's play. However, children who tend to be more confident and social, join in and find a way to contribute into the play, whether it be acting as a certain character in a sociodramatic play scenario or adding extra blocks to a building structure.

DR O'HARA: How do you help these kids [who over time have trouble with social-interaction or peer relationships]? And how do you advise other teachers to help them? Are there some tried and true strategies that seem to help them navigate the social realm?

V.T: We strive to teach children the importance of social and life skills through a positive discipline approach: 1. Help children feel a sense of connection (whether it be between teachers and children, and between children with other children); 2. Be mutually respectful and encouraging (kind and firm when that are being aggressive and need to be redirected); 3. Be effective with long-term in mind (consider what the child is thinking, feeling, learning and deciding in the moment); 4. Teach important social and life skills (respect, concern for others/empathy, problem solving and cooperation; and. 5. Invite children to discover how capable they are. This applies to helping children interact with other children and build peer relationships because we are meeting them where they are at by trying to understand the intent behind their actions, guiding them to practice social skills by problem solving and cooperating with other children until they are capable on their own.

Other strategies that we use is to provide children with different opportunities to engage with one another, especially if they are introverted. This may include placing children's tables next to one another, having children do a group project together and collaborating with one another. Teachers can acknowledge similar interests to help children connect and play with one another. Teachers can also help children engage in play but asking children what their friend can contribute to their play.

At our preschool, we instill in children that "we are all friends" because we are inclusive and want all children to feel welcome and included. This means that all children can play with one another because "we are all friends," so that friends do not get rejected. We do respect if a child wants to play alone and needs space from other friends. By acknowledging that children are all friends, this helps children who have trouble with social interaction feel included and know that they have children to play with.

DR O'HARA: What about self-control? How do you help children manage self-control, such as controlling aggressive behavior or delay of gratification?

V.T: Helping children with their self-control involves a lot of patience, talking through emotions, and providing different options. When children are frustrated and upset that they may not get what they want when they want it (delay of gratification), it is important for teachers to be right there with them to talk through these emotions to be a sense of calm and support. Some examples of how teachers can help children with their emotions as they practice self-control and delay of gratification include: "Sometimes we have to wait. But I can wait with you," or "I know it is hard to wait sometimes, but do you want to read a book with me until it is your turn with the toy?" or "I see you are frustrated. I am here to help you through these feelings."

When it comes to controlling aggressive behaviors, we use a positive discipline approach instead of using a punishment approach (focusing on the child being "bad"—rather than the child making and undesirable choice. Adult being responsible to control a child's behavior. Rely on fear or suffering for child to obey. Fosters anger, revenge, dishonesty, and disconnection). Teachers get to the root of the behavior (child was frustrated about ___), talking about the emotion ("I see that you are mad that __ took your toy. I would be upset too"), problem solve, ("If I was you, I would use my words to tell them instead of using my body"), and plan what to do next time, ("Next time, what do you think you can do instead?"). After the aggressive behavior and having a talk with the child, it is important that we do not make children say, "I'm sorry," as an immediate resolution to the incident. These words become meaningless. Instead, we have children check on the hurt child (whether they were hurt physically or emotionally), and say, "Are you okay? What can I do to make you feel better?" This helps the hurt child advocate for themselves, while the child who was aggressive, takes part in making them feel better (coming to a resolution). When aggressive behaviors are frequent, other methods may be used: meeting with parents to come with a plan, creating a behavior plan, etc.

DR O'HARA: What would you like parents to know/understand about supporting children's executive functioning to help them with their social development?

V.T: What I would want parents to know that sometimes the immediate and quick fixes to issues are not always the best way to support the child's executive function. For example, when a child is upset because they want something, parents typically give in and give it to them. This may be due to different motives (guilt from working, stress, parenting style, etc.). Although the quick give ins resolve the issue, children are not practicing delay of gratification or self-control when they do not have opportunities to practice these skills. Parents can acknowledge child's feelings, offer alternatives, and follow through with what they say (adults are instilling to children that words are important, and we mean what we say—this also builds trust with young children).

It is also important for parents to reiterate at home ways to be a friend and community member: being kind, welcoming all, helping those in need, etc. Parents are the greatest role model to children at this age, and it is important for them to impart these social and life skills at an early age.

Application and Reflection

1   What examples of behavioral inhibition (or lack thereof) did V.T. share? Based on these early indicators, what reactivity and behaviors might you expect from each preschooler when they reach adolescence?
2   Consider the examples provided regarding how teachers can support regulation. How might these supports change for children with different temperaments? Why?
3   Why might it be critical for teachers and school professionals to understand the cultural and familial context in determining how to support children best?

Early Interactions and Relationships

Although the ability of individuals to regulate their emotions is rooted in biology, experiences are critical to modulating those biological foundations. We now turn to one of the special experiences of infancy and how early interactions and relationships play a role in biological and brain development and are a critical part of the foundation upon which EFs develop.

Source: Photograph by author KDO.

Attunement and Dyadic Interactions

Parent's emotional expressions and emotional communication have been found to impact the development of children's ability to exercise and develop better inhibitory control. When caregivers are **attuned** to their infant's emotional needs it means that they are responding to their signals of emotion with behaviors and emotional expression that serve to ease that distress, or to mirror the positive emotions the infant is expressing. Very often, the infant will invite the caregiver into emotional **dyadic** exchanges, and research has shown that when the caregiver and infant engage in greater synchronicity of exchanges, over time this has a positive impact on the infant's developing self-regulation, and more specifically on the development of inhibitory control.

A notable set of studies using what is referred to as the **still-face paradigm** illustrate this co-regulation very clearly. In this example, caregiver and infant are placed in a face-to-face dyadic interaction, and after a time the caregiver is given the instruction to go into still-face and show no emotional expression or response to the infant's bids for attention. When this happens, and after multiple attempts to elicit a response from the caregiver, the infant becomes increasingly dysregulated. They begin to cry, sometimes lashing out, and often devolving into physical dysregulation such as drooling and losing control of their physical movements. However, once the caregiver returns to the exchange in a sensitive manner, the infant rapidly returns to a state of regulation.

Researchers often refer to this as indicating flexible dyadic interactions. In our day-to-day life, it is not every instant that a caregiver can respond in the most sensitive and attuned manner supporting **synchronous** interactions.

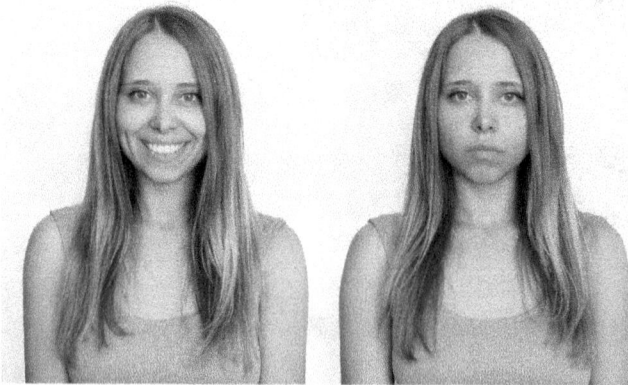

Source: Shutterstock.

Parents get busy, infants' needs can change drastically from day to day, and sometimes infants can be very difficult to console. In fact, it is not a single instance that sets the stage, but the cumulative impact of exchanges over time that contribute to infants' gradual ability to self-regulate and influence their growing EF abilities. For example, Tronick (2007) described how caregivers and infants go back and forth between states of mis-coordinated/asynchronous interactions that induce negative emotions and distress in the infant to states of coordinated/synchronous interactions that induce positive emotions and a reduction of anxiety and distress. He referred to this process as repair and noted that as each member of the dyad adjusts their behaviors and emotions to re-engage and move toward repair, the infant begins to develop regulatory skills and to cope with their distress in manageable ways.

These regulatory skills are dependent upon and play a role in development of EF. More broadly contextualizing the dyadic relationship, studies show that multiple aspects of parenting preschoolers predict improved EF, including use of less controlling language and greater provision of appropriate and sensitive support (Hughes & Devine, 2019). And yet, what happens when interactions are consistently mis-coordinated, as can be the case when a parent has depression? Maternal depression can cause difficulty in the ability to establish attunement, greater infant distress, and a much longer time for the dyad to reach face-to-face emotional synchrony (Feldman, 2007), and the extent of maternal depressive symptoms predict lower infant EF (Gueron-Sela et al., 2018), especially when mother-child interactions were harsh and punitive. When maternal depressive symptoms did not improve, these negative effects on EF remained at age 6 (Park et al., 2018).

And yet, there are continued long-term impacts of this affective asynchrony on child development, including psychophysiological (e.g., cortisol levels), emotional (e.g., empathy), cognitive and academic, and relational (e.g., attachment quality) factors across childhood and adolescence (Leclère et al., 2014). The ways in which maternal qualities affect child outcomes and EF is important to us as practitioners and advocates for healthy child and adolescent development. This research thus leads us to another critical component of early and formative relationships: attachment.

Attachment

Based on early interactions and their synchronicity, the bond formed between infant and caregiver has been referred to as the formation of an *attachment*. In addition to being critical for social and emotional function, attachment has been linked to cognition and EF. We will first describe attachment and some foundational terms, then discuss its relation to physiological and emotion reactivity, and finally links to brain structure and function, all with the goal of connecting these individual differences to EF through frontal lobe development.

FOUNDATIONAL TERMS FOR ATTACHMENT

The attachment bond is enduring, formed early in life, and adaptive, varying based on the manner and consistency with which caregivers respond over time. **Attachment theory** was first described by John Bowlby and his colleagues in the 1950's, and we have come to understand that healthy emotional development is rooted in the early formation of nurturing and trusting relationships between a caregiver and infant. Considering our previous discussion of attunement and its role in the development of self-regulation, this makes a lot of sense. In those relationships with a balance of stimulation and autonomy building, we would expect an increase in emotional regulatory functioning.

However, at its core, attachment security is a cognitive process that relies upon infants' growing working memory skills in which they must actively hold multiple pieces of information. Attachment **security** is characteristic of a dyadic relationship that includes a consistently responsive caregiver who provides a predictable source of stimulation and comfort for an infant (Bowlby 1969/ 1982). As young infants experience repeated interactions with their caregivers, they begin to form representations that signify their separateness from the caregiver and their place in the world as well as the predictability of the world and the people in it. We form these sophisticated mental representations called **internal working models** (IWMs (Bowlby 1969/1982)) of our relationships and ourselves across multiple contexts and interactions. IWMs provide humans with a representation of themselves and their skills, abilities, and worth in addition to providing a representation of others as a tool for interpreting behaviors and predicting responsivity (Bretherton, 1992).

Source: Shutterstock.

IWMs are implicit, in that parts of them cannot be accessed, and explicit, as we have overt ideas about ourselves and others that result from IWMs (Thompson, 2021). In fact, the prefrontal cortex activates differently when humans see or are comforted by an attachment figure versus an unfamiliar human (Laurita et al., 2019). It is possible that accessing emotional (hot) representations utilizes greater resources in working memory, thus taxing EF resources.

Of note, to experience distress upon a caregiver leaving, children must hold a representation in mind. As discussed in Chapter 2, infants need **object permanence** to find predictable patterns within these early relationships. With the onset of object permanence around 6 to 8 months, infants begin showing **separation anxiety** when the object of their attachment, usually a parent, is not present. They may cry intensely when the parent is out of their sight and continue to do so until the parent either returns or some other person (e.g., family friend), object (e.g., pacifier), or event (e.g., positive distraction) is able to sooth the infant's distress.

This process of separation and reunion, over time, creates the foundation for infants to begin to form their models, or cognitive representations about themselves and others in relationships. When the parent predictably returns and comforts the child, successfully alleviating their distress, the child begins to associate the attachment figure with stability and predictability, generally leading to increased attachment security and more positive internal working models of the self and other. **Secure attachment** is most commonly associated with the presence of a warm, responsive caregiver, and infants tend to be upset when the caregiver leaves but seek the caregiver for comfort upon return (Ainsworth et al., 1978). **Insecure attachment** (i.e., avoidant or ambivalent to the caregiver) is related to having an unpredictable or less responsive (less attuned) caregiver with infants who either actively avoid the caregiver or act inconsistently toward the caregiver, in neither case being comforted by them (Ainsworth et al., 1978). In any case, infants work to adapt to their environment by creating internal working models that provide accurate expectations of the world around them; that is, although in the United States, a secure attachment is considered most common, such a pattern of expectations about the other to be consistent, warm, and responsive would not serve a child well if they have an abusive caregiver, and instead, avoidance might serve them best.

PHYSIOLOGICAL AND EMOTION REACTIVITY

Beyond the experience of physical regulation and comfort from the caregiver, how does having formed a secure attachment impact emotional development over time? What mechanisms underlie the continued importance? And how does any of this relate to EF?

As we discussed earlier, in the first weeks of life, infants are regulated from the outside in a largely physiological manner. Caregivers help to support them in regulation of body temperature, breathing, and heartbeat, and soothe the infant to calm in times of distress. After this physiological, and largely unconscious regulation occurs, at around 6 to 8 months of life the infant begins to shift from physical/sensorimotor representations of their outside regulators (e.g., caregivers) to more cognitive representations of caregiving. Strongly linked to brain development, these representations of the caregiver and self are formulated to help the child emotionally regulate when they are upset or frightened.

Recall that every stress response begins with the individual's appraisal of the event or situation. Our experience in close relationships and the expectations we hold about others shape our appraisal of social and emotional interactions, and therefore whether we meet emotional situations with stress/arousal or with engagement and interest. Research on attachment security and emotion regulation has shown consistently that how individuals regulate their emotions in situations that trigger feelings about attachment is tied to past experiences with attachment. For example, children who were rated as *insecurely attached* at 12 months showed heightened stress response (e.g., higher heartrate and cortisol levels) during reunion with their caregiver, even though their behavior indicated disinterest (Spangler & Grossmann, 1993). In fact, although these children were the most physiologically distressed, they were the least likely to respond behaviorally to elicit caregiving. Related to this, similar indicators of high emotional reactivity were alleviated if there was a secure attachment (Gunnar et al., 1996). In other words, and despite overt behaviors, children with secure attachments appear to more smoothly and automatically regulate their physiological reactions to stress.

BRAIN STRUCTURE AND FUNCTION

In later childhood, attachment security has been correlated with different patterns of prefrontal activation during emotional regulation tasks. What do these different patterns mean? The right and left hemispheres of the prefrontal cortex underlie different motivational systems. The left frontal regions are activated during events or emotions related to "approach" motivation, such as joy, interest, and even anger, whereas the right frontal regions are activated during events or emotions related to "withdrawal" motivation, such as sadness or disgust (Davidson et al., 1990). O'Hara (2002), in an unpublished dissertation, found that attachment security was significantly related to frontal lobe patterns in 4- and 5-year-old children, with less secure children showing greater left frontal activity during reunion episodes. Consistent with attachment theory, this would indicate that those children were responding with approach motivation or anger. These different patterns of activity in the prefrontal cortex are directly related to EF throughout life.

Attachment security is not only related to patterns of brain function in the frontal lobe (Schore, 2001), but also with increased efficacy of specific measures of executive function in early to late elementary school (Regueiro et al., 2020). As discussed earlier, attachment involves interactions among infants' social, emotional, and cognitive systems. Similarly, EF, although often considered cognitive in nature, has also been discussed here as critical for self-regulation that involves both physiological and effortful control (Blair & Diamond, 2008). By consistently and warmly responding, caregivers may be promoting children's formation of self-regulatory skills, which buffer the stress response and thus mitigate associated deficits in EF (Gunnar & Quevedo, 2007).

Across development, attachment security is consistently related to improved EF. For example, Regueiro et al. (2020) found that more securely attached children, as measured at 15 months, showed better working memory, cognitive flexibility, and overall performance on a series of EF tasks in elementary school. What was surprising about these results was that measures of maternal support for autonomy did not explain the effect of attachment security but had an additional impact on children's EF. This indicates that the enduring bond and expectation of safety and security had an impact on children's EF abilities, even years in the future and even apart from other measures of parenting.

It is important to note that although much of this research has held up over time, most of the studies discussed thus far have been conducted with predominantly middle-class European-majority populations and so do not account for differences in cultural practices and values that may support alternative attachment styles as adaptive and successful for EF development. Furthermore, we have not examined how EF and emotional development occur in groups of individuals with developmental differences. We consider these next.

Contextual Foundations of Emotional Development

As discussed at the beginning of this chapter, the earliest roots of emotional development, or human basic emotions, are universal. This means that patterns related to both the subjective experience and the physiological response are consistent across cultures around the world (Izard, 1994). However, the development of EF as related to these emotions is shaped by culture as part of the intricate and life-long biology-environment connection. What are the mechanisms by which daily events, tasks, and values can impact such seemingly species-driven development? Some of what we understand comes from a recent theoretical framework known as **cultural neuroscience**, which looks to understand how cultural values and tasks shape and modify neural pathways related to emotion, cognition, and social development (Lin et al., 2018). We will refer back to this theoretical model for evidence of sociocultural effects on the internal processes introduced in this chapter, namely emotion regulation and attachment security.

Emotion and Reactivity

Cultures vary on the emotional qualities that they value within the society. For example, Ip, Miller, and colleagues (2021) described some Asian

Source: Shutterstock.

countries as promoting group cohesion and mutual support by socializing children to dampen their negative emotions. These cultures, in addition to other non-Western nations such as Iran, Turkey, and India, are considered collectivistic and thus interdependent on one another within the culture, and across many countries, collectivistic cultures support this **expressive suppression** (Ramzan & Amjad, 2017). Children developing in collectivistic cultures such as China and Japan show early and lasting positive outcomes related to suppressing their emotions both outwardly through facial expressions (Ip, Miller et al., 2021) and inwardly through emotion regulation. Further, research shows cultural differences in reactivity and cortisol; whereas Western samples display less cortisol reactivity with greater inhibitory control, non-Western samples show different patterns of reactivity with higher cortisol related to increased attentional control (Grabell et al., 2015). These patterns are consistent with cultural expectations for display of emotions (Ip, Felt et al., 2021).

In Western cultures, such as the United States and Germany, individuality and assertiveness are valued more highly than the collective group. Emotional expression is encouraged and demonstrated more freely (Ramzan & Amjad, 2017). Early measures of behavioral inhibition, or what we might refer to as "shyness" are more similar across cultures in infants (e.g., Bornstein & Cote, 2009), and as children spend more time exposed to the parenting and values of the culture, studies including participants as young as toddlers show higher behavioral inhibition in Eastern cultures such as South Korea and China as compared to Western cultures (Rubin et al., 2006). Therefore, inhibitory control may be linked to the context and values exhibited by the people around us.

Many theorists believe that the attachment process is common across cultures and that caregiver-infant bonding is based on an innate drive (Bowlby, 1969/1982), and responsive caregiving has been linked to attachment security across numerous nations (Mesman et al., 2016). However, there is variation in caregiving practices such as who cares for babies while the primary caregiver works in the home or outside the home, or with whom the baby sleeps, that can influence the trajectory of these attachments. Are there ways that differing attachments are adaptive to those culturally specific practices?

There is a body of research that has examined the caregiving practices within the social dynamics of the Israeli "kibbutz." In this societal arrangement, parents work in groups and live within those social arrangements while the children are raised in housing situations together. Research showed that in spite of spending less time with a primary caregiver, it was still maternal sensitivity that predicted attachment security (Sagi et al., 1995). Therefore, regardless of the cultural structure, the quality of the caregiver-child interaction is the predominant factor influencing attachment security. This research has been replicated among a wide array of cultures, such as the Efe people of Africa, which values multiple caregivers (Morelli & Lu, 2021).

Another cultural characteristic that has been examined considering EF and emotion regulation is the degree to which the self is construed as singular, or independent of others, or is seen as intertwined with the collective. This is related to cultural neuroscientific research on collective versus individualistic societies (e.g., Ramzan & Amjad, 2017). Research by De Greck (2012) illustrated that neurological responses to emotional faces varied between members of different cultures, especially as related to cultural construal of self. For example, angry facial expressions were more associated with greater neurological signs of distress in persons from China (a predominantly interdependent culture) than in persons from Germany (a predominantly independent culture). Researchers theorize that these different cultural perspectives affected the meaning of the angry faces, where those from China appraised these faces as threatening to the harmony of the group, and therefore were linked with greater personal distress. However, when the self is seen as independent of others, personal distress may not be experienced.

Careers and Executive Function

A variety of different careers can lead to supporting children's emotional development and the ways in which it interacts with EF and long-term outcomes. These can focus on buffering biological reactivity, support or training for caregivers on synchronicity or sensitivity, and coping strategies for children, for example. Specific careers that are particularly suited to serving children and families in these ways include teachers, counselors, social workers, health care workers, child life specialists, and occupational therapists, although this is by no means an exhaustive list of the many ways we can walk alongside children and families to support positive growth.

Summary

Emotional development is a complex process involving an intricate "dance" among various aspects of biology and environment. Development of the brain, and particularly the prefrontal cortex, is critical for both EF and emotional development. Although genes are programmed for brain development, it is individual differences in the environment over time that define how the brain actually develops. Physiological reactivity depends, in part, on how the brain develops, and behavioral responses to emotion and stress depend on how this reactivity is regulated. Further, interactions between caregivers and infants create a foundation upon which self-regulation and attachment bonds are formed, contributing directly to both prefrontal cortex development and EF function. Although there are universals in emotion development, regulation, and attachment, cross-cultural differences are important to consider and can ultimately affect biological processes, neurological development and modification, and behavior.

Further Resources

Blair, C., & Raver, C.C. (2015). School readiness and self-regulation: A developmental psychobiological approach. *Annual Review of Psychology, 66(1)*, 711–731. https://doi.org/10.1146/annurev-psych-010814-015221

Sapolsky, R. (2018). *The biology of humans at our best and worst.* Penguin.

Siegel, D.J., & Payne Bryson, T. (2012). *The whole-brain child.* Bantam Books.

Chapter 4

Social Cognition

The Interface between Cognitive and Social-Emotional Development

Early cognitive growth and representational ability, along with foundational social-emotional growth, are part of the intricate web of skills that coordinate more complex ways of interacting with the world. Building on our previous discussions of cognitive development and self-regulation of behavior, this chapter turns to the child's growing ability to represent and understand themselves and others in their social interactions. We will examine the ways that individual differences in biology and context are intertwined with children's burgeoning EF abilities to impact how they think about and navigate people in their increasingly complex worlds.

What is Social Cognition and How is it Related to Executive Function?

Children's social skills and abilities, how they get along with others, how they behave, and how they feel about themselves are markedly interconnected. **Social cognition** lies at the interface between children's representational skills and their prior social and emotional experiences. It encompasses their thinking about others and themselves as well as the behaviors that result from this thinking (Olson & Dweck, 2008). The ability and propensity for children and adolescents to develop social-cognitive skills, such as perspective-taking and empathy, and the EF skills children need to regulate these skills, relies on a number of overlapping factors. In this chapter we focus on how children develop and use their foundational understandings of themselves and others and the ways in which these developments both rely on and create boundaries for the development of EF in biological and social contexts into adolescence and early adulthood.

Agency Shapes Social Cognition

At the heart of social cognition is the human—the person who is thinking and acting by using their available resources. **Agency** refers to the ability to effortfully make things happen in the world (Bandura, 2001) and involves acting to control incoming perceptual information (Russell, 1996). As was

DOI: 10.4324/9781003131052-4

Source: Photograph by author KDO.

discussed in the previous chapter, early internal working models of the self and other are formed through early and ongoing infant-caregiver interactions that help infants create a representation of who they are and what they can do in the world. The idea of agency builds on this foundation by highlighting how the active role of the infant and their ability to elicit responses shapes brain development, physiology, and EF skills (Bandura, 1997). In fact, thinking is advanced as we act on objects with intentional, goal-oriented behavior (Rodriguez, 2022). This can include such actions as smiling at a caregiver, reaching for an object, or writing a paper for a class. Each involves the human controlling their behaviors to meet their goals, whether it be to obtain food from the caregiver, use a toy that was out of reach, or earn a degree and learn new ideas. Participating in each of these intentional and goal-oriented actions demonstrates agency and relies on EF—in this way, the two ideas are inseparable.

Research shows that both agency and EF serve to shape and be shaped by the prefrontal cortex (David et al., 2008). For humans to exert agency, they need EF skills to direct their attention, sustain focus, inhibit distracting thoughts and behaviors, maintain information in working memory, and think flexibility about how to reach their action goals. In situations when agency is lacking, such as in some environments of negative childhood experiences, brain function, physiological reactivity, and EF skills can be compromised (Zelazo & Carlson, 2020).

Biology and Experiences Work Together in Social Cognitive Development

Research on social and emotional development has increasingly focused on neurological underpinnings of what is referred to as the **social brain** (Adolphs, 2009), which grows as genes are expressed. The social brain is a set of specific brain areas and interconnections among them that help us to understand others. For example, when we look at the facial expressions of others, some brain areas are active, particularly the amygdala (critical to emotional reactivity) and hippocampus (essential for explicit memory). Other areas of the brain important in social development are the **orbitofrontal cortex,** a specific part of the prefrontal cortex that is sensitive to social rewards and punishments (Damasio, 2004) and the **insula,** which is a deeply rooted region of the brain that receives input from sensory areas and underlies our physical sense of self and knowledge of what we are feeling in our bodies. Together, these neurological regions create the foundation for our ability to connect with other people, feel what they are feeling, and share in their perspectives.

Recall that having genes does not mean they will be expressed; as with much of human development, these social regions of the brain are sensitive to social context (Adolphs, 2009). As discussed in earlier chapters, infants and young children use perceptual, cognitive, and emotional skills to interact with others and promote refining of connections within their social brains. Further, the complex social networks of adolescence that build on early foundations continue to show links among social, emotional, cognitive, and brain development (Blakemore, 2012). For example, research on neurological functions in adolescents shows that current social perceptions and expectations, which are strongly influenced by prior learning and experience, produce different activation patterns within these emotional sub-regions of the social brain (Silk et al., 2014).

Specific Domains of Social Cognitive Development

Emotion regulation is critical for the ability to balance feelings, thoughts, and biological reactions to the immediate context in order to successfully engage with the social world (Moadab et al., 2010). In fact, many theories of dysfunctional childhood behaviors and thoughts are related to having emotions that are too "big" or long-lasting for the individual to manage, such as depression or anxiety (internalizing behaviors) and overt aggression or conduct disorder (externalizing behaviors). As you read through each area of social cognitive development, draw upon your knowledge of the development of regulation within the earliest social contexts, changes in cognitive skills, and biological maturation to consider how they shape and depend on children's growing representational, social, and behavioral skills. Furthermore, consider how supporting children's EF development, thoughts, and behaviors can impact later social outcomes within the ever-changing context of the developing human.

Understanding of the Self

Earliest notions of self are rooted within the infant's sensorimotor systems, relying on integration and organization of sensory organs, such as hearing, vision, and touch. This organization and communication with the rest of the body is referred to as **interoception** (Seth, 2013). As the senses become integrated within the central and peripheral nervous systems, the infant begins to develop what is referred to as the **embodied self** or physical self, which is just what it sounds like—the self as represented only in the physical being, within sensorimotor functioning. For example, infants know from the first early months that their physical movements belong to them, but only through coordination with visual input on the effects of that sensation—such as figuring out that the hand in front of them is theirs—do they begin to show evidence of understanding their psychological self. For example, infants gradually begin to exert agency to use their physical self to make things happen, such as dropping things and waiting for someone to pick them up (I made that happen!).

The ways in which caregivers respond to this emerging agency in infancy and toddlerhood are stored and gradually accumulate in parallel with development of EF and representation, which together lay the groundwork for the later appearance of the **conceptual self** (Damasio, 1999). This more psychological understanding of the self—our thoughts and beliefs about our attitudes, characteristics, and what makes us who we are—begins to emerge around 3 to 5 years of age as concrete and observable characteristics (Harter, 2012). As children continue to use agency and represent themselves and others in the world, they form enduring ideas of their own **self-efficacy** and how successful they believe they can be in producing their desired outcomes (Bandura, 2018). Efficacy is based on self-reflection about specific abilities and serves as a motivator for future action (Bandura, 1997). These advancing social-cognitive skills provide foundations for a continuously more complex and abstract self-concept throughout adolescence.

The Role of Representational Skills

A critical social-cognitive skill for self understanding is representation, which develops in coordination with EF skills. As discussed in Chapter 2, the earliest representations demonstrate understanding that objects remain in existence

Awe, acrylic on canvas by Sydney Alexander.

even when out of sight (object permanence). A classic method for assessing object permanence, when the representation matches the environment (within the boundaries of the child's sensory and perceptual skills) is known as the **A-not-B task** (Piaget, 1954). In this assessment, an infant is presented with an attractive small toy and may even be allowed to play with the object. The experimenter then takes the object and places it underneath one of two cloths. But the experiment does not stop there. Imagine that after repeatedly hiding the object under the same cloth, the experimenter then places the object under a different cloth. *What do infants do in this case?*

Infants accurately reach for the object under this first cloth in the early trials of this task by about 8 months, showing object permanence, but they do not adjust their looking when the object is moved. This mistake looking in the old and more familiar location is called making the A-not-B error. Although there are great individual differences between infants of the same age, infants become better able to successfully reach for the object in the new location as they get closer to 12 months. After this, they continue to improve by succeeding after longer delays between hiding and being allowed to reach. Interestingly, using a variation of the typical A-not-B task requiring infants' looking behavior rather than reaching, Cuevas and Bell (2010) found that infants were successful as young as 5 months and that success improved gradually through 10 months. This suggests that the cognitive representation may be developed before the infant has developed the EF ability to inhibit their automatic reaching response (the one for which they had been rewarded previously).

Whereas object permanence simply requires representation of what was seen, A-not-B success requires multiple representations. To find the object, you would need to both hold in mind the new and currently correct location (working memory) while also inhibiting interference from the old and incorrect location. In fact, individual differences in working memory and inhibition as well as motor skills influence performance (Diamond, 1990). Because inhibitory control is both a cognitive and a motoric function, it is important to consider that they may develop at different paces. For example, consider the adolescent in an argument with their parent—they cognitively recognize they need to stop talking and just listen, but their actions may show they continue to argue.

Further supporting the role of the prefrontal cortex in A-not-B success is **comparative research** involving non-human primates (e.g., rhesus monkeys) who have undergone surgeries to remove specific portions of their brain. Specifically, neurons in the prefrontal cortex theorized to support working memory are

Source: Shutterstock.

active during representation of objects no longer present, and spatial location for these objects is impaired early in infancy when the prefrontal cortex is still organizing connections or with damage to specific areas in the prefrontal cortex (Diamond & Goldman-Rakic, 1989). In fact, even at the level of precise neurons in the prefrontal cortex, representation of specific spatial information occurs in different neurons within the prefrontal cortex and damage to these neurons impairs the ability to bring to mind those representations (reviewed in Goldman-Rakic, 1995). Thus, executive function is particularly critical to representation in allowing access to conscious knowledge of ideas, objects, or perceptions not currently present.

Self-Awareness

The onset and increased complexity of mental representations is theorized to underlie a number of social and emotional milestones. For example, separation anxiety begins to occur once infants represent their absent caregiver and feel upset at their lack of presence. Moreover, regardless of culture and environmental exposure, children across cultures begin to recognize themselves as distinct from other people as they become more mobile and gain cognitive and social skills. At the predictable age of 14 to 18 months, babies show **self-recognition**, which is recognizing yourself as separate from others. Many would agree this developmental milestone indicates the most basic evidence of the formation of a self-concept, and yet it does not indicate the full achievement of self understanding.

Self-recognition is often tested by researchers using the *rouge test*. Children are shown themselves in a mirror before placing a bit of makeup or a sticker on their face or forehead (Lewis & Brooks-Gunn, 1979). Children are then shown the mirror again to record their reactions. Prior to the emergence of self-recognition, they likely will touch the mirror, noting that "the other child" in the mirror has something on their face. However, once self-recognition is achieved, they touch their own faces, noting that they recognize that the child in the mirror is in fact, themselves. Children will also begin to identify themselves correctly in pictures after this time (Keenan et al., 2003).

Self-awareness requires this initial recognition, and yet it requires a greater meta-self-recognition; that is, knowing what one knows about the self (Lewis & Brooks-Gunn, 1979). To truly be self-conscious, we must be able to compare our own view of self to our expectations/goals or to see ourselves from someone else's perspective (Keenan et al., 2003). As children develop, they use these concepts to further refine their beliefs about themselves and others. They learn what they are good at, what they like to do, and how they ultimately feel about themselves. Although this work is cognitive in nature, social interactions play a role as others point out interesting aspects of the world, share stories and discuss personal and shared experiences, and react to children's behaviors (Thompson, 2015).

Preschoolers' estimations of their skills tend to be relatively inaccurate, as they believe they can run faster, jump higher, and perform a new skill perfectly the first time they try. As working memory skills increase and children engage in more complex thought as they interact with the environment and receive feedback from others, they adjust their beliefs about themselves and begin to compare themselves to others and see a more balanced self (Thompson, 2015). In this way, individual variability in the regulation and expression of self-conscious emotions such as guilt or shame are greatly impacted by a child's environment and culture, as well as their individual and familial dispositions and rapidly growing EF skills.

Identity

As adolescence arrives, it brings with it a growing awareness of the self and greater capacity for complex and abstract representational skills. It also facilitates formation of a stable identity rooted in self-concept. McAdams and Zapada-Geitl (2015) explained identity as developing in three facets:

1   The early understanding of the self as actor in the world involves a focus on defining roles in somewhat rigid ways to allow individuals to learn more about themselves and others;
2   Children then increasingly exert agency on their world, formulating expectations, goals, and plans for action;
3   We finally act as authors of our narrative self—reconstructing our life stories—and these continue to shape and be shaped by development and context.

The first two aspects of identity development fit nicely with our previous discussions about self-awareness, growth in complex emotions such as shame and guilt, and also the increasing role of EF in identity formation with age. As agentic youth see themselves with stable and consistent traits, they are also exposed to the broad views of society at the same time as the prefrontal cortex is organized and connected to better facilitate working memory and flexible thought. Adolescents (and into young adulthood) are faced with the task of reconciling who they know themselves to be with the expectations of society (Erikson, 1968), relying heavily on EF to integrate their social world with their cognitive selves.

Awareness of Others

As discussed in the previous section, infants first learn to differentiate themselves from their environment, such as learning they and their caregiver are not one (Piaget, 1954). From that time, the sense of self and other similarly rely on coordinated development of representational and EF skills and yet, they are separate concepts. As infants use agency to act on their environment to learn

Source: Photograph by author KWA.

about themselves, they are also learning about the other and how responsive and trustworthy they are (Bowlby, 1969). As they grow throughout childhood and adolescence, they use their experiences and burgeoning representational skills and self-concept to support more complex thinking about others. Note that although the self and other are tangibly separate beings, as has been shown, the understanding of the self is intricately tied to the other within community and so these ideas are difficult to separate.

Perspective Taking

Something most of us take for granted is the ability to understand what others are thinking and that it might be different from our own thoughts. This is not a skill that is present at birth, and in fact, research has shown us that there is a great deal of variability in humans' ability to read others' cues and detect the slightest nuances of others' changed perceptions or perspectives. Engaging in perspective taking may help to increase our ability and desire to feel with others and also to appraise others' behaviors and emotional reactions in a manner that helps us to regulate. Developmental and individual variability in these skills are dependent upon a number of factors, including EF maturation.

Developmentally, we know that the ability to take another person's perspective, or to "read their minds" takes time to develop and follows a trajectory tightly linked with other cognitive and neurological aspects of growth. For example, in the earliest stages of development, children cannot differentiate their own thoughts from those of others. As you read in Chapter 2, young children are limited in their ability to hold two representations in mind, and this is even more difficult when those representations are conflicting. This all relates to **theory of mind** (ToM), which is not a theory like those we have used to frame human development, but rather is a theory that each human individually devises based on their developmental experiences. It refers to how we understand the workings of our own mind and the minds of others; that is, our *theory* about how minds operate. It involves understanding our own mental states and that others can feel, think, or act differently (e.g., Perner, 1991). One example comes from the appearance-reality distinction discussed in Chapter 2, which stems from pre-schoolers' growing ability to understand that what they see right now may not represent what is real.

It is likely that the development of ToM takes time because of the extent to which it taxes working memory, and it is difficult to inhibit the more salient of the two representations—what they see or think or feel. In fact, much of communication involves both verbal language and non-verbal communication, as in the tone of voice or facial expressions—the basis of much of our social understandings depend upon this. ToM has been linked to children's dual representational abilities in such tasks as the scale model task from Chapter 2 as well as various EFs (Walker & Murachver, 2012). As preschoolers grow in their understanding of the mind, they also improve in skills of perspective taking, or the ability to comprehend and infer what other people are thinking based on their facial expressions, their eye gaze, or tone of voice. This ability is critical for the development of empathy, which will be discussed later in this chapter. Furthermore, ToM also pro-motes social and emotional development as it allows the individual to exercise goal-directed behavior, as they can hold the notions of that goal in mind (Blair & Raver, 2015). For example, when children have a contextual memory of events, places and people, their emotional response is different than if these things feel new to them.

Another way to consider the importance of this development is to consider the cognitive underpinnings. We often think of young children as **egocentric**, or not able to consider other people's points of view. This does not mean they are egotistical or selfish as we sometimes think of this word, but rather that they cognitively focus on their own view. This is a hallmark of the developmental stage that Piaget (1954) referred to as preoperational. A clas-sic example of this is the young child on a voice call with a grandparent, saying, "Grandma, look at this picture I drew!" Clearly, the grandmother is not currently in the room and cannot see the picture that the child is refer-ring to. Is the child being selfish and not thinking about Grandma? Certainly not! They likely care very much about other people, and yet developmental theory suggests that much of the reason for this behavior is that they cannot hold two different representations in mind at one time. With development of neurological systems, especially those within the prefrontal cortex, children develop more efficient working memory and flexibility in thinking, and therefore ability to hold both their own and other people's perspectives in mind at the same time.

Inhibitory control is also important in the development of perspective taking abilities. Research has shown that these developmental tasks follow a very similar trajectory and both engage the prefrontal cortex (Carlson & Moses, 2001). EF skills in both working memory and inhibitory control predict children's performance on ToM tasks that involve understanding differences between what they and others know (see Box 4.1 for an example). In line with these findings is the idea that children with ADHD or ASD have difficulty with both EF and social functioning. Many theories suggest that one reason is that they struggle to take other people's perspectives. However, recent research suggests that they perform equally well with typically developing children on ToM when the tasks are controlled for attention and inhibition (Mary et al., 2016).

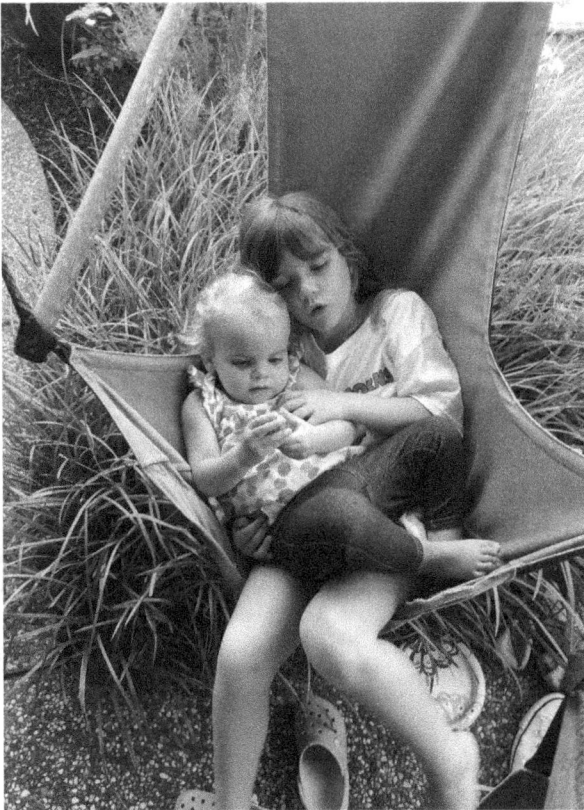

Source: Photograph by author KWA.

Box 4.1 False Belief Understanding

Setting the Stage

A classic measure of the development of theory of mind is referred to as the **false belief task**, in which a child is presented with an object that appears to be something that it is not. During the preschool years, children make marked improvements in false belief understanding, such that 3-year olds might insist they always knew the true identity of the object, whereas 5-year olds more accurately admit they initially believed something that is now known to be false (Frye et al., 1995).

The Research

The following example illustrates the difference in performance between a 4-year-old and a 6-year-old, modeled after this common false belief task (Perner, 1991). Note the clearly stated difference in their understanding that beliefs can be false and how it could lead to advances in social and emotional understanding and therefore, relationships.

Four-year-old exhibiting egocentrism on false belief task

Researcher presents a box that is labeled like a crayon box to the child.
RESEARCHER: What do you think is in the box?
CHILD: Crayons
RESEARCHER: Oh, okay you think there are crayons in the box?
CHILD: Yes
RESEARCHER: Okay, open it up and look.
Child opens the box to discover that inside the box are colorful ribbons.
CHILD: Oh, it's ribbons.
RESEARCHER: Before you opened it, what did you think was in the box?
CHILD: Ribbons.
RESEARCHER: Oh, so you always thought it was ribbons?
CHILD: Yes. Cause it's ribbons.

Note that this child initially stated there were crayons in the box and once learning the box contained ribbons, the child focuses on the current and true knowledge that the box contains ribbons and is unable to recognize their earlier representation was different.

Six-year-old exhibiting false belief understanding

Researcher presents a box that is labeled like a crayon box to the child.
RESEARCHER: What do you think is in the box?

Figure 4.1 False belief research illustration.

CHILD: Crayons
RESEARCHER: Oh, okay you think there are crayons in the box?
CHILD: Yes
RESEARCHER: Okay, open it up and look.
Child opens the box to discover that inside the box are colorful ribbons.
CHILD: Ribbons!
RESEARCHER: Before you opened it, what did you think was in the box?
CHILD: I thought it was crayons! But it's not! It's ribbons.

Note that this child initially stated there were crayons in the box and once learning the box contained ribbons, the child is able to keep in mind both the old and false representation of crayons in the box along with the current and correct representation that the box contains ribbons.

In a more advanced version of this task, children are asked one additional question, "If your friend came in right now and I asked them what was in the box, what would they say?" Note ToM and false belief understanding would allow the child to recognize that the new person would not share their own knowledge, and thus the friend would hold a false belief that the box contained crayons. The younger child would likely egocentrically state that their friend would believe there were ribbons, holding the single and most salient representation in mind. However, the older child would rely on more advanced representational skills to recognize that their own knowledge came from experience and that the friend, who did not have that same experience, would hold a different and false belief that there were crayons in the box, exhibiting false belief understanding.

Application and Reflection

1   Think about how ToM and false belief understanding (or lack thereof) could affect social or emotional interactions in a preschool setting. How might those working with preschoolers use their developmental knowledge to help children engage EFs to regulate emotions, engage in perspective taking, and participate in positive social interactions?
2   Developmentally, preschoolers are egocentric and this book has largely focused on strengths and adaptations of developing humans. Explain how this egocentrism can be considered a strength, helping preschoolers to adapt, learn, and engage at the appropriate cognitive and emotional levels.

EFs begin to have a dramatic impact on children's experience of emotional states, their self-concepts, and how they engage in perspective taking. For example, for a child to experience shame or pride, they must engage in social perspective taking and be able to view themselves from another person's perspective. They can attribute another person's actions to positive or negative intent, and this interpretation is based on social cues as well as past experiences, information they glean from their feelings, and their internal emotional states (Crick & Dodge, 1994). Adolescents continue to grow in these skills between 13 and 18 years of age, with greater perspective taking being linked to feeling better about oneself (Hall et al., 2021). This protracted developmental pattern highlights the importance of parents and professionals supporting continued growth in perspective taking.

Delay of Gratification

We have discussed how learning about ourselves and others, and how our minds work, relies on EF. Initially, infants expect their needs and desires to be met immediately, and yet their growing EF can be used in concert with developing knowledge to support more complex goal-oriented behaviors. The ability to suppress one's immediate desires for a later, more beneficial or larger reward is an important developmental ability referred to as **delay of gratification**. Delay of gratification is linked with important developmental outcomes related to school success, peer relationships, and down the road, even greater social skills. In the real world, infants have to wait for a caregiver to pick them up and preschoolers have to wait their turn to play with the toy, and the complexity of our goals and what will gratify us and the delay we must endure can increase as we age.

Classic research on delay of gratification engages children in a series of tasks in which they must wait for a larger reward (e.g., five candies) while in the presence of a smaller reward (e.g., one candy; e.g., Shoda et al., 1990). Generally, there is a delay imposed of a few minutes, and if the child can wait and not eat the candy in front of them, they get the larger reward. Children's behavior in this task changes as they get older, similar to other complex representational tasks like false belief. As you might imagine, children find the waiting quite stressful and often use different strategies in order to self-regulate. They might talk to themselves, or sing or rock back and forth, or physically avoid looking at the immediate reward. Physiological and observational measures before and during task performance have found that children best able to delay were the most physiologically reactive temperamentally and those that engaged in the greater number of self-soothing behaviors (Santucci et al., 2008). (For a fun break, search for "marshmallow experiment videos" and witness some of the kids' innovative strategies to delay gratification!)

When individuals cannot delay gratification and control their behavior in the interest of a greater goal, consequences can be much more drastic than not getting more candy or marshmallows. For example, a child who needs to finish homework, but reliably cannot delay the gratification of playing video games, will likely struggle with academic achievement over time. In fact, a body of longitudinal research has supported this idea, with lower self-control being related to negative outcomes such as defying rules and social norms even into adulthood (Moffitt et al., 2011). The ability to engage in self-control and delay gratification is also related to taking fewer risks in adolescence, like using drugs or alcohol, and those who are also higher in sensation seeking have the steepest adolescent increase in delay of gratification (Romer et al., 2010). This means that adolescents who are most inclined to seek out high arousal tend to engage their EFs and regulatory systems to match this over time to control this tendency. Consider these ideas in the context of emotional reactivity, as individual differences in regulation are dependent upon multiple systems coordinating over time.

There are a few ways that we can facilitate children's developing ability to delay gratification. First, to help children balance the emotional draw of the reward with their goal, one of the most commonly adopted strategies is distraction. For instance, to support the child who needs to do homework, removing any visual or auditory reference to the video console will allow them to focus on the task of homework without the heat of reward (video games) in their presence. Second, because the ability to delay is tied to both the development of inhibitory control and perspective taking, children can start to distance themselves from the reward by pretending to take another person's perspective. For example, White and colleagues (2017) had children imagine they were Batman, and found that the kids who were able to adopt that perspective were better able to delay gratification— even months later those same kids were better at delaying gratification! Consider how parents and professionals might use these strategies and knowledge of individual differences and rapid development of self-control in adolescence to support people of different ages to engage their inhibitory control to better meet their goals. And as we become better at self-control we also allow more mental space to think about others, which we turn to next.

Empathy

When you see a friend sitting, slumped over and crying, you may actually begin to feel sad and cry along with them. Based on your early experiences, emotional and representational development, self-awareness, and ability to take the perspectives of others, you are now holding in mind what you think your friend is thinking and feeling *and* you are physiologically responding to this representation. Nearly all definitions of **empathy** highlight the importance of perspective taking through the intersubjective emotional sharing that it requires, in that one adopts the subjective feelings of the other. Empathy goes beyond imagining another person's feelings and thoughts to understand what occurred to induce those feelings, recognize our potential role in the person's current state, and "feel with them." These empathic interactions help to shape and are shaped by our understanding of who we are in relation to others, who we like and who likes us back, what is right and wrong, and how we can act on these thoughts to promote the well-being of others.

Empathy can be defined as the ability to share emotional states with others, and it generally involves an affective component (e.g., feelings), a cognitive component (e.g., understanding other's perspectives), and a motivational component (e.g., a drive to care for others). According to Decety (2015), "empathy is also an interpersonal communication system that elicits response from others, helps to determine priorities within relationships, and holds people together in social groups" (p. 1). As such, empathy draws upon all

Source: Shutterstock.

components of EF that we have discussed thus far and also communicates important information to the individual about the social and emotional context. Empathy involves bottom-up processing, which is driven by the sensory experiences from the environment, but also effortful top-down processing, which is driven by higher-level cognitive functions such as inhibitory control and emotion regulation (Tousignant et al, 2017).

The earliest roots of empathy are theorized to be present from birth and include shared emotional responses, or **affective resonance**. Research on this phenomenon illustrates that in the first days of life, newborns can distinguish between their own cries of distress and those of others, and in fact they demonstrate greater distress to the cries of others (Decety, 2010). Research on this shared distress has illustrated that the neurological areas underlying self-reference to one's feelings, specifically the insula as was discussed in a previous section, as well as an area called the **anterior cingulate cortex** (ACC), are both activated when the baby is in distress themselves *and* in response to another's distress (Singer et al., 2004). Important to note about the ACC is that it lies at the interface of the limbic system and the prefrontal cortex; the transaction between the emotional and sensory bottom-up processes relies heavily upon the ACC to reach the prefrontal cortex and EFs.

This affective resonance becomes more sophisticated over time as the baby begins to understand feelings associated with different facial expressions and comprehend the nature of different social scenarios. Further components of empathy emerge early, and by 2 months of age infants experience themselves as a separate being from the environment. They respond differently to their own movements than those of another, although this is well before they are able to verbalize or illustrate mental representations of self. As the infant gains more agency, the interactions with caregivers begin to provide the foundation of this *social biofeedback* as the caregivers provide important mirroring during attunement with the infant (Gergely & Watson, 1996).

Developing empathy thus relies on cognitive and emotional growth within relationships, and empathy is increasingly associated with **prosocial behavior** as children gain social cognitive skills. Prosocial behavior is action designed to help another (Eisenberg et al., 1994). At the individual level, empathy relies upon the person to be able to share perspectives, but not become so overly aroused that they cannot regulate themselves. Therefore, a core ability in prosocial development is emotion regulation in the face of someone else's distress.

Further, empathy can be related to **moral reasoning**, which involves the societal understanding of what is right and wrong and the individual cognitive skill to reason about it from multiple perspectives to decide on the moral course of action. It may seem clear how feeling with another person by engaging in empathy would support more sophisticated moral reasoning; however, there is an alternative argument that empathy may actually interfere with moral reasoning. Think back to hot and cool cognition from previous chapters. Empathy requires sharing another's emotional experience, which makes this a hot representation and so it comes with the additional cognitive load of regulation. Moral reasoning would benefit from taking other perspectives, but adding this burden to EF, especially for developing infants and children, may be problematic. Further, imagine the burden of hot representation that would come from empathically feeling with the victims, family, and friends suffering from the most recent international tragedy. Perhaps instead, *sympathy* facilitates moral reasoning and could be more productive in such situations: with sympathy, we understand how someone else might be feeling, and reason about the morally correct actions to take, while not personally taking on those emotions (Decety, 2015).

Empathy continues to develop throughout childhood, building on social behaviors of the self and others, regulatory and EF skills, and increased capacity for moral reasoning. As children go through adolescence and into adulthood, their appraisal of negative experience is less dramatic, emotion processing areas of the brain less reactive, and their prefrontal cortex is more active in regions associated with cognitive control and EF (Decety & Michalska, 2010). Empathy develops from an innate and automatic sharing of affective responses, similar to the forms of infant imitation as we discussed in Chapter 3, to more modulated top-down EF processes of taking others' perspectives, making sense of them, regulating one's own emotional reactions to others' distress, and engaging in appropriate action. These aspects of empathy draw upon prefrontal cortex functions in an effortful top-down manner and to help modulate our reactions to other's emotions and help us to build social relationships. Figure 4.2 points out some important areas of the brain for emotion processing.

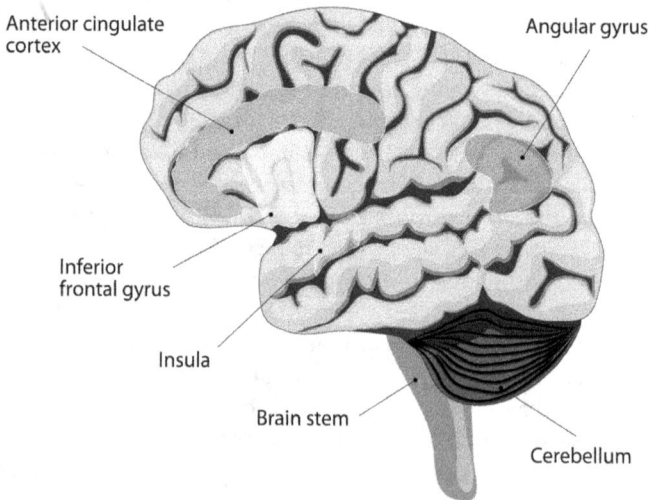

Figure 4.2 Emotion processing in the brain.
Source: Shutterstock.

Peer Relationships

All of the skills discussed so far in this chapter play a role in children's ability to engage with peers, which is among the most important social outcomes for human development. Having friends and feeling like a valued member of a social group is critical to our sense of self-worth, identity development, and well-being. Conversely, those experiencing negative peer interactions, such as increased peer-rejection and peer-victimization are more likely to develop lasting dysfunctional behaviors (externalizing; aggression, conduct problems) or thoughts (internalizing, anxiety and depression (Deater-Deckard, 2001)) and lower effortful control skills (Iyer et al., 2010).

A large body of research has supported the connection between EF and peer relationships (Holmes et al, 2016), all of which are tied to representational skills, perspective taking, and social and emotional functioning. For example, lower skills in ToM and perspective taking are related to more negative peer interactions, especially peer rejection and peer victimization (Fahie & Symons, 2003). Importantly, being able to regulate behavior and emotional arousal is critical to having successful peer relationships, as those children who struggle with self-control and behavioral regulation are at risk of alienating classmates and diminishing opportunities to form strong friendships (Blair et al., 2016). Research involving both preschoolers and primary school students suggests that children with poor self-control experienced more peer exclusion, and lower self-control was associated with later peer rejection. Further, adolescents who experience peer conflict engage in more risky behaviors, although it is important to note that having peer support can reduce the negative effects of conflict (Telzer et al., 2015).

What is particularly interesting in this research is that the relationship between EF and peer relationships appears to be reciprocal. Social interaction offers children and adolescents opportunities for learning and practicing important interpersonal skills and self-control, empathy and perspective taking, and scaffolding experiences that can affect working memory (Lecce et al., 2018). For example, dramatic play in childhood affects self-regulation, as children get the chance to envision social and emotional scenarios and explore their own ability to regulate the physiological arousal that comes with that (Walden & Smith, 1997). They get practice modulating their emotions and adapting their language and communication to fit the social context and relationships in the setting. Therefore, EF seems to influence peer relationships, and opportunities for positive peer interactions reciprocally affect the development of EF.

Recent research has asserted that perhaps one of the most important predictors of positive social emotional outcomes has to do with the internalization of prosocial behavior. For example, when children are motivated by their own internal representations of how they *should* behave and have the opportunity to practice these behaviors in both rituals such as circle-time at school or pretend play situations, they adopt these prosocial beliefs as part of their own scripts of how they *should* behave, which become habits. Caregivers can support these growing empathic connections through perspective taking skills. They can also promote play that affords the opportunity to develop agency, self-efficacy, and self-regulation strategies in the face of emotions, and EFs can be well situated to support positive peer relationships and prosocial behavior (Eisenberg et al., 2006).

Contextual Foundations of Social Cognitive Development

As has been a theme throughout this book, human development involves the dynamic transaction among individual characteristics and multiple levels of context over time (Thelen & Smith, 2006). Social cognitive development is no different from this general pattern, and this means that even children of the same age or living in the same difficult situation will react differently based on their own dynamic processes. Much of this has been included in our discussion as we have detailed the social-cognitive concepts of sense of self, perspective taking, delay of gratification, empathy, and peer relationships. Each of these social-cognitive domains relies on cognitive, emotional, and EF skills that unfold across the lifespan and thus show up in unique ways in each individual human. Rather than repeat these ideas here, we will provide an example of how a specific person-factor and then a specific context influences social cognition.

Person-Factor: Autism Spectrum Disorder

As we have discussed, social cognition helps us understand and predict who we are, how others think, feel, and behave, and how we fit in our world. We depend upon our developing social-cognitive skills to navigate relationships with others, and when these social cognitive skills lack maturity because of age or other challenges, it can be difficult to form and maintain relationships. Recall from Chapter 1 that a hallmark feature of people with ASD is problems with social communication and social interactions (American Psychiatry Association, 2013). Imagine how social interactions are for a child with ASD who has not yet learned how to read the expressions, body language, or emotional tone of others. People with ASD tend to struggle with ToM by taking an intellectual focus on relationships rather than understanding the other as one with potentially valid, but different, feelings and perspectives. People with ASD may seem unemotional and yet prosocial behavior is still entirely possible because they can use rule-based behaviors and moral reasoning. Amari from Chapter 1 is a great example—his mother reported that he is very engaged in social justice action.

Research has suggested for many years that EF difficulties are a central component in social difficulties in children with ASD. However, more recent neurological research in ASD has pointed out that EF difficulties may be an outcome and not a cause of these social difficulties. In fact, across children with and without ASD, inhibition, attention-shifting, and emotional control are related to behavioral dysregulation and social problems (Leung et al., 2016). And yet, specific to children with ASD, metacognitive strategies and higher order EFs, such as planning, are specifically associated with social functioning in children with ASD (Leung et al., 2016). This indicates that specific types of trainings may be helpful for children with autism to increase EF and thus, relational skills. For example, training on use of body language, tone of voice, and facial expression may induce a more metacognitive approach to social interactions.

Box 4.2 Social Cognition and Emerging Adulthood

Setting the Stage

E.M. is a 20-year-old working professional living local to her home. She received an early diagnosis of ADHD and then later she was diagnosed with ASD. She excelled in school, but struggled to feel motivated to earn high grades and sometimes, even to attend classes. E.M. is well-regarded by family members. She enjoys art and making people laugh.

Interview

DR O'HARA: What are your earliest memories of EF difficulties?

E.M.: Well, a big thing about EF problems is it does make you struggle with your memory. So, I don't have a lot of early memories of EF, but in school I had a lot of missing assignments. I struggled with initiation of tasks, and that was really noticeable in school.

DR O'HARA: What about as a little kid?

E.M.: I don't remember being a kid.

DR O'HARA: How did your family support you?

E.M.: I was lucky to get diagnosed with ADHD pretty early in life, because it's pretty underdiagnosed in women especially, so I was lucky enough to get diagnosed before the age of 10.

DR O'HARA: So your family helped you by getting you to doctors?

E.M.: Yes, and helping me to get on medication and reminding me of when I had to do things. That really helped. What didn't help was when I … (pause) forgot to do things, my mom would make me feel guilty about it. Instead of understanding that there is a pac man in my brain that just kind of "bop bop bop" makes me forget to do things …

DR O'HARA: So they didn't understand your condition that well, and didn't know how to motivate you?

E.M.: Yes.

DR O'HARA: How has EF affected your emotional well-being?

E.M.: It definitely contributes to feelings of guilt, for when you forget to do things, and people make you feel like you did it on purpose, but you didn't, you just forgot. Even ... it really drains your motivation and your self-esteem. Cause, like even if you want to do something, it can hinder you from doing it, and it makes it really hard to get out of bed in the morning. It makes it hard to get the motivation to do anything sometimes. It's definitely gotten worse over time, I'd say.

DR O'HARA: What has contributed to it getting worse, do you think?

E.M.: Uh, adding of responsibilities as I get older. Like I'm not legally required to go to school anymore, so ... (pause) ... sigh ... so it's kind of... there's no legally keeping me to a schedule. So it's my responsibility to find a job and keep a job, which are tasks of their own, and I ... so ... my mental health has definitely declined through the latter-half of my schooling, and after.

DR O'HARA: In what ways has it declined? What do you struggle with?

E.M.: Depression mostly. I got diagnosed with social anxiety in middle-school, but looking back that might have just been autism.

DR O'HARA: Autism-spectrum that went undiagnosed, molded into ADHD and social anxiety ...

E.M.: Yeah.

DR O'HARA: How has it affected your social development? And give some examples.

E.M.: Umm ... definitely, even if I want to start conversations with people, I don't have the energy to do it. And being able to pay attention enough to the conversation to build meaningful relationships is really, really hard. So I lose touch pretty easily with my friends.

DR O'HARA: You talked before about worrying about people not liking you ...

E.M.: Yeah, because I hear people complaining about people, "oh, I hate it when people flake on other people, or leave the on 'read'" or when people (sigh) they do this specific thing, and then I look back and go, "oh, I do that ..." But then you acknowledge ... you don't say it to the person's face. And I think, how do I know that they're not complaining about me doing that?

DR. O'HARA: So you're saying you have trouble making friends, and initiating social engagement, and then when you do ... you have trouble maintaining it?

E.M.: Yeah.

DR O'HARA: What is your advice for teenagers struggling with these problems? What would you tell them?

E.M.: I'd tell them, "You'll get through this. I know it seems like the world is ending, but it's not."

DR O'HARA: What advice would you give them ... what to do?

E.M.: What to do? ... umm ... have a designated person to just kind of poke you, and like hey, you were gonna do that! Hey, you were gonna do that! Ohhhh ... I was supposed to do that!!! yesss!!

DR O'HARA: Who does that for you?

E.M.: (laughs) Mostly my mom. Uh, but a friend can also be really helpful, like if you want to do homework, just doing homework in the vicinity of other people doing homework. Not even, it doesn't have to be doing it together, they don't have to be helping you they just have to be nearby. Like a reminder of what you're doing...

DR O'HARA: Like just setting up the situation to remind you ...

E.M.: Yes.

DR O'HARA: What about advice for their parents or teachers?

E.M.: Have patience. That's really the biggest advice to be patient with us ... to quote (comedian) "I also don't want me to be doing what I'm doing ..." (laughs).

DR O'HARA: (Laughs) ... okay. I hear you saying ...

E.M.: I hear you honking ...

DR O'HARA: What about helping them to manage their emotional health?

E.M.: Please start conversations with us ... you might have to take the lead on a lot of conversations. And words of affirmation are generally a good way to go.

DR O'HARA: What about specifically with EF? Not the social anxiety so much ...

E.M.: Lists!!! Like a whiteboard, in a space that's kind of out there. But like put things that may not be obvious to you, but that we will forget to do. Like, "eat food!" or "Brush your teeth!" Uhh ... remember you have to pee at some time. Drink water!"

DR O'HARA: What about interpersonally, what can they do? Like can they encourage you or force you to do things?

E.M.: That's not always the way to do it. Sometimes you're gonna drag your kid along and they're just gonna be miserable. And you didn't do anything wrong, you just have to be understanding and let your kid cool down. Cause, if something's overstimulating for them. This may be less EF and more just autism.

E.M.: Sometimes I can't tell the difference between under-stimulated and over-stimulated. Like "am I bored, or is there ... too much or is there too little? What is happening?"

DR O'HARA: And so that's kind of like the EF problems in autism?

E.M.: Yeah ... autism is the upper-barrier, and EF is the lower-barrier.

DR O'HARA: Okay, explain that.

E.M.: There's a lower barrier of under-stimulation in ADHD, there's a lower barrier of under-stimulation because we get bored really, really easily. So if we're under-stimulated things go south fast ... but with autism there is an upper barrier with overstimulation and if you get above that barrier, things go south fast ...

DR O'HARA: I see, so you have to zero-in on that perfect threshold ...

E.M.: Yeah, It's like flappy bird. In that it's really difficult and eternally frustrating for anyone trying to do it. It's gonna go wrong, and hope you don't throw your phone against the wall!!

Application and Reflection

1   E.M. has had many different challenges. Consider what she shared about her experiences with ADHD, ASD, anxiety, depression, and mood disorders.

    a   Which of these diagnoses are related to (or not) her inhibitory func-
tion? Are there specific examples from her narrative that you can
highlight to illustrate this?

    b   Which of these diagnoses are related to (or not) her working memory
and its capacity and speed limitations? Are there specific examples from
her narrative that you can highlight to illustrate this?

    c   Which of these diagnoses are related to (or not) her flexibility in
thinking? Are there specific examples from her narrative that you can
highlight to illustrate this?

2   After reviewing the interview, in what ways might E.M. exhibit strength from
within and in what ways does she share that her community and context supported her growth? As you reflect on this, consider your profession of interest
and how you might use what you have learned from this woman's experiences.

Context: Home

Self-awareness, social perspective taking, self-control, empathy, and peer relationships are important aspects of social-cognitive development, all relying of EF and
developing within the increasingly broad context as infants grow into adults. The
specific example of context we are using here is the home—it is the earliest context and one of the most lasting contexts for social cognitive growth. Developing
in a home that causes chronic distress has important implications for EF, biology,
and overall well-being (e.g., Andrews et al., 2021)—these contexts are discussed
elsewhere and so here, we focus on how homes of all economic or cultural backgrounds can provide tools for infants, children, and adolescents to use as they
develop in their ability to form and maintain social relationships.

    In the earliest weeks and months, the ways in which caregivers interact
with infants have lasting consequences for models of the self and other on
which much of social cognition is built (Bowlby, 1969). As top-down,
effortful processes develop, children become better able to represent more
complex ideas about people or objects out of sight, then about feelings or
behaviors out of sight, and finally, differentiate between what is real and
how that can be different from what is in the mind (DeLoache, 2004).
Play can be particularly important to engage in role-taking, try on behaviors without the same risk as in real life, and to learn from and model
behaviors (Piaget, 1954). It also provides a way to practice using working
memory, inhibition and regulation, and thinking in flexible ways
(Vygotsky, 1978). Ultimately, when children are encouraged to explore,
EFs and higher-order cognitive functions like metacognition increase
(Marulis et al., 2020). Although homes or early care centers do not need
sophisticated toys or learning activities, providing an emotionally and physically safe space for play is critical.

Source: Photograph by author KWA.

As social cognitive skills continue to flourish, children are better able to delay gratification by planning and using self-control, engage more complex representational skills to identify the emotions of others and feel with them, and engage in behaviors that promote social relationships. With a focus on the home, modeling and directly teaching strategies for regulation, talking about emotions and feelings to make explicit what is happening in the mind (Fivush & Nelson, 2004), and providing feedback on positive and negative relational skills promote EF and social cognition.

Careers and Executive Function

Within any context serving infants, children, youth, and families, social cognitive development is critical. Professionals working in hospital, therapeutic, educational, or home settings with infants and caregivers can foster attunement and agency. Occupational therapists can work on sensory integration to promote EF and create more space for engaging in social cognition. Additionally, across contexts this knowledge can be used to help children develop strategies for problem solving and regulation, including pausing to create time for planning and goal-setting, writing to decrease the load on working memory, and using play to teach new ideas in an engaging way (Hughes, 2023).

Adolescence is a period of great change in many ways. Puberty comes with changes in hormones and the body and continued rapid reorganization of the prefrontal cortex. Because of the importance of the prefrontal cortex in EF and social cognition, it is logically also a time of drastic change in those skills (Blakemore & Choudhury, 2006). Recall that we can process information more quickly, hold more in mind, and organize knowledge more efficiently in adolescence and beyond. And yet, adolescence is characterized not only by social-cognitive advancement, but also a renewed sense of egocentrism (Piaget, 1954) and increased risk-taking behaviors. In fact, one theory for increased risk-taking behaviors involves remodeled neurotransmitter systems in the brain that require greater levels of inhibitory control (Steinberg, 2008). Taking a Systems theoretical approach, professionals partnering with adolescents and emerging adults can capitalize on the strength of their clients' complex representational skills while also recognizing the need for those skills to become coordinated for synchronous function.

Summary

Social cognition is the result of days, weeks, months, and years of biological, emotional, and cognitive growth within a context. It helps us to know who we are and forms the foundations on which we will ultimately define our own identities. Social cognition comes together to help us understand other people, what or how they are thinking, and whether we feel similarly. This growing self-awareness and perspective taking graduates into self-control as we learn that we do not always get what we want, and so goals may require waiting to achieve. Our greater representational abilities and increased working memory, inhibitory control, and cognitive flexibility help us to understand what others are feeling and use this understanding to think about right and wrong and how to behave to achieve our goals. All of this comes together in one of the most critical outcomes of childhood—forming peer relationships. We all come into the world with a different set of biological and contextual resources, and it is through the interplay of these resources that we are all unique. Leveraging these resources can provide parents and professionals the opportunity to walk alongside humans at any age to support well-being.

Further Resources

Thompson, R.A. (2018). *Social-emotional development in the first three years: Establishing the foundations.* Edna Bennett Pierce Prevention Research Center, Pennsylvania State University.

Gottlieb, A., & DeLoache, J. (2016). *A world of babies: Imagined childcare guides for eight societies* (2nd ed.). Cambridge: Cambridge University Press.

Chapter 5

Applications of Executive Function within Careers that Involve Direct Work with Children, Adolescents, and Families

Previous chapters detailed what EF is and how it is interrelated to biological, emotional, social, and cognitive development in typically developing children and those at promise. Recall from Chapter 1 that *at promise* is a term used to focus on the developmental potential of people who might encounter difficulties (e.g., Swadener, 2012). This chapter discusses specific ways parents and professionals can facilitate EF in various contexts through direct interactions. The next chapter will provide suggestions for affecting infants, children, adolescents, and families indirectly though alterations in contextual factors.

Theoretical Model for Application

To frame our discussion of application, we will emphasize the importance of developmental processes highlighted in systems-like theories of development. Bronfenbrenner and Morris (2006) argue for the dynamic and transactive role of the person in multiple nested contexts engaging in interactive processes over

Source: Shutterstock.

DOI: 10.4324/9781003131052-5

time. The term *dynamic* highlights the importance of changing and adapting over time, and *transactive* emphasizes that each part both impacts and is impacted by all other parts. Recognizing *multiple nested contexts* underscores the different ways humans interact with direct contacts and how even indirect or outer contexts (parent's job, policies around education) play a role in human development. In adapting this model to human development in diverse groups of children and families, there is a recognition of the critical role of the **context** in which a **person** participates in **processes** over **time**, illustrated in Figure 5.1. Of note, over the course of the development of a human, the person becomes more complex because of the constant interaction between and within multiple contexts, and knowing these intricacies will allow parents and professionals to identify when, where, and how to best support EF development and thus, human development as a whole.

Context

Contexts of development can be intimate, such as a family, or increasingly broad to include neighborhood, social structures, laws, and societal and cultural norms (Bronfenbrenner & Morris, 2006). The family level, which can be a particularly important and insular context for marginalized youth, provides values, socialization, socio-economic status, and contributions to development of assets and competencies for healthy development and coping (Garcia Coll & Szalacha, 2004). As we know, these factors are directly relevant to how EF develops and can provide guidelines for how professionals partner with families in promoting healthy development. These more intimate contexts will be considered further within later sections of this chapter.

Considered as one of the broadest levels of context has typically been culture, providing societal norms and practices, and for people who have been marginalized by racism, segregation, and environments that inhibit their healthy development, this level can be particularly important in also potentially providing a culture of adaptability and environments that promote individual strengths (Garcia Coll & Szalacha, 2004). Moreover, some theorists suggest that culture embeds ways of learning and that passing such ways and tools to new generations occurs within communities, but at the individual level as they engage in processes (Gutiérrez & Rogoff, 2003). These broader contextual levels will be considered further in Chapter 6. Before moving on to the role of the individual, it is important to note the importance of this theoretical perspective for professionals working with children, teens, and families in diverse settings as they work to foster individual strengths by engaging with communities to learn their ways of doing and their needs to provide effective policies and practices in working with various communities.

Person

The person brings with them the biological foundations, behavioral proclivities (tendencies), and their lived history (Bronfenbrenner & Morris, 2006).

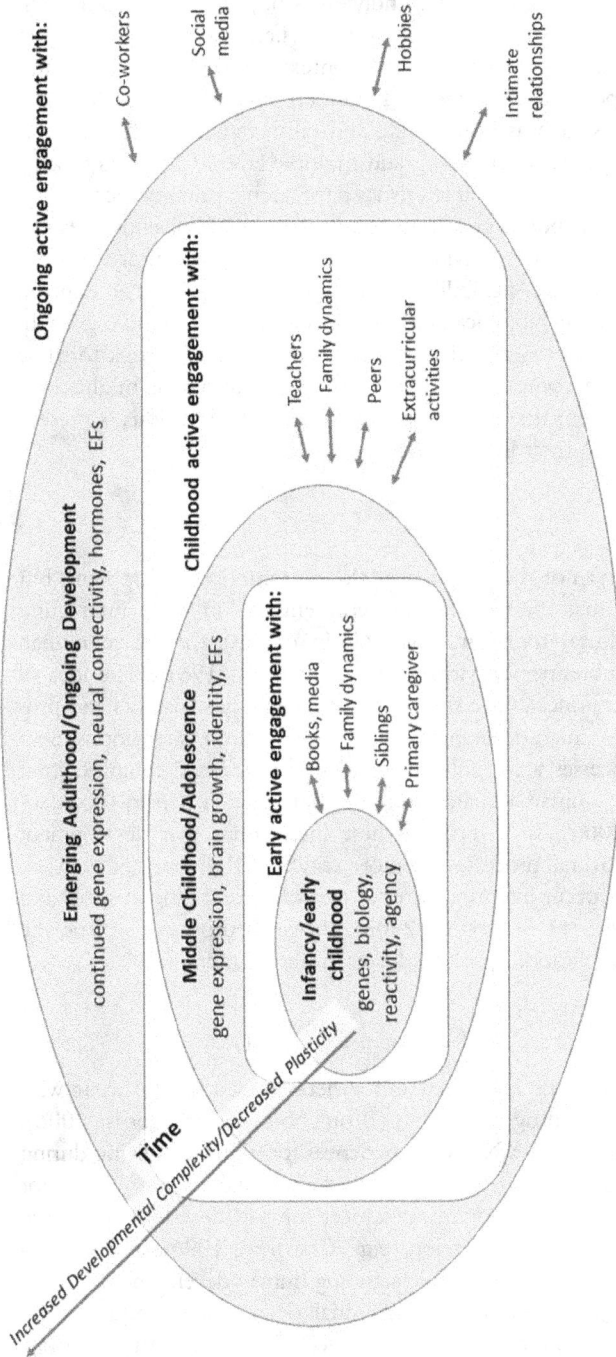

Figure 5.1 Time radiates outward from infancy/early childhood. As internal developmental proclivities of the individual interact with the environment through active engagement of the developing human with their context, those internal proclivities become more complex and serve as foundations for subsequent engagement with the environment. Adult EFs are based on these ongoing interactive processes over time, and parents and professionals can support interactive processes at any point in development.

Source: Based on models by Bronfenbrenner, Garcia Coll, Rogoff.

Important, then, is the recognition that individuals have membership in multiple cultural or identity groups at the same time (i.e., intersectionality), and this creates multiple and overlapping nested contexts, which then affect individual practices and personal characteristics (Gutiérrez & Rogoff, 2003). And so, child characteristics such as health, age, and temperament both influence, and are influenced by, these overlapping and multiple layered contexts (Garcia Coll & Szalacha, 2004). Person characteristics have been a primary focus of the first four chapters of this book, providing details about the behaviors, resources, and demands brought by individuals as they develop inhibitory control, working memory, cognitive flexibility, and higher-level executive control, within the context of their biological, emotional, social, and cognitive growth. Practical suggestions made later in the current chapter will refer back to these person characteristics in context, and illustrate how professionals might draw upon these within a **strengths-based** approach, seeing the individual's present state as an adaptation to their lived history.

Process

It is neither the context nor the person that alone promotes development, but rather, the processes that the person repeatedly engages in while interacting with the people, cultural tools, and symbols in context that drive human development (Bronfenbrenner & Morris, 2006; Vygotsky, 1981). The idea of **proximal processes** provides a nice theoretical model for how parents and professionals can support human development within these direct interactions. Specifically, proximal processes are regularly occurring, increasingly complex, joint interactions between a human and an object, symbol or other person (Bronfenbrenner & Morris, 2006). It is through these interactions that development occurs, and in fact, proximal processes are more critical to development than the context alone and may occur intentionally or as part of participating in social and cultural activities (Gutiérrez & Rogoff, 2003). Proximal processes will be the focus of many of the applications presented later in this chapter.

Time

Timing is critical at both the individual and societal level; changes occur with historical time and with ontogenetic time (Bronfenbrenner & Morris, 2006). **Historical time** provides a set of shared experiences for individuals living during that period, such as significant historical events and availability of technology. For example, increased use of technological tools over the past decades impacts the way humans think, interact, and develop (e.g., Crawford, 1996), and so considering historical timing is critical to understanding human development.

Ontogenetic time is the course of individual development, highlighting milestones reached by a human throughout development. For instance, once a human reaches puberty, there are associated physical, hormonal, and cognitive changes that are expected at that time (e.g., Worthman et al., 2019). Of note, ontogenetic time has been a major focus of this book thus far as we discussed different developmental periods and changes that occur in person characteristics of biology, emotion, and social and cognitive understanding, as this book is written to be applied within the modern 21st century. The careers discussed within these pages largely focus on ontogenetic development as well; although historical time will be discussed briefly in the next chapter as related to the "big picture" and as critical for professionals working with groups of people who share a common history of interacting within their world with a common set of tools (Gutiérrez & Rogoff, 2003).

Executive Function and Proximal Processes in Real World Professions

The goal of this book is to apply our knowledge of EF to the real world with humans experiencing a variety of conditions that affect and reflect EF. This can include humans of various ages exhibiting typical individual differences as well as those overcoming challenges, such as infants who have signs of autism, preschoolers experiencing trauma, children with learning disabilities, teens undergoing serious medical procedures, or emerging adults facing housing insecurity. Let's quickly review what we know about the first eight years of life:

1   the brain, and particularly the prefrontal cortex, is increasing in complexity, connectivity, efficiency, and function;
2   function of the prefrontal cortex is directly related to improvements in inhibitory control, working memory, and cognitive shifting during the preschool years;
3   episodic memory improves greatly in accuracy and completeness during the preschool years;
4   language plays a critical role in learning appropriate social and cultural tool use and shapes cognition and EF;
5   the prefrontal cortex is formed and modified based on early experience, including synchronous interactions with caregivers and a trusting and secure early relationship;
6   self-regulation is governed by EF as emotions, physiological reactivity, and knowledge of the self and other grow;
7   increased emotional and cognitive skills draw on EF to support more complex understandings of the self, other, and how to interact with the world around us.

This book takes two approaches to apply the knowledge in previous chapters. On the one hand, some professions operate within the external layer of the contextual model and can have broad but *indirect* effects on human development. Discerning the role of EF across domains and over time will assist

Source: Shutterstock.

professionals in developing practices, policies, expectations, and laws that adequately promote emotional, physiological, social, and cognitive growth. On the other hand, understanding EF development will assist professionals with *directly* supporting strong EF skills in clients. That is, some professions work directly with developing humans and their families by engaging in proximal processes that support strengths and develop assets. The remainder of the current chapter will focus on some of these direct and micro-level careers, and for the sake of clarity, we have divided them into five contexts: Education, Psychological and Mental Health, Government and Law, Health Care and Physical Well-Being, and Home.

Education

Education is a broad context that includes a variety of careers that require an understanding of EF to effectively and directly interact with children and youth. Whereas some subjects in school might be assessed and treated separately (if reading is a particular challenge, students may work with a reading specialist), EF is broader and cuts across subjects as it affects those over-arching control functions that apply to multiple academic domains (Bierman & Torres, 2016) and across phases of life. Many existing resources focus on educators' understanding of EF and integration of this knowledge with their practice (see Additional Readings at the end of this chapter); however, in this section we provide explicit connection to material from previous chapters for those working within the field of education. Some careers in this field include infant and toddler caregivers, teachers, administrators, education specialists (special education teachers), and paraprofessionals and aides.

In the school context, students spend hours trying to focus attention, learn, link new and old ideas, and organize knowledge in way it can be recalled and even transformed into new ideas. In this way, emotion and behavioral regulation, attentional control, working memory speed and capacity, and flexibility of thinking affect when and how children learn to read, write, and perform mathematical functions (e.g., Cortés Pascual et al., 2019). The *person* (student) must be engaged with the *process* (person interacting with material) within this educational *context* over *time* in order to think in increasingly complex ways. Thus, educators with knowledge of interrelations can make specific applications to teaching, learning, and creating a safe and inclusive environment within the classroom, school, and community. The more educational professionals know about EF and its role in learner behaviors, the better they can support students' success across educational contexts.

Early Childhood Education

The field of early childhood education serves the specific needs of infants, preschoolers, and young children aged 0 to 8 years. As prior chapters have shown, early childhood provides a foundation for later EF and thus is a topic of critical concern for social and cultural development across emotional, regulatory, social, and cognitive domains. We can add to this knowledge some specific information about how EF supports academic performance. As discussed briefly in Chapter 2, EF, early math skills, and emerging literacy serve one another during the preschool years (Blair & Razza, 2007). Learning is highly regulated by motivation to engage with the material, and so educational professionals who create environments that invite children to take an active role in their own learning and a context that encourages and fosters connection between the school with homes, neighborhoods, and communities may best serve students. For example, a play-based environment that is heavily supported with classroom tools and by teachers who scaffold student application improves EF in the early years (Diamond et al., 2007). Tools in such a classroom include drawing and pretend play across the curriculum, which helps students self-regulate and apply EF to learning (Bodrova & Leong, 2006).

Because temperamental effortful control is related to EF, it is also considered a more biologically rooted trait and thus supporting greater effortful control within the early classroom setting may differ according to the child. We have learned that self-regulation (as measured by temperamental effortful control) predicts better academic performance (Blair & Razza, 2007). Consider the sensitive child who is higher in behavioral inhibition and needs a quiet setting versus the preschooler lower in behavioral inhibition who is less reactive and thus can handle or even crave more "busyness." A classroom environment would be inclusive and promote healthy development by providing a learning context with varied opportunities for attuned interactions with professionals and peers, and greater EF can actually reduce stress and promote learning (Cumming et al., 2020).

Diamond and Lee (2011) reviewed numerous techniques to administer in an early childhood classroom and provided specific observations on the most successful supports. First, improvement is greatest for those with more challenges (e.g., low income, ADHD) and when implemented consistently with increasing challenge and across academic subjects. Second, EF training can be implemented seamlessly in typical classroom structures and does not require a specialized teacher, but rather someone who is invested in learning and providing developmentally appropriate supports. Finally, to be developmentally appropriate and inclusive of a variety of student needs, training or support needs to be implemented without requiring long periods of sitting (remember young kids are still developing their ability to sustain attention and inhibit behaviors!).

Elementary and Secondary Education

EF in early childhood predicts academic performance later in life; and yet, EF continues to mature and be modified according to experience. As EF improves, it continues to relate directly to academic performance, with working memory most broadly related to academics, and inhibition and flexible thinking varying depending on task and age group (Spiegel et al., 2021). Elementary and secondary education begins to broaden the social world and also encompasses the biological changes associated with puberty in adolescence, causing a cascade of physical, emotional, and cognitive changes as well. Administrators, teachers, extended care aides (before or after school), paraprofessionals and support staff, and education specialists supporting students with mild, moderate, or extensive support needs are some of the professionals that work directly with students in Kindergarten through secondary school.

Whether a child enters formal schooling with strong EF or needs further support, training is helpful. Many studies show that general training in working memory, or even training on a specific aspect of working memory (i.e., visuo-spatial or phonological) can have broad and lasting effects on other EFs as well as relational, behavioral, emotional, and cognitive outcomes. These effects can be particularly pronounced for children with attention deficits (e.g., ADHD), but can bolster students from all backgrounds (Diamond, 2013). For example, training within an elementary classroom setting in visuo-spatial and phonological working memory over a period of five weeks produced lasting improvements across domains, including over-arching EFs such as inhibition and self-regulation (Berger et al., 2020). This training was a paid service, however, and may be challenging for teachers to implement without funding. Other studies have found similar results by using free apps (e.g., Judd et al., 2021). An important takeaway from this research is that consistent training in working memory can be a worthwhile curricular element in elementary and secondary schools.

Interesting findings relate improved EF to some specific physical activities that could be inclusively and systematically offered within a school setting. For example, Tae Kwon Do (versus other physical education activities) has been linked to improved cognitive and behavioral regulation and working memory, especially in middle childhood (Lakes & Hoyt, 2004). Although Tae Kwon Do requires special training and may not be feasible for many schools to implement, other school-based mindfulness practices have improved EF. Specifically, practicing yoga predicts improved EF (and mental health) both at home and in the classroom across neurodiverse and typically developing students (Hart et al., 2022).

Source: Shutterstock.

Higher Education

Post-secondary education in colleges, universities, and trade schools continues to rely on and foster EF. Careers within these settings include instructors, support staff (e.g., advisors, peer mentors), and outreach professionals. Post-secondary students use EF to plan classes and set goals, manage their time and resources, attend to learning materials and inhibit distractions, regulate emotions and behaviors, and use memory and language to think abstractly and transform their knowledge. Evidence for EF and higher education falls primarily into two categories:

1 Typically developing students with varying levels of EF show greater levels of concentration, time management, and test taking skills and lower regulation with lower EF (Petersen et al., 2006); and
2 Students with particular challenges to EF exhibit specific problems in academics as well as marked improvement with training. For example, in

university students with ADHD, inattention is particularly problematic for academic success (Henning et al., 2022). In students with special needs, executive function and self-regulation are among the top predictors of success and completion (Moriña & Biagiotti, 2021).

Some practical applications of this knowledge that involve direct interaction with students can occur at programmatic and classroom levels. Within institutional programs, support staff and outreach professionals work with students to understand course schedules and available tools and physical and mental health training, particularly to help students plan schedules and work toward goals (e.g., Parker & Boutelle, 2009). Within the classroom, institutions can arrange the classrooms with learning tools and spaces that permit clarity, lack of distraction, and multiple modality instruction to help regulate inhibitory control, regulation, and optimize working memory. Instructors can help students adjust to learning independently as well as use engaging materials, which should promote active learning to improve concentration (Burke & Ray, 2008), and materials should vary according to subject to support abstract thinking.

Box 5.1 School Administration as a Microsystem

Setting the Stage

Mason Combe (M.C.) is an administrator in a diverse region of Southern California. He grew up near the area in a middle-income household with his two parents and two siblings. Upon graduation from high school, he moved about an hour away to attend college and earn his Bachelor's degree in Physics. He began teaching high school physics upon graduation, while also earning his single-subject teaching credential. He later went on to earn his MA in Education (emphasis on Educational Administration) and then Ph.D. in Leadership Studies. After his years as a high school teacher, he moved into administration as a vice principal, and he currently serves as principal for a K-8 school.

Interview

DR ALEXANDER: What is your field and how long have you been in this field?

M.C.: I am currently working in my 27th year as an educator. I taught for a year in my home town, then I moved to a nearby district high school and taught there for almost 20 years. I left my teaching position to serve as "teacher on special assignment" at a newer, virtual school, where I oversaw the entire program, essentially as the administrator, but without the title or pay.
(laughter)

After 2 ½ years there, I got a job as an assistant principal at a district middle school, and then 3 years later I was promoted to principal of a local elementary school. Due to the pandemic, demand for the virtual school I had previously served at was very high, so I took a position as the principal of the newly relaunched school. I am currently there as the principal for TK-8 grades.

DR ALEXANDER: You started in the field as a teacher. Can you tell us about that?

M.C.: I started teaching as soon as I graduated from college, without any experience or any training. I taught for one year at a high school near the one I attended myself, with a schedule of four periods of integrated science and one period of biology for students who had failed the previous year. It was challenging for two main reasons.

I did not have the proper training; I started teaching straight out of college. I drew from my experience as a student, which did not align with the student population I was serving. As a student, I took mostly honors courses; the courses I taught were college preparatory, but not advanced or honors.

Also, integrated science required knowledge of all the sciences and I only felt equipped to teach the physical sciences. Teaching biological and earth sciences was challenging. Another difficulty was the lack of a textbook to help guide the course. I was surprised to find out there wasn't a "playbook" to help guide you through what to teach each day.

DR ALEXANDER: Wow, that is a lot for a first-year teacher. How did it go after that?

M.C.: In my second year of teaching, I moved to a different district, and so a different high school. There, I taught integrated science and AP Physics. (Advanced Placement (AP) courses prepare high school students for a standardized exam that awards university level credit, depending on the score earned and university later attended.) There was definitely a difference in the students who took AP Physics compared to the students who took integrated science.

DR ALEXANDER: Can you describe your student body and your co-workers?

M.C.: My first school had very diverse student demographics. The school had the highest percentage of Hispanic students—I'm guessing, but it was probably around 60% and about 10% African American students. There was also a high percentage of students who were classified as low socio-economic. I did not fully understand the challenges those students faced. I remember being appalled that only 3 students had completed my homework assignment. I know now that those students probably had many barriers to completing homework that were out of their control. Most students learned only when they were in school. Student attendance was inconsistent.

DR ALEXANDER: Was the student population similar the next year, when you went to the other high school?

M.C.: When I first started at the next high school, the population was completely different. There were many class sections of honors and AP classes. Many students had strong support at home and the resources to get extra help if needed. However, student demographics here changed over the 20 years I was there to look a lot closer to the population I served during my first year.

DR. ALEXANDER: And what did your virtual program look like when you served on special assignment? That was before COVID, so things were probably different.

M.C.: The student population at the virtual school was unique. There were two "schools." One was dedicated to full time enrollment. There were only about 120 students in the program. Most of the students were there for social reasons—either they just didn't fit in at an in-person school, or they had anxiety or other issues that made it difficult to attend in person.

DR ALEXANDER: You have sought out a lot of training and schooling since those early years. How does your experience and knowledge help you now?

M.C.: Over my career, I have come to realize that limited resources, individual differences, and executive functioning have a tremendous impact on student learning and growth. Students with limited resources face a few different challenges. Some of them do not have the resources for supplies or extra things that make it easier to work. At that time some students had a computer to type out assignments, others did not. Some students did not have experiences that help you learn. For example, when I made a reference to what it was like at the beach, some students could draw on their experience of going to the beach, while others could not.

Every student has their own story. There are many factors that will limit the students' ability to concentrate in class, complete homework, stay organized, control their emotions, and the list goes on and on.

DR ALEXANDER: That must have changed the way you approached your job.

M.C.: As a teacher, I always tried to get to know my students, so I could understand their situation. But, it was difficult when I had about 180 students. Getting to know the student personally will help to paint a picture of the challenges a student might face.

Many students operated at different levels of executive function. Students with high executive function were definitely the top students in the class. They would complete all their assignments, had the social skills to work well in a group, and knew when to stay quiet and when to speak up. One of the critical aspects of teaching, that may be underestimated, is the ability of the teacher to know their students' strengths and weaknesses. When the teacher knows the challenges a student faces, they are equipped to help the student grow.

DR ALEXANDER: You moved into administration. Can you tell us about that?

M.C.: As the assistant principal in my first official role at the middle school, I was responsible for just about all aspects of a typical school administrator. However, discipline and attendance dominated my time. Through discipline and attendance investigations, it became clear that the root cause of many issues was a lack of some essential skills. A student who got into several fights did not know how to avoid those situations. A student who was sent to the office almost every class period—I'm exaggerating a little, but we definitely had "frequent flyers"—lacked the ability to listen and focus on what the teacher was explaining, or the activity they were working on.

As a result of my role, I began to realize that teachers needed more training to help them deal with discipline differently. We made a big push for teachers to get to know their students on a personal level to understand their limitations and barriers to success. In addition, we aimed to teach students more skills that help them improve as an academic student. We used many of the strategies prescribed in the AVID program. (Advancement via Individual Determination (AVID) is offered in partnership with schools primarily in the United States to promote students' attainment of the skills and confidence to pursue college.)

As a principal, I have had more of a role in guiding organizational goals. One critical aspect of school that we are trying to improve through the virtual model is the ability to individualize instruction.

DR ALEXANDER: How do your knowledge and experiences help you in this role?

M.C.: As an assistant principal and principal, I have seen a broader view of the limited resources available to some of our students. It was always a challenge to balance what the teacher viewed as lazy or irresponsible with the reality of the students' home life. For example, a teacher might have a strict policy about bringing items to class and send the student to the office for failing to bring the required material because the student is considered defiant for refusing to follow clear instructions from the teacher. However, learning more about the students' stories, one might discover they are not able to bring the items to school for valid reasons.

Similarly, students who lack some skills may have a difficult time working with other students or in certain class settings. Part of the role of assistant principal is working with the most challenging students (usually related to poor behavior in class). Many times, you could relate the behavior to an attention-seeking issue. Successfully helping students with behavior issues requires a good relationship with the student. I had a few girls who would frequently get in fights or approach other girls with the intent to fight. After working with them, I had a few make me a promise that they would not fight again, or they would at least seek me—or a supervisor—out to help them through the issue. It was satisfying when students did that, because it meant that they wanted to change.

When I was able to get several staff members to understand the challenges and they created a plan to address the issues, it really helped turn the tide of school culture. Some students attended small group sessions with a licensed therapist, others had regular check-ins with a trusted adult.

DR ALEXANDER: Is there an experience or course you had in high school or college that you feel motivated you or sticks with you somehow?

M.C.: The most impactful experiences in college courses were from teachers or professors who made a personal connection, or those who inspired me to make a positive difference.

DR ALEXANDER: Are there any experiences you might share that involved watching a student or colleague grow to better use their executive functions?

M.C.: There are many, but I will just give you a few here.

One student struggled with getting in a lot of fights. She used to fight as her main mechanism for dealing with conflict. Over the course of two years, we had her in a small group learning about ways to self-regulate and think differently when conflict arose. She developed over time to recognize that other students persuaded her to get into fights by reporting that someone was talking about her. When they reported someone "talking sh**" about her, she would approach the other student confrontationally. At that point it was a no-win situation. The other student would deny the claim and want to defend herself from the accusation. Things would usually escalate from there into an eventual fight. Once the student learned some ways to deal with rumors and ways to manage her behavior, she never got in a fight again.

Some students needed organizational skills. I remember one parent-teacher-student conference where the student had almost all of the completed assignments from the quarter in his backpack. When asked why he didn't turn them in, he did not have a good answer. In the end, part of the problem was that he was disorganized, part of it was that he was unaware that the assignment was due (even though it was always clearly written on the board and announced in class). We gave him a few simple tips for keeping himself organized and set up a buddy system to make sure he was held accountable for turning in his work. Over time, his behavior changed and he turned things in on time.

I have had many cases of students with a lack of impulse control. In most cases the student was attention seeking, but in other situations, the student needed constant reminders to make it through a period without doing something to disrupt the class. In one extreme case, a school counselor took the student under her wing and had him report to her every day for one of his class periods. The student would be sent to the office multiple times per day (from many different teachers). The counselor worked with him daily for months; over time he managed to completely change his behavior. I remember that she would come to me at the end of the day and say "He made it through the day without getting sent to the office once!" She was so excited. When he was able to make it through class without any disruptions, he was learning more, too. His grades dramatically improved.

Application and Reflection

1   Think about your own high school experiences. Is there a student (or yourself!) who you could see struggling with academics or behavior or just needing attention? What did they do that makes you think of them as you answer this question? How might you link executive functions, such as working memory, inhibition, and cognitive flexibility to these behaviors? Explain.

2   Again, think about your own experiences in high school. How have teachers handled disruptions? How have they treated fellow students who did not keep up, either by not turning in work or by doing poorly on exams? How can you

apply, in these situations, what you know about the development of executive function and emotional, social, cognitive, and biological changes? Explain.

3   Often, administrators must serve as teachers for many years before being hired as an administrator. Based on the professional growth you read about in M.C.'s interview, describe three potential reasons for this.

Mental Health

Mental health is "a state of mind characterized by emotional well-being, good behavioral adjustment, relative freedom from anxiety and disabling symptoms, and a capacity to establish constructive relationships and cope with the ordinary demands and stresses of life" (American Psychological Association, 2023). Let's unpack this in light of the previous few chapters. Being healthy means being okay with how you are feeling, and this includes physiological and cognitive assessments of emotion, requiring working memory to think about and put together various aspects of emotion, inhibitory control to stop intrusive thoughts, and higher order cognition to regulate thoughts, stress, and anxiety. Also, it means behavior regulation and appropriate adjustment to various people and contexts, with inhibitory control preventing automatic reactions, cognitive flexibility supporting a variety of coping strategies and behavioral solutions, and working memory to choose one. Creating and maintaining productive relationships depends in part on emotional, cognitive, and behavior regulation, as well as attachment, empathy, memory, and language. Mental health thus relies critically on EF.

Keep in mind that what mental health means at any given age must change over the course of development. Preschoolers have limited regulatory skills and self-awareness, and yet they can cope and use cultural tools to promote mental health, such as using inner speech to remind themselves to inhibit a behavior or thought (Vygotsky, 1987). Even infants who are highly reactive can cope to limit perceptual intake by turning their head or moving away from overstimulation. As humans grow, their biological and physiological processes may remain inhibited or reactive, and yet teens and adults can draw on experiences, strategies, and coping skills to stabilize their emotional responses and reframe their perceptions and attributions. It is important, then, to consider mental health as developmentally appropriate adaptation, using the knowledge from all of the previous pages to inform what is a developmentally appropriate *process* for a *person* within a specific *context* at any given *time*. Professionals that focus on mental health can provide early intervention, social services, and counseling, for example.

Social Services

Social services are provided with public funding to help people who are developing in a disadvantaged or vulnerable context or situation. Services can be provided as a buffer for children and adolescents in such situations, and

Source: Photograph by author KWA.

services also may be provided to support a change in the context, and therefore developmental trajectory of infants, children, or youth. Previous chapters have emphasized the importance of the environmental and biological/physiological contexts on EF development. Many aspects of social services aim to bolster the context in which humans grow to highlight strengths within themselves, their families, neighborhoods, schools, and cultures.

Social services can operate in a variety of settings, such as the home, school, or hospital, and so the way in which EF is related to the profession may depend on the context. Early interventionists work with infants and toddlers and their families before they enter school. They can work with caregivers to synchronize consistent interaction when a caregiver may not have learned that themselves while growing up—this is known to foster EF development. Further, professional collaboration is beneficial when it occurs both formally and informally, and is an important part of service (Tschannen-Moran et al., 2007).

Child welfare services works with families to promote mental and physical welfare for minors aged 0 to 18 years. They sometimes remove children from their homes to provide a safe space for them to develop if children are found to be in situations of psychological or physical harm, which creates stress and chronic activation of the sympathetic nervous system and lasting effects on prefrontal cortex and EF development. Some practices required of caseworkers and agencies burden the system and prevent effective support, requiring a change in policies and practices of agencies (Font & Gershoff, 2020). Despite this, social services provide early intervention for low-income families to promote EF and school readiness (see previous section on "Education" for tips for related professions). And, social workers can be employed in a variety of settings to support psychological well-being of clients in homes, hospitals, and schools. Relying on principles provided here, such as promoting secure attachments, individualized care, adequate nutrition and stress reduction, and nurturing interactions with cultural tools, social workers foster EF.

Counseling

Additionally, in the context of mental health, it is important to understand how multiple facets of EF are intertwined with the mind, body, and behavior. Counselors or therapists can serve in a variety of contexts to support healthy emotional, social, and cognitive well-being. For example, in educational settings, counselors support EF by working primarily with students on regulation and behavioral strategies during the early years, and scheduling and time management in secondary and higher education contexts. Counselors also help students to identify careers and create goals and plans to reach them, thus directly coaching EF.

Some infants, children, youth, and emerging adults face challenges and seek out counseling for therapeutic support. Recognizing the importance of mental health across contexts, counselors can be found in many settings outside of schools, such as private offices, hospitals, group homes, and detention centers. Therapeutic settings may be one-on-one or group based. Across settings, counselors supporting mental health build rapport with their clients to later address specific needs. Techniques with children may involve play therapy to help maintain their attention and reduce physiological stress while sharing

Source: Shutterstock.

memories, using language, and learning new coping strategies (Wong et al., 2022). In such settings, counselors can help alter **cognitive attributional biases,** or help individuals to reframe the meaning of events and situations such that they are able to alter their appraisal of events and the intent of others' that they feel have harmed them. This approach focuses on the top-down processing related to emotion regulation as was discussed earlier.

Government and Law

Most legal cases revolve around identifying right from wrong and bringing justice to balance. Professionals in this field, thus, are concerned with protecting rights to achieve justice. The legal system is not generally a place where EF is trained to grow in children, but rather knowing about EF skills at various ages into adulthood can help these professionals provide developmentally appropriate services.

Legal fields related to human development and who directly interact with clients include police officers, judges, attorneys, child advocates (e.g., *Guardian Ad Litem*), and a host of support staff. Each has opportunities to directly interact with children and families and support EF development by provision of resources or rely on knowledge of EF to direct their expectations and services. Police officers are one of the first group of professionals that children encounter when entering the legal system, as police officers and detectives gather evidence, conduct interviews, and make arrests. After that, although judges are to remain impartial in an attempt to enact justice, attorneys are responsible for upholding the rights of their client. Prosecuting attorneys are responsible for bringing action before the court on behalf of their client, who is accusing another person of breaking the law and violating their own rights. In the case of a defense attorney, the charge of the professional is to defend the accused client's rights and allow their side of the story to be heard. Child advocates can be legally appointed to serve children in the legal system, primarily looking out for their welfare as a minor.

Children as Victims or Witnesses

When children are victims of crimes, they must rely on a host of EF skills to convey their accusations. First disclosure is often to an adult closer to the child or adolescent, which can then involve social services and police officers and, if evidence warrants it, contact with attorneys and other legal professionals. It is critical from the point of initial disclosure to limit suggestion and simply listen to the child's account of their experience. As we know, memory can be dependent upon EF skills while perceiving the event, encoding the event for long-term memory, and retrieving the event by binding multiple contextual details into single, accurate episodes. Of note, physiological and cognitive stress can re-occur each time the child recalls their victimization, and thus needs to be regulated along with the experience.

The gradual development of the prefrontal cortex and EF skills is not necessarily associated with children's ability to provide accurate reports of victimization, but rather is related to being less detailed in reports and more susceptible to suggestion (Schaaf et al., 2008). Of note, studies show that children can be even less likely to spontaneously create false memories than adults (Otgaar et al., 2019) and in some situations, provide highly accurate memories even a decade after the experience (Alexander et al., 2005). With age, children also become increasingly able to understand Theory of Mind and how to differentiate things they dreamed or wished for or pretended about, from reality. They can better inhibit these alternatives, maintain reality in working memory while also regulating their stress, and think about the importance of telling the truth. Some legal agencies have established interviewing centers so that all parties can be present for a single, trained interviewer to ask the child questions, limiting repeated interviews and opportunities for suggestions and source monitoring errors (Otgarr et al., 2019).

Minors as Perpetrators

Sometimes, minors (children under 18) are accused of committing crimes. Committing a crime involves both a cognitive component—understanding what is right and wrong—and a behavioral component—controlling (or not) one's behavior to be consistent with those beliefs. If children *feel* along with another person, or empathize, they are less likely to engage in behaviors that hurt the other person (Eisenberg et al., 2004). However, once accused, professionals involved in the case must be mindful of the developing EF skills of the accused. Social pressure and false evidence during interrogations can elicit false confessions, with younger adolescents more at risk than older adolescents and emerging adults

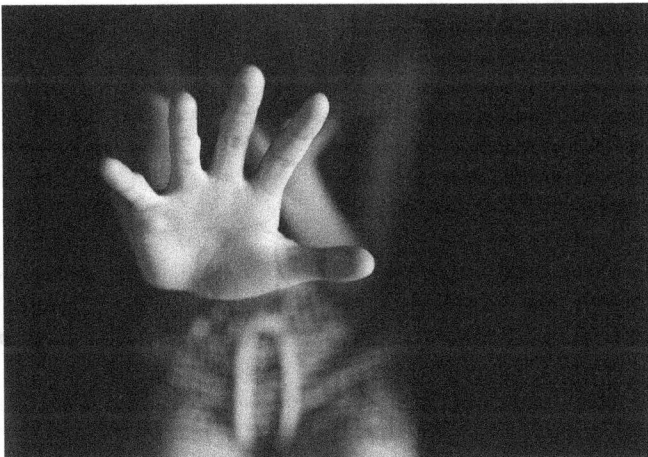

Source: Shutterstock.

(Redlich & Goodman, 2003). In those situations, EF can be inefficient to inhibit the overwhelming urge to end the interrogation, and may not allow for higher EF skills to operate, such as planning and working toward the larger goal of avoiding prosecution or punishment. Attending to the limitations of children of different ages can allow legal professionals to obtain evidence that can be used in court without concern for violating the rights of the accused.

Box 5.2 Trauma Informed Care and Human Development

Setting the Stage: Theories

Theories of how executive function impacts behavior are valuable; however, *using* those theories to inform practice can be challenging. As we have seen throughout this book, research and practice support the idea that using knowledge and experience with EF has real and lasting positive outcomes. One area this is particularly relevant for is the situation of ongoing stress or trauma, even long after the stress has ended.

Evidence

Research shows early trauma or ongoing stress or disadvantage can cause lasting effects on epigenetics, brain structure, neural function, hormones, and consequently, thought, behavior, and feelings (e.g., Sapolsky, 2012). Evidence shows that EF skills are directly related to trauma exposure, especially when the trauma was family based (DePrince et al., 2009), as can be for many children. This lower EF is then responsible for regulating emotions, controlling behaviors, and managing distracting thoughts and sensory experiences. The ongoing emergence of EF within the traumatized individual can be increasingly hindered without intentional support (see Figure 5.2).

Practice

Trauma-informed care acknowledges that all individuals have potential trauma backgrounds and proposes that high-quality support should be provided in a universal manner to all individuals. That is, rather than providing a specific intervention for one group, this approach works to effortfully infuse the supportive and inclusive practices into the culture of the organization and all services it provides. Human services provide a range of supports to children, adolescents, and families through many of the various careers discussed in this chapter. Using a framework that inclusively provides care relevant to various backgrounds can help to alleviate some current inequities in long-term outcomes, especially of some of our most marginalized groups. Further, understanding human development will help professionals at each level to design care settings that serve the developmentally unique needs of different age groups (Jones et al., 2016).

Specifically related to EFs, professionals in early care settings should be mindful of creating environments that nurture growth, trusting relationships and strong social and emotional foundations. Caregivers and professionals should be sensitive to the egocentrism and lack of emotion and behavior regulation characterized by toddlers and children in the preschool years (Jones Harden, 2015). Later, professionals can provide inclusive supports by acknowledging that behaviors are adaptations to previous experiences. In other words, professionals should approach youth services with the goal of building on their strengths rather than "fixing" them; this includes creating safe spaces that welcome youth, being transparent with goals and processes, and fostering a positive self-concept (National Center on Domestic Violence, Trauma, and Mental Health, 2019). Given the increased likelihood of teens to engage in risky behaviors (e.g., substance abuse), partnering with older children and adolescents in building EF skills such as organization, decision making, and helping them think flexibly about potential risks will benefit youth from all backgrounds.

Moreover, it is important to recognize that EF training and support does not always generalize from the context in which it is fostered (Diamond & Lee, 2011). That is, if youth are coached to improve their working memory in math contexts, this does not necessarily help their reading comprehension. To improve long-term outcomes, professionals across fields must coordinate to serve infants, children, youth, and families, and this becomes critical for children with trauma in their background. For example, a child (regardless of trauma background) can benefit from basic services to ensure food and shelter as well as a safe and loving environment to promote social and emotional well-being and brain development. That same child will need academic services that support individual differences in EF and thus behaviors and academic skills. Offering a variety of services through many of the agencies mentioned in this chapter would allow the child to utilize those that best meet their needs, including recreational activities, mindfulness training, or individualized coaching. Such wrap-around services allow those with trauma backgrounds to avoid being re-traumatized by a special need for services because such services are available and encouraged for all.

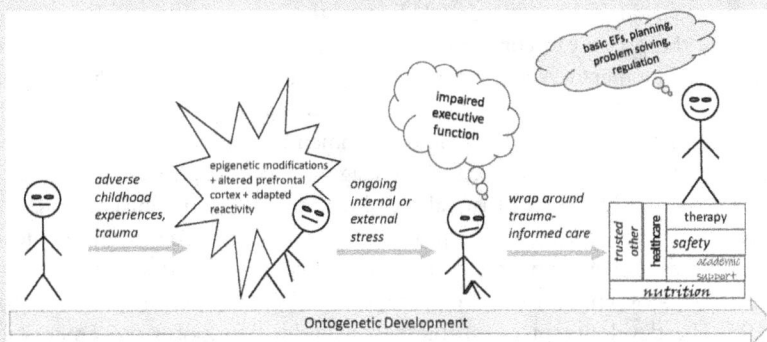

Figure 5.2 Breaking the trauma cycle.
Source: Based on Ortiz & Sibinga, 2017.

Figure 5.2 illustrates the idea that trauma and adverse childhood events cause toxic stress. This weighs on the individual through the physiological and psychological response to stress (and repeated and chronic stress). This can lead to lasting changes in epigenesis, brain structure and function, and EF, ultimately resulting in lasting adulthood outcomes such as depression or disease. Engagement with trauma-informed support or services, such as mindfulness training (Ortiz & Sibinga, 2017) and numerous other services provided by professionals listed in this chapter, can alleviate these consequences and promote EF skills that support emotion and behavioral regulation as well as higher cognitive function. If left unsupported, and because of epigenesis and learned patterns, continued difficulties with EF re-occur in future generations and can create and maintain marginalization.

Application and Reflection

1　Note that EF has been found to be more challenged when trauma occurred within the home. Why do you think this is? Consider biological, emotional, social, and cognitive links in your explanation.
2　Thus far, we have discussed professionals supporting EF in educational, mental health, and legal contexts. For each of these three contexts, describe one career and how professionals in that career might take a trauma-informed approach in their direct interactions with clients.
3　What are the mechanisms by which support and services can buffer the effects of trauma on EF?

Physical Health and Care

Physical health covers a wide range of biological functions, and a large number of the professionals supporting physical health are in the medical field. This can include professionals working in a hospital setting as well as those in therapeutic settings that can be in educational, home, and private settings. The physical factors of the *person* can change the *context* in which they engage with people, and the developmental *time* during which physical care is provided dictates some of the skills available for that *proximal process*. Earlier, we discussed how EF influences and is influenced by brain development, nutrition, physiological stress, and hormones. We also discussed how engaging in certain physical activities such as yoga and Tae Kwon Do, that calm and direct behavior, might bolster EF.

Here, we elaborate on an additional area of physical growth: motor development. Researchers and practitioners have recently learned about the synergistic link between motor development and EF (McClelland & Cameron, 2019). The development of motor skills includes fine motor movements utilizing small muscles (e.g., writing) and gross motor skills that use large body muscles (e.g., running) and each involves a level of coordination with other senses. For example, visuomotor skills rely on coordinating what is seen with movement. Studies consistently show that motor development and training is related to cognitive improvements, academic achievement, and EF and that inhibitory control and visuomotor coordination act in a compensatory nature: relative strength in one of these compensates for lacking in the other (Cameron et al., 2015).

Medical Settings

Entering into a medical setting can be preventative, meaning there is not a known problem but the goal is health maintenance, or diagnostic or corrective, when an individual is experiencing a problem. In this context, we can encounter professionals who provide patient care and support, such as doctors, nurses, and assistants. Like in legal settings, the goal is not usually long-term improvement of EF skills, but professionals who understand developing EF skills and related individual differences can better serve their patients. Specifically, a doctor who talks to a child to build rapport and describes what they will do beforehand is addressing the stress of a child who may be in a novel situation. When we are in new situations, our working memory can more easily be overloaded with all of the details, and such uncertainty can induce fear.

Similarly, nurses and care professionals who give inoculations (i.e., shots) can gauge the child's level of reactivity and inhibitory skill and provide individualized support, knowing that all children do not have the same needs, particularly when dealing with those of different ages and backgrounds. Interestingly, increased distress during inoculations is moderately related to children's inhibition, and children were more overtly distressed when their parent was more avoidantly attached (Alexander et al., 2002). In other words, children with lower inhibitory

Source: Shutterstock.

control and insecure attachments may need greater support from medical staff during medical procedures. To address this need, some hospitals have Child Life Specialists who work directly with children and families to provide knowledge and increased coping strategies, often through therapeutic play (Jenkins et al., 2023).

Therapeutic Settings

Other health care professionals can work outside of the hospital setting in schools, homes, and private offices. Such professionals include physical therapists, occupational therapists, speech-language pathologists, and audiologists, to name just a few. Understanding EF skills and their interrelation with other aspects of development is critical for these professionals working with individuals experiencing a challenge in motor or sensory function. For example, occupational therapists that understand the link between EF and motor skills might include goals for motor skills with the purpose of enhancing EF (Cramm et al., 2013). They might also use games and motor exercises that require appropriate levels of working memory and engage cognitive flexibility and problem solving.

On the other hand, physical therapists working with toddlers to move their bodies benefit from understanding the limited EF of toddlers, much as medical professionals do, so they can engage young children who lack aspects of inhibitory control and working memory. For example, they may use play-based exercises to engage young clients and be prepared to repeat actions more than with their adult clients. Further, in attempts to better recognize the whole human, physical therapists can also promote restoring EF within physical therapy sessions meant to repair damage (Studer, 2007).

Source: Shutterstock.

Home

The home setting often involves many of the professionals discussed thus far, and yet many hours of the day are spent within the home or organized by someone in the home. This section addresses some of this, and how the home provides a foundational *context* for the rest of development, with the *person* engaging in selected *processes* within and related to the home, with a reliance on the home lessening across developmental *time*.

Caregivers and Families

One critical role we have not yet addressed in this application chapter is the role of the immediate caregivers and family in fostering EF development. Of note, many of these roles were discussed in previous chapters as caregiving is related on the most basic levels to prenatal nutrition and brain development, infant attunement and attachment, and ongoing socialization of values, cultural tools, and experiences. In early childhood, parental scaffolding and providing enriching environments is related to increased EF; however, interestingly, this association relies on children's language skills (Fay-Stammbach et al., 2014). In other words, it appears that parents who provide stimulating contexts for development and regular, appropriately challenging support produce children who are more skilled in early language skills, and greater language skills are related to higher EF. Added to what we already know about parental sensitivity relating to lowering cortisol and increasing EF (Blair & Ursache, 2011), and as with many other developmental concepts, parenting and EF have a complex relationship.

Furthermore, the decisions parents make for children and the way they interact can affect EF. As we discussed earlier, household chaos and lack of responsive parenting are related to poorer EF (Andrews et al., 2021). Also, although some research shows negative effects of video gaming, close examination of specific aspects of some games (e.g., fast-paced, interactive, rapidly changing) are related to enhanced EF skills, such as attention, working memory, and creativity (Granic et al., 2014). Parental monitoring and care are just some examples of how parents can facilitate EF development through their regular interactions and the experiences they provide and restrict for their children.

Engaging with Local Opportunities

Immediately outside the home, and somewhat dependent upon the culture and values within the home, children venture out into their neighborhoods and communities. There are opportunities to directly foster EF in these contexts as well. For example, professionals working in parks and recreation may provide enrichment via sports, gymnastics, and crafts that provide exercise for children's motor skills, challenging but engaging opportunities for working memory, and occasions to practice emotion and behavior regulation. Such professionals can use their knowledge of EF to enhance engagement by providing developmentally appropriate spaces to meet and to set appropriate expectations and rules.

Linking Concepts to Real People

In Chapter 1, we learned about Amari from his mother, Leigh. Amari was diagnosed early with autism and has worked with a variety of specialists. Now that we've covered so many person characteristics throughout the book, let's think about his case and some of the directly interacting professionals and advocates who might have benefitted his EF development.

In Chapter 2, we read about Joe, who was described as a bright student who struggled with focus. Similarly, E.M. told her story in Chapter 4 as a young adult who grew up with ADHD and various other diagnoses related to her mental health. Across biological, emotional, social, and cognitive domains, different professionals and advocates have had the opportunity to partner with Joe and E.M. to bolster their EF and healthy development. Consider some of the professions qualified to support these developing humans, such as teachers and counselors.

Both Chapter 3's interview with a preschool teacher and the current chapter's interview with a school administrator support the critical importance for those working directly with infants, children, adolescents, and families, of understanding EF, how it develops, and how it is interlinked with all other aspects of human development. It is only when professionals are knowledgeable, collaborative, child-centered, and proactive that our children will be supported to their full potential, and the pages of this book highlight how individual people can have drastic impacts on a single child through direct, ongoing proximal processes.

Summary

Direct interactions with infants, children, adolescents, and families must incorporate awareness of the context of growth, factors of the person, their ongoing proximal processes, and the timing of the interaction. A variety of professionals have the opportunity to work with and support EF development by engaging with humans in the educational, mental health, legal, physical health, and home settings. In order to most effectively support EF development within and across these settings, professionals must collaborate with one another to provide optimal services and they each must approach their students, clients, patients, and offspring in ways that promote development of the whole human.

Further Resources

Diamond, A. (2014, November). Turning some ideas on their head. [Video]. TEDxWestVancouverED. www.youtube.com/watch?v=StASHLru28s

Diamond, A. (2012). Activities and programs that improve children's executive functions. *Current Directions in Psychological Science, 21,* 335–341. doi:10.1177/0963721412453722.

Meltzer, L. (2010). *Promoting executive function in the classroom.* Guilford Press.

Chapter 6

Advocating for Developmentally Appropriate Policy, Outreach, and Well-being

For most of this book we have focused on information most relevant to those working directly with children and families. However, it is just as important to look at this information from another, perhaps higher-level perspective, as all levels of society and culture impact growth and development. The focus of this chapter is two-fold: first, we discuss the importance of the less direct social and cultural forces that impact homes and the workforce and the children and families they serve; and, second, we examine how EF plays a critical role in helping the developing person to actively change these larger structures. Various contexts in which professionals may advocate are discussed; specifically, educational, mental health, law and government, physical health, and the home.

Theory and Context Revisited

The Bio-ecological model described by Bronfenbrenner and Morris (2006) illustrates the intricate way that human development is nested within different *systems,* or ecologies. In the previous chapter, we discussed the person, process, context, and time, with an emphasis on the person and process. The current chapter more specifically focuses and elaborates on the idea of context. For most of this book, we have focused on the **microsystem** levels of analysis, which is the human in direct interaction with other people and objects—such

Source: Shutterstock.

DOI: 10.4324/9781003131052-6

as parents and teachers—and how that human changes over the course of time. We have briefly touched on the idea of the **mesosystem**, which is the way that microsystems interact. This happens when parents and teachers, both of whom are in direct contact with the developing human, engage with one another. These interactions can be collaborative and productive or they can be combative and harmful (or anywhere in between). When a therapist and social worker collaborate to find solutions for the foster child they are serving, they likely produce more comprehensive outcomes.

Outside of these systems are aspects of society and culture that developing humans may never directly experience, and yet these aspects also assert forces on children's growth and development. That is, society, culture, and other indirect influences can affect the places children live, learn, and grow, the tools available for them to engage with, and also the people who are in those spaces and using those tools with them. These outer systems are not as often considered by developmental scientists, and yet they have great power to shape developmental processes (Rogers & Way, 2021). Moreover, critical to understanding the role of these outer circles of influence is the idea of **bidirectionality**—that these outside factors influence individual development *and also* that individual development influences those outside factors. In other words, the child can have ideas and behaviors within their microsystems that then change the way others think and act, which over time can even change the way culture and society reflect and function.

The first of these outer ecologies is the **exosystem,** which includes entities or contexts just outside of the microsystem (that is, they don't directly interact with the person), but that directly interact with an element of the microsystem (Bronfenbrenner & Morris, 2006). For example, a child does not directly interact with the parent's co-workers even though the parent interacts directly with both the child and their workplace and co-workers. Even without proximal processes directly with the child, parental workplace stress, relationships, and satisfaction may alter the way the parent engages in interactions with the child. Likewise, interactions between the parent and child will influence how the parent engages with their work. An alternative example can be seen when professional development opportunities provided for teachers affect how teachers design curriculum and manage their classroom. This affects the child without the child actually experiencing the professional development.

Surrounding these contextual systems is the **macrosystem,** which consists of the broad values of a society and cultures. It consists of political systems, social norms, and welfare policies, for example. The value that a society or culture or family places on work, education, and families filters into policies and practices supporting each of these structures, and these ideologies can be particularly powerful and resistant to change (Garcia Coll et al., 1996). Laws, government structures, and public funding dictate the availability of various opportunities at inner contextual levels. For example, a society that has as a core value equal access to education across gender, ability, and social status might publicly fund and provide government structure and maybe even laws related to promoting and supporting education for all. These macrosystem ideologies would create opportunities for specific types of jobs in administration, leadership, and curriculum design in the exosystem, trickling inward to teachers and specialists providing direct services in the microsystem. In the continuous bidirectional developmental process, the person then influences their teachers and specialists, who collaborate and advocate to administrators and policy makers, who sometimes advocate for societal change in the macrosystem.

Important to note is that the person, in the center of all of these ecologies, changes over time. Each person factor is unique to a snapshot in time, embedded within each of these contexts and interacting with elements of the context. Add to this idea the fact that the other people and contexts are changing constantly as well. This is a reminder that human development is the result of a **dynamic** process, characterized by continual change. These dynamic changes

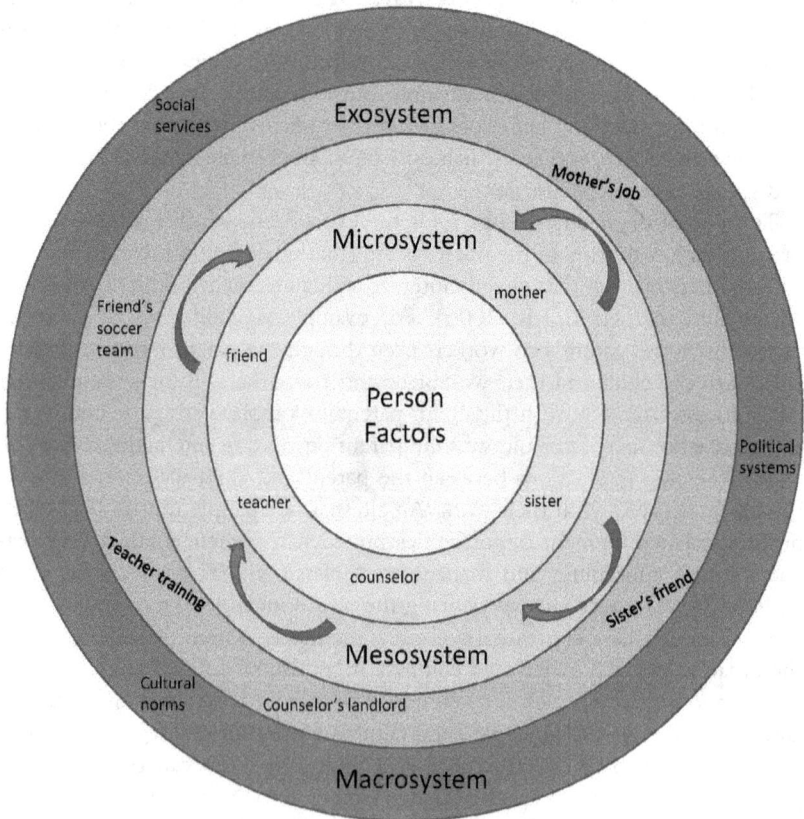

Figure 6.1 Bio-ecological model of nested contexts.
Source: Adapted from Bronfenbrenner & Morris, 2006.

may be stable and follow a consistent pattern over time, or they may be unstable and result from abrupt or drastic events within the individual and their contexts. For example, for children developing in the year 2020, the onset of widespread concern about the COVID-19 pandemic created instability in many lives. In fact, researchers found evidence that parts of the exosystem—those aspects of the child's environment that used to be out of reach—entered the child's microsystem (Frankel & Sampige 2022). What this means is that the parent's job, for example, which used to be outside of the child's immediate contact, was then brought into the home when many parents continued their work at home to accommodate safety and health concerns. The child then had direct opportunities for interaction with the parental workplace environment.

Box 6.1 Policy, Funding, and Language

Setting the Stage

Partnering with professionals who work directly with children and families provides a context for a multi-layered, strengths-based approach to EF development. This is an interview of TV, a pediatric speech-language pathologist who works with young children ages zero to three. She earned her Master's degree and certificate of clinical competence in speech language pathology. TV shares with us how she works within the constraints of society and limited funding, providing insight into how professionals who work *indirectly* with children and families can be a critical part of supporting EF.

Interview

DR O'HARA: When we think of our community responsibility for supporting children's developing EF, what are some of the critical considerations?

TV: One major concern is that the funding for early intervention, and especially for multi-disciplinarian assessments and treatment is drying up in California and other states which previously funded early intervention. Now we are seeing children only able to get services covered by insurance and only for situations with highly visible and multiple disabilities. Those covered by the state need to have a medical component, such as a genetic or medical syndrome. There's growing concern for children with invisible disabilities, like we see in children struggling with EF, to get services. (ASD and Sensory Processing are no longer covered.)

DR O'HARA: So I hear you saying that we need more focus on early intervention.

TV: Absolutely. When we can identify children early who may be developing differently, or who we may predict will have trouble with EF, research shows that the outcomes are much more positive. In the current direction, letting this funding dry up, more of these children will not get the support that they need. Research shows that early intervention is key to helping children lead healthy and happy lives and that it helps parents learn how to parent more effectively.

DR O'HARA: When you say "**invisible disabilities**," what do you mean? Who are these kids?

TV: When we think of "disabilities" we usually think of those that have obvious physical impairments and require support, such as a wheel chair. Other more visible impairments could be cognitive in nature which affect one's ability to learn. However, there are a lot of kids with disabilities that "fly under the radar" for a long time and these children go undetected and more importantly, unsupported appropriately in school. Sometimes these children are very quiet and don't make a big fuss, don't draw a lot of attention, and even may be doing okay in school. When the amygdala is engaged, these children are in flight, fight or freeze. Those in freeze are considered easy and therefore do not get support as easily. Those in fight or flight cannot be ignored quite as easily but they are often pushed off as "behaviorally challenged" and the parents are made to feel as though they are at fault. The profile is still within the invisible disability range, however, as according to most schools as they are "good students." But this is the case when properly regulated, which often requires schools to have funding to help support neurodiverse students.

DR O'HARA: What can we do as a society? As teachers, policy-makers, and clinicians to help make sure these kids get the support that they need?

TV: We need funds for continued early intervention as a means of saving multiple costs later down the road. And we need funding for schools to have proper training for teachers for neurodivergent students. We also need funding for para-educational support (and livable wages) in the school system.

Application and Reflection

1 TV repeatedly mentions the importance of funding. Given what we know about language development and EF skills, let's ask the government for a small grant to start a program to support language and EF.

   a First, choose an age group. Is your program for infants? Children? Teens?
   b Provide three specific things you would set up in your program that would strengthen and facilitate both language and EF in that age group.
   c Now explain why the government should fund your program. How will it have far-reaching impact? And be inclusive and serve diverse needs?

2 TV introduced the idea of invisible disabilities. What does this mean and why is it relevant to our understanding of EF development. What other invisible disabilities have we talked about in this book that might leave some students excluded from being supported?

Supporting Executive Function in the Real World

How is all of this related to executive function and promoting regulation and flexibility in thinking? These outer contexts have much to contribute to this conversation! Professionals have many opportunities to use knowledge of EF to ensure their leadership and advocacy promotes well-being. Further, the bidirectional nature of these contexts suggests that the individual can ultimately transform aspects of their culture (Vélez-Augusto et al., 2017). Building on their individual agency, growing humans can use **proxy agency** to influence others to use tools and resources inaccessible to the individual, which can ultimately result in **collective agency** that consists of the joint resources and tools to strive together toward change (Bandura, 2018). In other words, the person can become a catalyst for change in the exosystems and macrosystems. We will start here with a focus on how professionals working within the child's macrosystems and exosystems can use knowledge of EF to support human development. Later, we will use this understanding to turn focus toward how the individual at the center of these contexts can leverage their EF skills to influence the outer contexts in which these professionals work.

Macrosystem Influencing Executive Function: Role of Society

We will start at the broadest level of context: Macrosystem. Encompassing cultural values and support systems, this level structures inner contexts. For example, consider ideologies surrounding people with special needs, such as Down's syndrome or Autism Spectrum Disorder. The value placed on these humans by their social and political structures will dictate opportunities afforded them throughout development and across contexts. When laws and policies mandate hiring practices for individuals with special needs, employers and human resources departments align practices that support employment (Borghouts-van de Pas & Freese, 2021). You might imagine how implementation of such policies would ultimately impact microsystem interactions that promote knowledge, skills, learning, and EF with teachers, parents, and peers even from the earliest age. The more macrosystem professionals who know and appreciate the importance of children's EF and the supportive mechanisms therein, the more our external structures can support children's growth and development.

Before diving into more ideas about how those in the macrosystem can apply their understanding of EF development to promote regulation and individual control, we consider a more recent thought about how remote the macrosystem *really* is. Some researchers argue that because the macrosystem is so integrally tied to culture, its influence is not as indirect as once thought (Vélez-Agosto et al., 2017). For example, because culture provides structure for interactions, language, and tools, children do, in a sense, directly interact with culture (Vygotsky, 1981). Moreover, institutional embodiment of systems of social stratification, race, and gender enter the microsystems of human development through their direct influence on availability of cultural tools, experiences, and people and also in the ways in which they shape perceptions of the self within these contexts (Garcia Coll et al., 1996). Keep in mind that, although we turn back to considering the macrosystems as residing in the outer circle of indirect effects, the boundaries among contexts and the developing human are fluid.

Language and Cognition, Executive Function, and Values in Society

Within the previous chapters, we have discussed how ideologies of the macrosystem, such as political systems and cultural norms, guide policies and practices that are institutionalized and thus filter down to influence how individuals develop. In some ways, cultural norms are passed on via various tools, such as language (Kramsch, 2014), which provides a structure for thought. Culture, through language, thus has the potential to influence children's use of EFs such as inhibition (Carlson & Beck, 2009) and working memory (Baddeley et al., 2021). For example, young children use private speech and older children and adults use inner speech to guide themselves through maintaining information, preventing action, and transforming thought (Vygostky, 1981).

In representing abstract concepts, cultural ideas may have an even greater potential to influence language and thus, thought. For example, how one talks about time can change based on the language spoken, and this cultural influence changes the way these people think about time. This is illustrated in Mandarin Chinese speakers who can use vertical spatial language (up/down) to describe time (e.g., using words translated to mean "climb" and "descend"), whereas American English speakers use horizonal spatial language (back/forward; e.g., using words like "forward" and "back" (Boroditsky, 2001)). Although this may seem like a minor distinction, consider the trickle down (and up) effect of such a long-term linguistic variation and how working memory and spatial and temporal (i.e., time) representations might differ.

But, how do *ideologies* of the macrosystem filter in to ultimately affect the person? One example comes from bilingualism. Although bilingualism has been found to exert benefits on EF and other areas of cognitive development (Bialystok et al., 2012), societal ideologies had long kept bilingualism from being fostered in the U.S. consistently during the past century (García & Torres-Guevara, 2021). In fact, historically, children who spoke languages other than English in the U.S. were placed in classrooms speaking a language they could not understand, leading to high rates of identification of these children as needing remediation and performing poorly in school. In some states, views of bilingualism have become more representative of the science and support learning multiple languages early (García & Torres-Guevara, 2021). The impact of societal ideology on individual development is clear. When bilingualism was not valued, children speaking languages other than

Source: Shutterstock.

English were at risk for being outcast from mainstream society and education; whereas, when bilingualism is valued, children speaking multiple languages are appreciated for their skills. In the former, a deficit model conveys to the child and their supporters that they and their community are inadequate, whereas a strengths-based approach acknowledges the asset of multilingualism and supports the child in valuing themselves and their community's cultural wealth (Yosso, 2005). Both ideologies have a cascade of other effects, and these effects are not limited to the U.S., but have been identified in other nations such as England (Safford & Drury, 2013).

In historical reviews, some of the most impactful professions for linking the macrosystem to more direct developmental contexts can vary. Within the government, the President of the nation, advisors, and policy analysts and lobbyists, in addition to Supreme Court Justices and lawmakers at lower levels use cultural values to create and advocate for policies. These individuals are guided by the ideologies of the culture in how they decide it is best to promote positive human development, and understanding the importance of, and multiple influences on, EF development can guide these professionals. To read more about how all of these professions played a role in policies around bilingual education in the U.S., check out the review by García and Torres-Guevara (2021).

Regulation, Executive Function, and Values in Society

Culture can also greatly affect emotion and the development of regulation, as detailed in Chapter 3. Displaying emotion may be encouraged or discouraged depending on cultural standards, and over time people tend to show how they are feeling according to those social norms (e.g., Ekman et al., 1969).

Throughout development, and particularly as EF increases, children learn and practice these norms through participation in shared cultural activities with individuals in their microsystems who have been influenced by outer contextual layers (Gutiérrez & Rogoff, 2003).

Overarching societal values can also seep down to the level of the person by affecting the exosystems and then microsystems. One example can be seen in how our understanding of emotion regulation and executive function have changed according to the way children in society were valued and expected to behave. Historically, children around the world were expected to "be seen and not heard," meaning they were expected to behave, contribute when asked, and otherwise be somewhat invisible. This would have required a great deal of regulation of emotion and behaviors from very early ages, and yet we have discussed throughout this book the extent to which these skills develop during childhood. How have values changed, and how is this related to changes in views of regulation and EF and the supports provided by professionals for regulation and EF?

Examining the previous century of scientific writing about emotion regulation, Post and colleagues (2006) provide some insight. Some of the earliest psychological writing about regulation, early in the 1900s, held views that regulation was unconscious and automatic, with the exception of "bad" behaviors that were intentional. You might imagine with this societal and scientific view, how professionals might support human development by trying to remove the will of the child who misbehaved. Experts told parents and teachers to use corporal punishment to stamp out misbehavior (Forehand & McKinney, 1993). Gradually, children were more protected by legislation and prevented from working and then required to attend school, and along with these changes came laws against corporal punishment (Forehand & McKinney, 1993). At this same time, scientific psychological research transitioned from a focus on using external punishment and reward systems to considering instilling an internal fear response in the 1950s, and finally moving into current times where the individual person, their cognition, and EF are all part of how we understand and promote regulation (Post et al., 2006). Along with these changes in societal values of children and perspectives on discipline come different ways in which professionals and parents support children's emotion and behavioral regulation.

Relationships, Executive Function, and Values in Society

Cultures define relationships, from the earliest parent-child relationship to peer interactions and intimate relationships and marriage, and so they also contribute to the way a person defines themselves and others. Cultural differences have been found in Theory of Mind and how children talk about their own mental state (Taumoepeau, 2019). Further, people in more collectivist cultures that foster interdependence appear less able to effortfully engage empathy when faced with people who threaten the harmony of the group (de Greck, 2012). Their brain activation shows the same pattern: These adults are more likely to engage brain areas related to regulation (i.e., prefrontal cortex) and less likely to activate cortical areas responsible for perspective taking (de Greck, 2012). Given limits to EF resources, people who expect harmony and avoid negative emotions in collectivist societies may need to choose to regulate their own negative emotion about threat rather than concerning themselves with the feelings of the person posing the threat.

It is important to consider how changes in ideologies and values might result in changes in how EF and cognitive flexibility are promoted, and specifically in how people take perspectives. Recall from Chapter 4 that perspective taking requires complex representational abilities, as we must hold in mind our own thoughts and feelings while at the same time, consider another person's thoughts and feelings. Perspective taking and empathy develop substantially and are highly dependent upon EF as we work to understand and feel what we think others are feeling.

Although historical evidence shows empathy has long been valued by society, *who* we are encouraged to have empathy for and *how* we support its development has been dictated by societal ideologies. For example, the work of Kenneth Clark highlights economic and racial inequities, and for decades he called for, and designed, systematic methods of increasing empathy to overcome these divisions, as it would force people to find commonalities that promote perspective taking (e.g., Clark, 1971). Although most would agree that empathy is a social value that should be fostered, there is disagreement based on potential situations with multiple sides and moral issues (Jordan et al., 2016), and so promoting cultural wealth and individual well-being remains a task involving flexible thinking and EF.

Source: Shutterstock.

Exosystem Influencing Executive Function: Role of Indirect Effects

We can now consider how these broad ideologies support exosystem structures. The exosystem includes contextual structures in which the child is not an active participant, but that influence the child's experiences through the way they affect other people, places, or things (Bronfenbrenner & Morris, 2006). As discussed earlier, values and ideologies shape policies and laws, and yet how those policies and laws are carried out, and also how microsystem professionals are trained and supported, depends on the exosystem layer of professionals. Careers within the exosystem thus have the potential to affect individual EF development, within the contexts of education, mental health, government and law, physical health and well-being, and the home.

Education

In the previous chapter, we discussed how direct interactions between educational professionals and developing humans can strengthen EF within the microsystem. Now, we turn to consider how those people and objects within the child's microsystem are shaped by the exosystem, further situated within the macrosystem. At the micro-level, teachers, classroom support professionals, and education specialists are regulated by macro-level policies set by local, state, and federal agencies in support of overarching values. Imagine the school system that values engagement and using education to transform boundaries and practice freedom (hooks, 1994)—the classrooms, hiring practices, and available trainings would look very different from a school system valuing conformity. The ways in which these policies are administered and micro-level professionals supported are dictated by exo-level professionals.

In a variety of ways, people within the exosystem can positively affect children's microsystems. Community members can serve on their local, county, and state Boards of Education, which addresses issues of funding, hiring, firing, facilities, and curriculum directions. Staff in district, county, and state offices, such as superintendents and their associates, administrators, curriculum specialists, principals, and counselors shape the school climate, the types of events that take place at the school, the funding, the support the teachers are given, and even who the teachers are. For example, El Zaatari and Maalouf (2022) explained that a school concerned with standardized test scores might adopt curriculum and teaching strategies that support strong test performance, therefore dictating students' micro-level processes.

The neighborhood in which the school is placed can be part of the exosystem, as it can dictate such minor aspects of the school day as playground noise levels as well as major aspects of children's schooling, such as perceived safety going to and from school. Knowing the importance of a positive school climate and how to create one, the critical role of play in human development, and how safety is a foundation for learning are a few ways educational professionals can promote development of cognitive and behavioral regulation, working memory, and cognitive flexibility (Piccolo et al., 2019). For example, when holistic research is considered, funding may be allotted for Community Resource Centers within school sites, a place where families can get academic resources but also support with housing, food, and health services.

When community members and professionals know the importance of early EF development and environments that support healthy brain development, practices will be consistent with research. How can we ensure those in the exosystem know the research on EF and its critical role in the educational context (if they are not reading this book!)? Alazmi and Alazmi (2022) outlined a plan to effectively communicate research to educational policy-makers by becoming a part of the process, providing consistent collaboration, and also evaluating the effectiveness of the policy or program. To provide you with a successful example of a program designed with research collaborators—you may be familiar with the Head Start program, which is a federally funded preschool program that was designed to promote school readiness for low-income children. It was pioneered by Bronfenbrenner, the same researcher we have been referring to in the structure of the contexts for development. He was involved in formulating the project and ultimately evaluated it to show lasting positive effects (Bronfenbrenner, 1974) that helped to maintain it as a federally funded program still today.

Mental Health

Children's mental health spans across all of the contexts discussed in this book, so the exosystems discussed here may cross professional lines and affect micro-level professionals in a variety of settings. As has been established by the research presented thus far, mental health is critically tied to EF, both by EF allowing individuals to regulate and think flexibly about their own thoughts and those of others as well as mental health improving biological, physiological, and cognitive underpinnings of EF. Here, we focus on the exosystems, held between the macrosystem values, policies, and stigmas about mental health and direct interactions with the microsystem.

One way in which the exosystem can affect children's EF within the area of mental health is by providing support for micro-level professionals in this field. Across contexts, counselors and therapists have a high rate of burnout and attrition; that is, they are more likely to leave the job or switch careers than other careers (McCormack et al., 2018). Some of the most cited reasons for leaving this career or experiencing burnout include high caseloads and lack of support from the workplace (e.g., feeling their work is valued and perceiving the work environment as positive (Bardhoshi & Um, 2021)). Emotional exhaustion is also a major factor involved in burnout, and this seems to be increased with greater workload, more paperwork, and overinvolvement with clients (Maslach et al., 2001). All of this suggests that professionals who set regulations on caseload (e.g., state, county, and city officials and policy-makers) as well as administrators who obtain funding to reduce workload, streamline practices to avoid unnecessary paperwork, and create a positive and affirmative work environment will facilitate retention. Retention of high-quality mental health professionals will also provide relational consistency for clients, and likely enhanced EF and mental health. All of this occurs within the macro-level values and depends on whether society is willing to prioritize mental health and de-stigmatize a need for mental health support.

Another way the exosystem can play a role in enhancing children's EF skills via mental health is by providing programs that allow parents to provide a supportive family environment. Funding for welfare, food pantries, thrift stores, and special services for women with infants and those experiencing domestic violence end up allowing the parent to be more present and enriching with their child. Professionals in these exosystems can direct, serve on a board, or work at a non-profit or government agency that provides services. And when mental health care is incorporated into such services, parents indicate they are less stressed and feel more adequate as parents (Klawetter et al., 2020), which we know from research on attachment and parent attunement, affects children's foundational EF skills. This is another reminder that the value that society places on mental health in the culture, in part, specifies the funding that will be provided for such services. Including mental health trainings along with existing services and making resources widely available (e.g., suicide hotlines, low-cost prescriptions) could be part of the support provided outside children's reach, but affecting those who care for and serve them.

Source: Shutterstock.

Government and Law

> *Consider young Trent, who was removed from his home because social services deemed it an unsafe environment in which to grow. He is now a 2-year-old toddler in foster care, but he struggles with emotion and behavior regulation, likely related to his early trauma. He keeps getting moved from home to home, as the caregivers feel unequipped to handle his dysregulated behaviors. Because of his young age, he is not allowed to provide input into his case. He has a team of professionals that work directly with him to support and advocate for him, but just outside of these micro-systems are the regulations, legal professionals, and laws that shape Trent's experiences. How can we work to promote children's EF within the exosystems of the legal and social welfare system?*

Judges, attorneys, private agencies that support foster and adoptive families, workplace regulations for foster and biological parents, and public and private agencies that provide services and support to children in the welfare system all have the potential to influence children's EF development. And yet, many of these professions require little, if any, training on human development. The decisions that are put into place about what is best for the child will ultimately dictate the micro-level processes that occur in the child's life. These decisions relate to how involved the child is in the court case, the information and preparation for legal proceedings, and ultimately, the outcomes (Weisz et al., 2013). Such impact would apply to children in the legal system across contexts, including contested cases of divorce and custody, child welfare, and cases in which the child is accused of committing a crime. See Box 6.2 for more about this.

Another example of how the exosystem relates to children's EF through law and government is parental leave, as regulated by laws as well as workplace policies. In a recent study, mothers who were offered paid leave, versus those who took similar amounts of time off work with unpaid leave, had toddlers with greater language skills. Moreover, by examining data from across the U.S. on parental leave for the past two decades, regardless of paid status, researchers showed positive health effects from maternal leave specifically (Khan, 2020). Policy makers who are aware of the research on EF and the importance of early caregiver-child interactions can support such policies and related funding to promote EF within the exosystem. Moreover, to raise awareness lobbyists, analysts, and other professionals educated about EF and development can make research accessible and advocate for funding, training, and best practices within children's microsystems.

Box 6.2 Teens, Stereotypes, and the Legal System

Setting the Stage

Brenton, a 15-year-old Black teen, headed out one Sunday morning to apply for a job. He didn't know it, but outside a nearby hotel, someone had been shot and killed earlier that day. Police felt Brenton fit the description and arrested him, taking him to the scene of the crime. The witness, who was also threa-tened at the time of the murder, immediately and confidently identified the teen sitting in the back of the police car, Brenton, as the killer. Brenton was taken to the police station, where he confessed to committing the murder verbally and then signed a confession. Easy case, right? Having an eyewitness *and* a confession makes the work of the prosecutors easy! Wrong! There are some other things to consider in this case …

The Research

Several lines of research relate this situation to EF as we consider the guilt of this teen. First, the **cross-race effect** (CRE) may be relevant. CRE occurs when people are better able to accurately identify a person of their own race than they are a person of another race. In a seminal field study, Brigham and colleagues (1982) found that Black and White adults exhibited this pattern, and that measures of earlier experiences interacting with the other race improved accuracy. It seems that humans look more at features of same-race faces, whereas we look at the face as a whole, without details, for other races. As an example of the role of EF here, note how familiarity and experiences might allow more space in working memory for processing features.

Second, **binding** can play a role in both eyewitness memory and in resisting suggestive or coercive interrogation techniques. Binding is the term for tying together different aspects of event memories within the episodic buffer of working memory. Binding occurs for different features of the face, but also the location of the event in space and in the world, and improvements in this skill are evident even in preschool (Sluzenski et al., 2006) and beyond. Under con-ditions of stress, working memory could be compromised because the limited capacity is involved in emotion regulation and self-preservation in addition to event details (Mitchell & Phillips, 2007).

Third, individuals can be **suggestible** to a different extent depending on situational and personal factors. Suggestibility decreases with age, as individuals are better able to resist false details and separate them from the facts. Not surprisingly, as resisting suggestion requires stopping yourself from the natural response to agree with the speaker, the EF of inhibition has been linked to the accuracy and ability to resist suggestion (Schaaf et al., 2008).

Revisiting the Case

Let's revisit Brenton, who is now sitting in court in front of a jury. Evidence of the eyewitness testimony and his own confessions is presented. The jury may expect at that point for it to be an easy conviction. But as we said earlier, there are other considerations. His age makes him particularly vulnerable to coercion; in fact, Brenton reported (and pictures supported) that he was beaten until he confessed. He also reported that investigators interviewing him threatened his family, and there was no evidence of investigators gathering other evidence, such as Brenton's whereabouts earlier that day. As you know, adolescents' EF is still developing, especially in skills that would help them avoid irrelevant information, control their emotions, plan and think about consequences, and take other perspectives. Add to this lack of maturity the physical harm, threats to his family, and pure fatigue after an exhausting, emotional 12 hours of interrogation that would likely wear down even the strongest of adults. EF is an effortful process, and so to engage Brenton's EFs he would need to have the mental energy to engage in these top-down EF processes. Also consider that his working memory would likely have been holding a lot of irrelevant information related to his fear and unfamiliarity with the people, place, and situation.

But, did he do it? What about the eyewitness? One important thing to remember about episodic memory is that it uses EFs in the active storage and retrieval processes. Despite our perception that we make an objective copy of the event in our minds, this process of encoding (and retrieval) involves recon-struction of the event, and we know hot EF (involving emotion, as would be the case for this eyewitness watching someone be murdered) can function differently. Because the eyewitness was white, we must consider the cross-race effect. Also, when we have experiences, the features of the event bind with preconceived biases if those biases are not effortfully inhibited. It is quite likely all of this came into play as this white tourist confidently made an erroneous report.

In the end, Brenton was acquitted by the jury, and a new trial convicted two other men with a confession and fingerprints on crime-related objects. Had the investigators been aware of or exercised caution surrounding these limitations in EF regarding teens, emotion, and memory, and limitations in eyewitness memory, these tragic accusations may have been avoided. In fact, police and interviewer training programs have been shown to be quite effective when implemented (e.g., Ginet & Py, 2001).

Applications and Reflections

1   Let's assume the eyewitness did his best to identify the perpetrator of the crime. What aspects of the situation in which he identified the Brenton as the suspect may have contributed to his inaccuracy? How might this be related to EF?

2   Brenton knew he did not commit the crime, and yet he confessed verbally and then signed a statement. How would EF contribute to an adult better resisting false suggestions than this teen? What factors of the situation make it difficult for anyone's EF to function adequately in this situation? Why?

3   What exosystems and macrosystems played a role in the way Brenton was treated? How could the micro-level professionals have been supported by these outer contexts to avoid many of the problems that resulted?

Physical Health and Care

Supporting the physical health of developing humans can involve many professionals, including those in the medical field as well as nutritionists, community food banks, and athletic coaches. Although some may have expertise in human development, this is not required for all in these fields. For example, worldwide, medical professionals working with children and families are not always trained on best practices with children and how to adapt procedures for patients of different ages (Walsh et al., 2015). In part, because of the lengthy training some of these professionals undergo for their primary area of knowledge (e.g., dietary needs and cellular biology), it may not always seem feasible to require yet another training on a specific patient population. However, hopefully at this point in the book, you as a reader see it is essential that such professionals working with children and caregivers have such knowledge! How can exosystem policies and practices ensure developmentally appropriate training and services for professionals working directly with children and adolescents?

The manner in which these institutions are run plays a critical role and is guided by professionals in the exosystems. Hospital administrators make decisions about continued training required of their staff, the areas in which those trainings are allowed, and whether staff are expected to truly specialize versus work across various settings, age groups, and medical specialties, all of which affect how staff rate their workplace environments (Buckley et al., 2022). Community-based and school-based athletic activities have directors (who are also guided by policies of their larger organizations and the individuals creating those) who hire coaches and athletic trainers, and if they are not required to

Source: Shutterstock.

have knowledge of human development, they may be able to display exquisite skill at the sport while not making it any more accessible to their athletes. Providing even informal training and guidelines about youth development leads to more positive outcomes for children in community athletic programs (McDonald et al., 2010). This may include a variety of techniques, such as practice guidelines about how many instructions athletes of different ages can hold in mind, how distractible they will be over time, and how much they can contribute to and be motivated by, the game. In the absence of proactive directors, administrators, and leaders, microsystem professionals will not reliably have the skills needed to promote children's well-being.

Of course, larger macrosystem issues play a role in policies and funding individuals have within the exosystems. Whether the government funds quality healthcare for all and the value society places on fitness, nutrition, and physical health play a role in overall physical health and well-being.

Home

The home is the primary location of many microsystems for human development, and yet just outside of the home is the community and its city council and neighborhood norms, parent(s) workplaces and support systems, and sibling(s) schools, friends, and jobs if not shared by the child. The way in which these exosystems support a positive home environment have great potential for impact on EF development. The expectations parents experience in their workplaces can affect their expectations of their children and thus how they interact with them on a daily basis (Pearlin & Kohn, 1996). For example, if a parent is expected to be highly autonomous at work, take initiative, and be self-sufficient, they may bring home similar expectations in their parenting. Another exosystem factor is community violence, which can affect human development even when not witnessed or experienced directly. It can increase parental stress (Wang et al., 2020) and cause chronic stress in children and affect how they think about the world (Cicchetti & Lynch, 1993).

These potentially negative factors within the exosystem do not prevent children from experiencing positive outcomes, as also within the exosystem are professionals who may provide supports. For example, law enforcement, community outreach, and non-profit agencies can reduce and even eliminate violence by providing positive activities and resources to those engaging in violence and increasing neighborhood cohesion (Markowitz, 2003). Figure 6.2 provides a model of the multiple ecosystems in disadvantaged neighborhoods who lack supportive ecologies. Note the changes at any level—the microsystem of parents and teachers, exosystem of city recreational services and outreach, or macrosystem of neighborhood cohesion and collective efficacy—would change all levels of the context in which the person is developing.

Neighborhood cohesion may increase when community members feel belonging (outside of the violence) and change the values the community

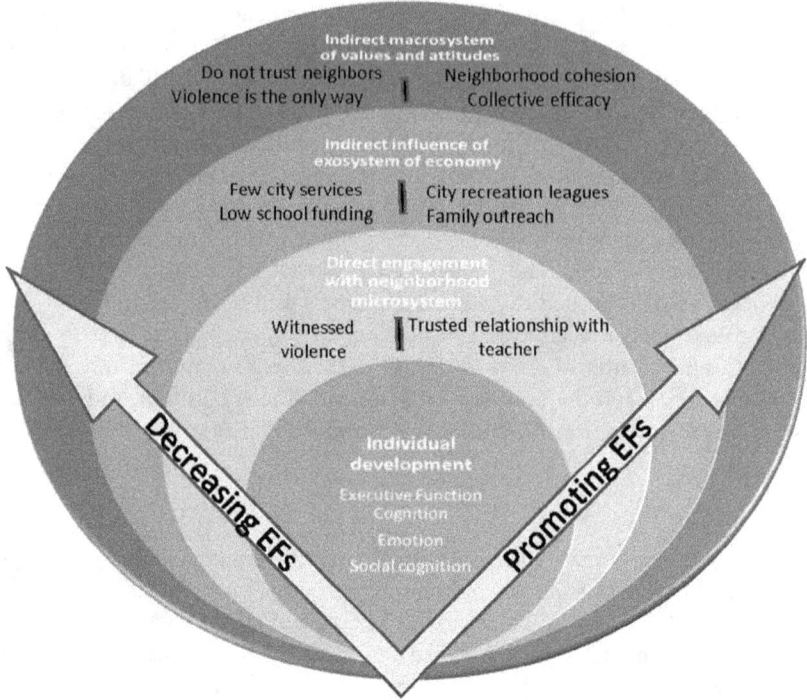

Figure 6.2 Neighborhood context for development.
Source: Adapted from Markovitz, 2003.

places on violence and one another. Community structures that facilitate positive formal and informal ways to belong (e.g., sports, clubs, mentorship) may increase cohesion, reduce violence, and reduce the negative impact of that violence on youth outcomes. Recall from Chapter 4 that efficacy refers to the beliefs we have about what we can accomplish, and **collective efficacy** applies this idea to the community; it is a belief that working together will create positive outcomes. One way to foster this would be to provide parents with resources; social support helps parents cope and exhibit more collaborative parenting qualities (Koeske & Koeske, 1990). Directors and administrators of community outreach groups, services to provide parenting classes and resource centers, and mental health resources for parents can greatly enhance parents' ability to cope with community violence and promote positive child outcomes (Wu & Xu, 2020). All of the professionals working within these exosystems can benefit from understanding the critical role of the home and family in EF development across the lifespan.

Full Circle of Bidirectionality: The Person Can Change Ideologies and Social Structures

Within this book, you have found detailed explanations and evidence for numerous career pathways that can affect all aspects of EF development, but here we will turn directly to the person in the center of the model to consider how they exert direct and indirect effects on outer contextual circles. We focus on how people engaging in their local and worldwide communities, through such activities as community service and activism, can change not only their microsystems, but also their mesosystems, exosystems, and ultimately, macrosystems. On the one hand, such engagement affects EF development and cascading other outcomes of the person and future generations of people. These changes would mirror the effects previously discussed and so are not a focus of this section. On the other hand, much of this engagement requires use of the EF of these developing humans. It is this latter idea that serves as the focus of this section, with an emphasis on how professionals can support the development and use of person EF skills to support their development into **agents of change**; that is, people devoted to advocating and actively pursuing transformation in places, ideologies, and values.

Macrosystem values that guide society are sometimes so engrained into culture that individuals scarcely notice the effect these ideologies have on their thoughts and behaviors. Societal values of the family, development, and health shape the systems we use to care for one another through social welfare systems, allocation of funding, and election of political leaders. For example, earlier we discussed how a change in cultural attitudes toward bilingualism was related to changes in policies, practices, and micro-level contexts in which children directly interact. How did the change in ideologies arise? It is possible time alone caused the change, but it is more likely that people at the center created change gradually.

Diversity, Equity, and Policy

In recent years, societies around the world have begun to recognize racism and exclusionary practices more explicitly, and it is because of individuals speaking out that awareness has increased and cultural shifts are occurring. Important to note is that many policies and practices are so embedded within the culture and internalized by marginalized individuals that they are not recognized as changeable and in fact, making change can feel quite inaccessible to individuals who are marginalized by those policies (Jones, 2020).

Increasing evidence and historical and sociological knowledge of the deep roots of racism within our systems of government and education and its long-term impact have become more widely acknowledged (e.g.,

Source: Shutterstock.

Rothstein, 2017). Mounting evidence has indicated that systemic racism and discrimination on the basis of gender, ability, religious beliefs, and/or sexual orientation, for example, have a tremendous impact on developing minds and bodies and particularly affect EF skills (e.g., Ozier et al., 2019). For example, experiencing a lifetime of discrimination may create situations of chronic and acute stress and ongoing coping and monitoring that affect brain development and challenge productive EF skills. Therefore, when we consider the role of policy in promotion of human development, we must also consider the actions, laws, and enforcement practices that work to dismantle discriminatory systems within the multi-layered contexts of development.

Worldwide, efforts are being made to create more equitable and inclusive environments that support diversity. Consider the importance of EF, particularly cognitive flexibility, in adopting and promoting such a value. Growing up within an ideology that does not acknowledge and support the human rights of a group of people makes it more likely that people will continue to perpetuate this cycle (Snyder, 1981). To break the cycle, individuals must use EF to effortfully inhibit thoughts and actions that are discriminatory, engage in perspective-taking and hold multiple ideas in mind, some of which may conflict with their own beliefs, and create new solutions to transform the way they and others think about the world. In fact, a study of adults who participated in a program that guided them through engaging their EFs to combat stereotypes showed long-term transformation in **implicit biases** (Devine et al., 2012), those beliefs we hold without even consciously recognizing them and yet they affect our decision making and behavior.

When macro- and exo-level structures support the availability of such programs, and individuals are interested in engaging with them, successful change in ideologies may occur. Changes involve cognitive systems and potentially transforming stereotypes and group representations, finding ways to re-shape learned behaviors and re-evaluate memories that shape current thinking, and engaging language in ways that promotes the self to adopt inclusive ideas and actions. Additionally, emotional systems may be transformed using top-down and effortful processing to make explicit feelings and consider early experiences. And social and relational systems must also be evaluated to engage empathy. All of these use EF, and all of this effortful processing is more likely to occur in adolescence and beyond because of the development of EF.

In efforts to frame development in ways that promote agency and action, we need to reconsider our views of resistance to status quo. Rogers and Way (2021) suggest that our evidence of child development displays many examples of a natural adaptation for resistance as opposed to more frequently discussed socialization or adaptation to societal expectations. They argue that framing human development as socialization alone perpetuates social inequalities and institutionalizes cultural ideologies. **Resistance** is a concept long used regarding issues of oppression, but rarely in concert with human development. Rogers and Way (2021) argue that humans either resist or accommodate to norms and ideologies as socialized into the macrosystem. Resistance as a just and moral strategy can be applied to inclusion across many factors, including gender (Gilligan, 2011), race (Comeaux et al., 2021), and ability (Gabel & Peters, 2004).

Resistance can sometimes be associated with moral actions and disobedience. Opposing unjust practices and decisions made by those in positions of power can result in civil disobedience. This can be considered immoral by some, because by nature they go against the laws in place (Turiel, 2003). Thus, key to promoting the development of resistance might be fostering critical thinking about honesty, and recognizing blurry lines between rules that can and cannot be broken. All of this requires EF skill:

1   inhibitory control of emotions, behaviors, and thoughts to identify biases and choose alternative action, and also to inhibit social conformity when it promotes injustice;
2   working memory, by maintaining multiple perspectives, working to be empathic, and using representational skills to transform ideas; and
3   cognitive flexibility to recognize that all evidence is not equal and to generate new solutions and new ways to engage others in those solutions.

Taking a Global Perspective

Another major societal concern has been taking care of the limited resources of our planet. Although recycling programs have long been in place, a disproportionate use of oil resources and emissions and trash have contributed to a crisis: global warming. Global warming has been blamed for climate changes, odd weather patterns, melting polar ice caps, and it has been said that a continuation of the pattern as it currently progresses will result in an end to the world as we know it. Developmentally, research has shown children are more likely to be involved in a solution when they have adequate knowledge of the scientific problem (Lester et al., 2007). But, how is this related to EF?

Executive function plays a role in this activism in ways that draw on skills similar to those in the previous section; and yet, the nature of this problem is different. First, to see the problem, one may need to take perspectives, consider alternative viewpoints, and trust the knowledge of others who have more training in the area. As one acknowledges the problem, and to generate potential solutions, one needs to effortfully learn and organize their knowledge, engage in flexible thinking and planning of their actions, and collaborate and create solutions with others. Finally, to become part of the solution, one must commit to change. This requires inhibition of some actions and perhaps thoughts, considering multiple solutions and determining which is most feasible to implement, and planning and carrying out the actions. And thus, opportunity for influence is contained within the microsystems of the home and classroom, exosystems in which the curriculum is developed, standards for students are set, and community organizations provide structure, and macrosystems of values about resources.

Source: Shutterstock.

Example of Resistance: Dr. Martin Luther King, Jr.

An example of a person who used EFs to exert change on their multi-layered contexts across their own development as well as historical time is Dr. Martin Luther King, Jr. Dr. King was a young Black man who died arguing for peaceful means to change (Carson & Lewis, 2023). He grew up in a two-parent home, with both his father and grandfather serving as Baptist preachers. He was raised in a neighborhood considered middle class and safe. Dr. King was well educated, entering college at age 15, and then attending seminary, during which he learned about the work of Ghandi and Protestant Christian scholars, and then he went on to earn his doctoral degree at Boston University. Dr. King became a pastor, married, and had four children.

He was known to be a gifted speaker, and quickly became a leader in the Civil Rights Movement. After being jailed for leading a peaceful protest in Birmingham, Alabama, he was admonished by his fellow clergymen in 1963, and replied to them with a plea for them to join him. "Injustice anywhere is a threat to justice everywhere." He argued for "constructive tension" and "creative maladjustment," similar to the idea of resistance that we discussed earlier. Although he experienced discrimination and multiple jailings and was assassinated in 1968, he was widely known and respected by national leaders.

In 1967 Dr. King was invited to address psychologists at a meeting of the American Psychological Association, and he challenged this group to consider some forms of conflict and dissonance as healthy. He called professionals and scientists to promote change in systemic discrimination:

> The problem is deep. It is gigantic in extent, and chaotic in detail. And I do not believe that it will be solved until there is a kind of cosmic discontent enlarging in the bosoms of people of good will all over this nation [...] [T]here are some things in our society, some things in our world, to which we should never be adjusted. There are some things concerning which we must always be maladjusted if we are to be people of good will. We must never adjust ourselves to racial discrimination and racial segregation. We must never adjust ourselves to religious bigotry. We must never adjust ourselves to economic conditions that take necessities from the many to give luxuries to the few. We must never adjust ourselves to the madness of militarism, and the self-defeating effects of physical violence.
>
> (King, 1968)

To peacefully protest and lead, Dr. King engaged many EF skills in his social justice work. This involved inhibitory control of cognition and behaviors, regulating emotion and preventing oneself from acting on the anger and injustice occurring. This method involved holding many ideas in mind, within a constantly stressful context of discrimination and risk. And, his ideas exhibited a great deal of cognitive flexibility as he promoted new solutions to old problems. He used planning, strategies, and linguistic skill to advance his efforts and engage others in his call to action.

Within his microsystem, he exerted change by speaking out within his church, in his interactions with his wife and children, and boldly in public settings. He encouraged those in his microsystem to engage with one another to further action, thus promoting meso-level change. These effects trickled outward to the exosystems. He organized and inspired multiple marches and rallies that he did not necessarily attend himself. All of these efforts were designed to dismantle laws, policies, and practices that promoted segregation, lack of voting rights, and violations of human rights. The macrosystems espousing these issues are still undergoing transformation as a result of Dr. King's actions even though he is no longer with us. Laws have been changed, and practices and policies that support continued efforts to create equality are in place.

Linking These Concepts to Real People

In the previous chapter, we remembered Amari from Chapter 1. As a child with autism, he has certainly been impacted indirectly by some of the professions discussed thus far. Attitudes about autism within the larger society affect how he thinks about himself and others and regulates his emotions. Policies that provide funding for his services may vary based on cultural values, which will directly impact how he develops. Further, the interview with a speech pathologist in the current chapter focused on how policies and government affect children's access to resources. By informing contextual levels and appreciating cultural diversity, professionals have a great deal of influence over the way in which we support human development in our society and ongoing.

Recall Joe, whose case of ADHD was discussed by his teacher in Chapter 2 and E.M., who shared her continued journey with ADHD through childhood, adolescence, and emerging adulthood in Chapter 4. The context in which they are developing continues to indirectly affect their access to resources, such as the types of training their teachers and counselors receive, the quality of services in their schools and communities, and the value society puts on their well-being, all of which trickle into the developing person.

Finally, we shared the example of Dr. Martin Luther King, Jr. leveraging his EF to resist acceptance of inequalities. Professionals in his microsystems, exosystems, and macrosystems somehow provided contexts that promoted his personal resources. This support may have been intentional, by explicitly working to provide him with enriching experiences, or it may have been unintentional, by creating contexts that interacted with his predispositions to bring out his inner strengths in spite of what was around him. Regardless, he engaged his cognitive and behavioral inhibition, working memory, flexible thinking, creativity, and planning to use his agency with outer contextual layers; a bidirectional process possible for all developing humans and one that is increasingly likely when professionals provide intentional and explicit support of executive function development.

Summary

In this chapter, we have provided a broad view of the various ecologies in which humans develop. At the macrosystem level, there are societal values and systemic services. At the exosystem level, we have the systems that are supported by this external framework, and the systems that form the way professionals interact directly with children. We have provided suggestions for ways this occurs today as well as ideas for invoking change where one sees injustice or inequities. EF is necessary to serve the developing humans we interact with, it is needed to make decisions about and learn how to do so, and it is vital to being the change we want to see in the world.

Further Resources

Hammond, A.L. (2014). *Culturally responsive teaching and the brain: Promoting authentic engagement and rigor among culturally and linguistically diverse students.* Sage.

Lerner, R.M. (2007). *The good teen: Rescuing adolescence from the myths of the storm and stress years.* Crown Publishing.

References

Abelson, R.P. (1963). Computer simulation of "hot cognition". In S.S. Tomkins & S. Messick (Eds.), *Computer simulation of personality* (pp. 277–298). Wiley.

Adams, A.-M., & Gathercole, S.E. (2000). Limitations in working memory: Implications for language development. *International Journal of Language & Communication Disorders*, 35(1), 95–116. https://doi.org/10.1080/136828200247278.

Adolphs, R. (2009). The social brain: neural basis of social knowledge. *Annual Review of Psychology*, 60, 693–716.

Ainsworth, M.D.S., Blehar, M.C., Waters, E., & Wall, S. (1978). *Patterns of attachment: A psychological study of the strange situation*. Lawrence Erlbaum.

Alazmi, A.A., & Alazmi, H.S. (2023). Closing the gap between research and policy-making to better enable effective educational practice: A proposed framework. *Educational Research for Policy and Practice*, 22(1), 91–116.

Alderson-Day, B., & Fernyhough, C. (2015). Inner speech: Development, cognitive functions, phenomenology, and neurobiology. *Psychological Bulletin*, 141(5), 931–965. https://doi.org/10.1037/bul0000021.

Alexander, K.W., Goodman, G.S., Schaaf, J.M., Edelstein, R.S., Quas, J.A., & Shaver, P.R. (2002). The role of attachment and cognitive inhibition in predicting children's memory for a stressful event. *Journal of Experimental Child Psychology*, 83, 262–290.

Alexander, K.W., Quas, J.A., Goodman, G.S., Ghetti, S., Edelstein, R.S., Redlich, A.D., Cordon, I.M., & Jones, D.P.H. (2005). Traumatic impact predicts long-term memory for documented child sexual abuse. *Psychological Science*, 16(1), 33–40. https://doi.org/10.1111/j.0956-7976.2005.00777.

American Psychiatric Association (2022). *Diagnostic and statistical manual of mental disorders* (5th ed., text rev.). https://doi.org/10.1176/appi.books.9780890425787.

Andrews, K., Atkinson, L., Harris, M., & Gonzalez, A. (2021). Examining the effects of household chaos on child executive functions: A meta-analysis. *Psychological Bulletin*, 147(1), 16–32. https://doi.org/10.1037/bul0000311.

Arnsten, A.F.T. (2009). Stress signalling pathways that impair prefrontal cortex structure and function. *Nature Reviews Neuroscience*, 10(6), 410–422. https://doi-org.proxy.lib.csus.edu/10.1038/nrn2648.

Arterberry, M.E., & Albright, E.J. (2020). Children's memory for temporal information: The roles of temporal language and executive function, *Journal of Genetic Psychology*, 181(4), 191–205. doi:10.1080/00221325.2020.1741503.

Atkinson, R.C., & Shiffrin, R.M. (1968). Human memory: A proposed system and its control processes. In K.W. Spence & J.T. Spence (Eds.), *The psychology of learning and motivation*:II (pp. 89–195). Academic Press. https://doi.org/10.1016/S0079-7421(08)60422-3.

Atkinson, R., & Shiffrin, R.M. (2016). Human memory: A proposed system and its control processes. In R. Sternberg, S. Fiske, & D. Foss (Eds.), *Scientists making a difference: One hundred eminent behavioral and brain scientists talk about their most important contributions* (pp. 115–118). Cambridge University Press. doi:10.1017/CBO9781316422250.025.

Baddeley, A.D. (2002). Is working memory still working? *European Psychologist*, 7(2), 85–97. https://doi.org/10.1027/1016-9040.7.2.85.

Baddeley, A. (2012). Working memory: Theories, models, and controversies. *Annual Review of Psychology*, 63(1), 1–29.

Baddeley, A., Hitch, G., & Allen, R. (2021). A multicomponent model of working memory. In R.H. Logie, V. Camos, & N. Cowan (Eds.), *Working memory: State of the science* (pp. 10–43). Oxford University Press. https://doi.org/10.1093/oso/9780198842286.003.0002.

Bahrick, L.E., Lickliter, R., & Flom, R. (2004). Intersensory redundancy guides the development of selective attention, perception, and cognition in infancy. *Current Directions in Psychological Science*, 13(3), 99–102. https://doi.org/10.1111/j.0963-7214.2004.00283.x.

Bailey, J.O., & Bailenson, J.N. (2017). Considering virtual reality in children's lives. *Journal of Children and Media*, 11(1), 107–113. doi:10.1080/17482798.2016.1268779.

Baillargeon, R., & DeVos, J. (1991). Object permanence in young infants: Further evidence. *Child Development*, 62(6), 1227–1246. https://doi.org/10.2307/1130803.

Baldwin, D.A. (1995). Understanding the link between joint attention and language. In C. Moore & P.J. Dunham (Eds.) *Joint attention: Its origins and role in development* (pp. 131–158). Erlbaum.

Balogun, O.O., Dagvadorj, A., Anigo, K.M., Ota, E., & Sasaki, S. (2015). Factors influencing breastfeeding exclusivity during the first 6 months of life in developing countries: A quantitative and qualitative systematic review. *Maternal & Child Nutrition*, 11(4), 433–451. https://doi.org/10.1111/mcn.12180.

Bandura, A. (1997). *Self-efficacy: The exercise of control.* W H Freeman/Times Books/Henry Holt.

Bandura, A. (2001). Social cognitive theory: An agentic perspective. *Annual Review of Psychology*, 52(1), 1–26.

Bandura, A. (2018). Toward a psychology of human agency: Pathways and reflections. *Perspectives on Psychological Science*, 13(2), 130–136. https://doi-org.proxy.lib.csus.edu/10.1177/1745691617699280.

Barac, R., & Bialystok, E. (2012). Bilingual effects on cognitive and linguistic development: role of language, cultural background, and education. *Child Development*, 83(2), 413–422. https://doi.org/10.1111/j.1467-8624.2011.01707.x.

Bardhoshi, G., & Um, B. (2021). The effects of job demands and resources on school counselor burnout: Self-efficacy as a mediator. *Journal of Counseling & Development*, 99(3), 289–301.

Barkley, R.A. (1997). Behavioral inhibition, sustained attention, and executive functions: Constructing a unifying theory of ADHD. *Psychological Bulletin*, 121(1), 65–94. https://doi.org/10.1037/0033-2909.121.1.65.

Barkley, R.A. (2006). *Attention-deficit hyperactivity disorder: A handbook for diagnosis and treatment* (3rd ed.). Guilford Press.

Baron, L.S., & Arbel, Y. (2022). An implicit-explicit framework for intervention methods in developmental language disorder. *American Journal of Speech-Language Pathology*, 31(4), 1557–1573. https://doi.org/10.1044/2022_AJSLP-21-00172.

Bauer, P.J., & Dugan, J.A. (2020). Memory development. In J. Rubenstein, P. Rakic, B. Chen, & K.Y. Kwan (Eds.). *Neural circuit and cognitive development* (2nd ed.; pp. 395–412). Academic Press.

Berger, E.M., Fehr, E., Hermes, H., Schunk, D., & Winkel, K. (2020). The impact of working memory training on children's cognitive and noncognitive skills. *NHH Dept. of Economics Discussion Paper*, 9. http://dx.doi.org/10.2139/ssrn.3622985.

Berkes, J., Raikes, A., Bouguen, A., & Filmer, D. (2019). Joint roles of parenting and nutritional status for child development: Evidence from rural Cambodia. *Developmental Science*, 22(5), e12874. https://doi.org/10.1111/desc.12874.

Berninger, V.W., Abbott, R.D., Abbott, S.P., Graham, S., & Richards, T. (2002). Writing and reading: Connections between language by hand and language by eye. *Journal of Learning Disabilities*, 35(1), 39–56. https://doi.org/10.1177/002221940203500104.

Bialystok, E. (2001). *Bilingualism in development: Language, literacy, and cognition*. Cambridge University Press. https://doi.org/10.1017/CBO9780511605963.

Bialystok, E., Craik, F.I., & Luk, G. (2012). Bilingualism: consequences for mind and brain. *Trends in Cognitive Sciences*, 16(4), 240–250. https://doi.org/10.1016/j.tics.2012.03.001.

Bierman, K.L., & Torres, M. (2016). Promoting the development of executive functions through early education and prevention programs. In J.A. Griffin, P. McCardle, & L.S. Freund (Eds.), *Executive function in preschool-age children: Integrating measurement, neurodevelopment, and translational research* (pp. 299–326). American Psychological Association. https://doi.org/10.1037/14797-014.

Bjorklund, D.F., & Causey, K. (2017). *Children's thinking: Cognitive development and individual differences* (6th ed.). Sage.

Blair, B.L., Gangle, M.R., Perry, N.B., O'Brien, M., Calkins, S.D., Keane, S.P., & Shanahan, L. (2016). Indirect effects of emotion regulation on peer acceptance and rejection: The roles of positive and negative social behaviors. *Merrill-Palmer Quarterly*, 62(4), 415–439.

Blair, C., & Diamond, A. (2008). Biological processes in prevention and intervention: The promotion of self-regulation as a means of preventing school failure. *Development and Psychopathology*, 20(3), 899–911.

Blair, C., & Raver, C.C. (2015). School readiness and self-regulation: A developmental psychobiological approach. *Annual Review of Psychology*, 66, 711–731.

Blair, C., & Razza, R.P. (2007). Relating effortful control, executive function, and false belief understanding to emerging math and literacy ability in kindergarten. *Child Development*, 78(2), 647–663.

Blair, C., & Ursache, A. (2011). A bidirectional model of executive functions and self-regulation. In K.D. Vohs & R.F. Baumeister (Eds.), *Handbook of self-regulation: Research, theory, and applications* (pp. 300–320). Guilford Press.

Blakemore S.J. (2012). Development of the social brain in adolescence. *Journal of the Royal Society of Medicine*, 105, 111–116. https://doi.org/10.1258/jrsm.2011.110221.

Blakemore, S.J., & Choudhury, S. (2006). Development of the adolescent brain: Implications for executive function and social cognition. *Journal of Child Psychology and Psychiatry, and Allied Disciplines,* 47(3-4), 296–312. https://doi.org/10.1111/j.1469-7610.2006.01611.x.

Bodrova, E., & Leong, D.J. (2006). The development of self-regulation in young children: Implications for teacher training. In M. Zaslow & I. Martinez-Beck (Eds.), *Future directions in teacher training* (pp. 203–224). Brooks-Cole.

Borghouts-van de Pas, I., & Freese, C. (2021). Offering jobs to persons with disabilities: A Dutch employers' perspective. *Alter,* 15(1), 89–98.

Bornstein, M.H., & Cote, L.R. (2009). Child temperament in three U.S. cultural groups. *Infant Ment Health J.,* 30(5), 433–451. doi:10.1002/imhj.20223.

Bornstein, M.H., Putnick, D.L., & Lansford, J.E. (2011). Parenting attributions and attitudes in cross-cultural perspective. *Parenting, Science and Practice,* 11(2-3), 214–237. https://doi.org/10.1080/15295192.2011.585568.

Boroditsky, L. (2001). Does language shape thought? Mandarin and English speakers' conceptions of time. *Cognitive Psychology,* 43(1), 1–22.

Bos, K.J., Fox, N., Zeanah, C.H., & Nelson, C.A.III (2009). Effects of early psycho-social deprivation on the development of memory and executive function. *Frontiers in Behavioral Neuroscience,* 3, 16. doi:10.3389/neuro.08.016.2009.

Bowlby, J. (1969/1982). *Attachment and loss: Attachment* (Vol. 1). Basic.

Bracha, H.S. (2004). Freeze, flight, fight, fright, faint: Adaptationist perspectives on the acute stress response spectrum. *CNS Spectrums,* 9(9), 679–685.

Brandes-Aitken, A., Braren, S., Swingler, M., Voegtline, K., & Blair, C. (2019). Sustained attention in infancy: A foundation for the development of multiple aspects of self-regulation for children in poverty. *Journal of Experimental Child Psychology,* 184, 192–209. https://doi.org/10.1016/j.jecp.2019.04.006.

Bretherton, I. (1992). The origins of attachment theory: John Bowlby and Mary Ainsworth. *Developmental Psychology,* 28, 759–775.

Brigham, J.C., Maass, A., Snyder, L.D., & Spaulding, K. (1982). Accuracy of eye-witness identification in a field setting. *Journal of Personality and Social Psychology,* 42(4), 673.

Bronfenbrenner, U. (1974). Is early intervention effective? *Teachers College Record,* 76 (2), 1–19. https://doi.org/10.1177/016146817407600202.

Bronfenbrenner, U., & Morris, P.A. (2006). The bioecological model of human development. In R.M. Lerner & W. Damon (Eds.), *Handbook of child psychology: Theoretical models of human development* (pp. 793–828). Wiley.

Buckley, L., Berta, W., Cleverley, K., & Widger, K. (2022). Exploring pediatric nurses' perspectives on their work environment, work attitudes, and experience of burnout: What really matters? *Frontiers in Pediatrics,* 10, Article 851001. https://doi.org/10.3389/fped.2022.851001.

Burke, L.A., & Ray, R. (2008). Re-setting the concentration levels of students in higher education: An exploratory study. *Teaching in Higher Education,* 13(5), 571–582.

Burnham Riosa, P., Chan, V., Maughan, A.L., Stables, V., Albaum, C., & Weiss, J.A. (2017). Remediating deficits or increasing strengths in autism spectrum disorder research: A content analysis. *Advances in Neurodevelopmental Disorders,* 1, 113–121. https://doi.org/10.1007/s41252-017-0027-3.

Buss, K.A., Schumacher, J.R.M., Dolski, I., Kalin, N.H., Goldsmith, H.H., & Davidson, R.J. (2003). Right frontal brain activity, cortisol, and withdrawal behavior in 6-month-old infants. *Behavioral Neuroscience*, 117(1), 11–20. https://doi.org/10.1037/0735-7044.117.1.11.

Buyanova, I.S., & Arsalidou, M. (2021). Cerebral white matter myelination and relations to age, gender, and cognition: A selective review. *Frontiers in Human Neuroscience*, 15, Article 662031. https://doi.org/10.3389/fnhum.2021.662031.

Cabeza, R., McIntosh, A.R., Tulving, E., Nyberg, L., & Grady, C.L. (1997). Age-related differences in effective neural connectivity during encoding and recall. *NeuroReport* 8 (16), 3479–3483.

Cain, K., Oakhill, J., & Bryant, P. (2004). Children's reading comprehension ability: Concurrent prediction by working memory, verbal ability, and component skills. *Journal of Educational Psychology*, 96, 31–42. doi:10.1037/0022-0663.96.1.31.

Callaghan, T., & Corbit, J. (2015). The development of symbolic representation. In L. S. Liben, U. Müller, & R.M. Lerner (Eds.), *Handbook of child psychology and developmental science: Cognitive processes* (pp. 250–295). Wiley. https://doi.org/10.1002/9781118963418.childpsy207.

Cameron, C.E., Brock, L.L., Hatfield, B.E., Cottone, E.A., Rubinstein, E., LoCasale-Crouch, J., & Grissmer, D.W. (2015). Visuomotor integration and inhibitory control compensate for each other in school readiness. *Developmental Psychology*, 51(11), 1529–1543.

Cantor, P., Osher, D., Berg, J., Steyer, L., & Rose, T. (2019). Malleability, plasticity, and individuality: How children learn and develop in context. *Applied Developmental Science*, 23, 307–337. doi:10.1080/10888691.2017.1398649.

Carlson, S.M., & Beck, D.M. (2009). Symbols as tools in the development of executive function. In A. Winsler, C. Fernyhough, & I. Montero (Eds.), *Private speech, executive functioning, and the development of verbal self-regulation* (pp. 163–175). Cambridge University Press. https://doi.org/10.1017/CBO9780511581533.014.

Carlson, S.M., & Meltzoff, A.N. (2008). Bilingual experience and executive functioning in young children. *Developmental Science*, 11(2), 282–298. https://doi.org/10.1111/j.1467-7687.2008.00675.x.

Carlson, S.M., & Moses, L.J. (2001). Individual differences in inhibitory control and children's theory of mind. *Child Development*, 72(4), 1032–1053.

Carlson, S.M., & Zelazo, P.D. (2008). Symbolic thought. In M.M. Haith & J.B. Benson (Eds.), *Encyclopedia of infant and early childhood development* (pp. 288–297). Academic Press.

Carlson, S.M., Moses, L.J., & Hix, H.R. (1998). The role of inhibitory processes in young children's difficulties with deception and false belief. *Child Development*, 69(3), 672–691.

Carson, C., & Lewis, D.L. (2023, April 27). Martin Luther King, Jr. *Encyclopedia Britannica*. www.britannica.com/biography/Martin-Luther-King-Jr.

Cartwright, K.B. (2008). Introduction to literacy processes: Cognitive flexibility in learning and teaching. In K.B. Cartwright (Ed.), *Literacy processes: Cognitive flexibility in learning and teaching* (pp. 3–18). Guilford Press.

Case, R., Okamoto, Y., Griffin, S., McKeough, A., Bleiker, C., Henderson, B., & Stephenson, K.M. (1996). The role of central conceptual structures in the development of children's thought. *Monographs of the Society for Research in Child Development*, 61 (1-2).

Casey, B.J., Cohen, J.D., Jezzard, P., Turner, R., Noll, D.C., Trainor, R.J., Giedd, J., Kaysen, D., Hertz-Pannier, L., & Rapoport, J.L. (1995). Activation of prefrontal cortex in children during a nonspatial working memory task with functional MRI. *NeuroImage*, 2(3), 221–229. https://doi.org/10.1006/nimg.1995.1029.

Casey, B.J., Glatt, C.E., Tottenham, N., Soliman, F., Bath, K., Amso, D., Altemus, M., Pattwell, S., Jones, R., Levita, L., McEwen, B., Magariños, A.M., Gunnar, M., Thomas, K. M., Mezey, J., Clark, A.G., Hempstead, B.L., & Lee, F.S. (2009). Brain-derived neurotrophic factor as a model system for examining gene by environment interactions across development. *Neuroscience*, 164(1), 108–120. https://doi.org/10.1016/j.neuroscience. 2009.03.081.

Casey, B.J., Tottenham, N., Liston, C., & Durston, S. (2005). Imaging the developing brain: What have we learned about cognitive development?, *Trends in Cognitive Sciences*, 9, 104–110. https://doi.org/10.1016/j.tics.2005.01.011.

Chi, M.T.H. (1978). Knowledge structures and memory development. In R.S. Siegler (Ed.), *Children's thinking: What develops?* (pp. 73–96). Erlbaum.

Chiappe, P., Hasher, L., & Siegel, L.S. (2000). Working memory, inhibitory control, and reading disability. *Memory & Cognition*, 28(1), 8–17. https://doi.org/10. 3758/BF03211570.

Cicchetti, D., & Lynch, M. (1993). Toward an ecological/transactional model of community violence and child maltreatment: Consequences for children's development. *Psychiatry*, 56(1), 96–118.

Clancy, B., Darlington, R.B., & Finlay, B.L. (2001). Translating developmental time across mammalian species. *Neuroscience*, 105(1), 7–17. https://doi.org/10.1016/ s0306-4522(01)00171–00173.

Clark, K.B. (1971). The pathos of power: A psychological perspective. *American Psychologist*, 26(12), 1047–1057. https://doi.org/10.1037/h0032217.

Cole, P.M., Armstrong, L.M., & Pemberton, C.K. (2010). The role of language in the development of emotion regulation. In S.D. Calkins & M.A. Bell (Eds.), *Child development at the intersection of emotion and cognition* (pp. 59–77). American Psychological Association. https://doi.org/10.1037/12059-004.

Comeaux, E., Grummert, S.E., & Cruz, N.A. (2021). Strategies of resistance among racially minoritized students at a Hispanic-serving institution: A critical race theory perspective. *Journal of Higher Education*, 92(3), 465–498.

Cortés Pascual, A., Moyano Muñoz, N., & Quilez Robres, A. (2019). The relationship between executive functions and academic performance in primary education: Review and meta-analysis. *Frontiers in Psychology*, 10, p. 1–18.

Courchesne, E., Mouton, P.R., Calhoun, M.E., Semendeferi, K., Ahrens-Barbeau, C., Hallet, M.J., Barnes, C.C., & Pierce, K. (2011). Neuron number and size in prefrontal cortex of children with autism. *Journal of the American Medical Association*, 306(18), 2001–2010. https://doi.org/10.1001/jama.2011.1638.

Cowan N. (2016). Working memory maturation: Can we get at the essence of cognitive growth? *Psychological Science*, 11(2), 239–264. https://doi.org/10.1177/ 1745691615621279.

Cragg, L., & Nation, K. (2010). Language and the development of cognitive control. *Topics in Cognitive Science*, 4, 631–642. doi:10.1111/j.1756-8765.2009.01080.x.

Craik, F.I.M., & Lockhart, R.S. (1972). Levels of processing: A framework for memory research, *Journal of Verbal Learning and Verbal Behavior*, 11(6), 671–684. https:// doi.org/10.1016/S0022-5371(72)80001-X.

Cramm, J.M., Strating, M.M., Roebroeck, M.E., & Nieboer, A.P. (2013). The importance of general self-efficacy for the quality of life of adolescents with chronic conditions. *Social Indicators Research*, 113, 551–561.

Crawford, K. (1996). Vygotskian approaches in human development in the information era. *Educational Studies in Mathematics*, 31, 43–62.

Crick, N.R., & Dodge, K.A. (1994). A review and reformulation of social information-processing mechanisms in children's social adjustment. *Psychological Bulletin*, 115(1), 74.

Crick, N.R., & Dodge, K.A. (1996). Social information-processing mechanisms on reactive and proactive aggression. *Child Development*, 67(3), 993–1002. https://doi.org/10.2307/1131875.

Crivello, C., Kuzyk, O., Rodrigues, M., Friend, M., Zesiger, P., & Poulin-Dubois, D. (2016). The effects of bilingual growth on toddlers' executive function. *Journal of Experimental Child Psychology*, 141, 121–132. https://doi.org/10.1016/j.jecp.2015.08.004.

Cuevas, K., & Bell, M.A. (2010). Developmental progression of looking and reaching performance on the A-not-B task. *Developmental Psychology*, 46(5), 1363–1371. https://doi.org/10.1037/a0020185.

Cumming, M.M., Bettini, E., Pham, A.V., & Park, J. (2020). School-, classroom-, and dyadic-level experiences: A literature review of their relationship with students' executive functioning development. *Review of Educational Research*, 90(1), 47–94.

Cusick, S.E., & Georgieff, M.K. (2016). The role of nutrition in brain development: The golden opportunity of the "first 1000 days." *Journal of Pediatrics*, 175, 16–21. https://doi.org/10.1016/j.jpeds.2016.05.013.

Damasio, A.R. (1994). Descartes' error and the future of human life. *Scientific American*, 271(4), 144–144.

Damasio, A. (1999). *The feeling of what happens: Body and emotion in the making of consciousness*. Harcourt College Publishers

Damasio, A.R. (2004). Emotions and feelings: A neurobiological perspective. In A.S.R. Manstead, N. Frijda, & A. Fischer (Eds.), *Feelings and emotions: The Amsterdam symposium* (pp. 49–57). Cambridge University Press. https://doi.org/10.1017/CBO9780511806582.004.

Daniels, M.C., & Adair, L.S. (2005). Breast-feeding influences cognitive development in Filipino children. *Journal of Nutrition*, 135(11), 2589–2595. https://doi.org/10.1093/jn/135.11.2589.

Darwin, C. (1872). *The expression of the emotions in man and animals*. John Murray. https://doi.org/10.1037/10001-000.

Davidson, R.J., Ekman, P., Saron, C.D., Senulis, J.A., & Friesen, W.V. (1990). Approach-withdrawal and cerebral asymmetry: Emotional expression and brain physiology: I. *Journal of Personality and Social Psychology*, 58(2), 330–341. https://doi.org/10.1037/0022-3514.58.2.330.

Davies, P.L., & Gavin, W.J. (2007). Validating the diagnosis of sensory processing disorders using EEG technology. *American Journal of Occupational Therapy*, 61(2), 176–189. https://doi.org/10.5014/ajot.61.2.176.

Day, J.J., & Sweatt, J.D. (2011). Epigenetic mechanisms in cognition. *Neuron*, 70(5), 813–829. https://doi.org/10.1016/j.neuron.2011.05.019.

De Bellis, M.D. (2005). The psychobiology of neglect. *Child Maltreatment*, 10(2), 150–172. https://doi.org/10.1177/1077559505275116.

DeCasper, A.J., & Fifer, W.P. (1980). Of human bonding: Newborns prefer their mothers' voices. *Science*, 208(4448), 1174–1176. https://doi.org/10.1126/science.7375928.

DeCasper, A.J., & Spence, M.J. (1986). Prenatal maternal speech influences newborns' perception of speech sounds. *Infant Behavior & Development*, 9(2), 133–150. https://doi.org/10.1016/0163-6383(86)90025-1.

Decety, J. (2010). The neurodevelopment of empathy in humans. *Developmental Neuroscience*, 32(4), 257–267.

Decety, J. (2015). The neural pathways, development and functions of empathy. *Current Opinion in Behavioral Sciences*, 3, 1–6. https://doi.org/10.1016/j.cobeha.2014.12.001.

Decety, J., & Michalska, K.J. (2010). Neurodevelopmental changes in the circuits underlying empathy and sympathy from childhood to adulthood. *Developmental Science*, 13, 886–899. https://doi.org/10.1111/j.1467-7687.2009.00940.x.

Deater-Deckard, K. (2001). Annotation: Recent research examining the role of peer relationships in the development of psychopathology. *Journal of Child Psychology and Psychiatry and Allied Disciplines*, 42(5), 565–579.

de Greck, M., Shi, Z., Wang, G., Zuo, X., Yang, X., Wang, X., Northoff, G., & Han, S. (2012). Culture modulates brain activity during empathy with anger. *NeuroImage*, 59(3), 2871–2882.

DeLoache, J.S. (1991). Symbolic functioning in very young children: Understanding of pictures and models. *Child Development*, 62, 736–752.

DeLoache, J.S. (2004). Becoming symbol-minded. *Trends in Cognitive Sciences*, 8(2), 66–70. https://doi.org/10.1016/j.tics.2003.12.004.

DePrince, A.P., Weinzierl, K.M., & Combs, M.D. (2009). Executive function performance and trauma exposure in a community sample of children. *Child Abuse & Neglect*, 33(6), 353–361.

Depue, B.E., Burgess, G.C., Willcutt, E.G., Ruzic, L., & Banich, M.T. (2010). Inhibitory control of memory retrieval and motor processing associated with the right lateral prefrontal cortex: evidence from deficits in individuals with ADHD. *Neuropsychologia*, 48(13), 3909–3917. https://doi.org/10.1016/j.neuropsychologia.2010.09.013.

Devine, P.G., Forscher, P.S., Austin, A.J., & Cox, W.T. (2012). Long-term reduction in implicit race bias: A prejudice habit-breaking intervention. *Journal of Experimental Social Psychology*, 48(6), 1267–1278.

Diamond, A. (1990). Developmental time course in human infants and infant monkeys, and the neural bases of, inhibitory control in reaching. *Annals of the New York Academy of Sciences*, 608(1), 637–676.

Diamond, A. (2013). Executive functions. *Annual Review of Psychology*, 64, 135–168. https://doi.org/10.1146/annurev-psych-113011-143750.

Diamond, A., & Goldman-Rakic, P.S. (1989). Comparison of human infants and rhesus monkeys on Piaget's AB task: Evidence for dependence on dorsolateral prefrontal cortex. *Experimental Brain Research*, 74, 24–40. https://doi.org/10.1007/BF00248277.

Diamond, A., & Lee, K. (2011). Interventions shown to aid executive function development in children 4 to 12 years old. *Science*, 333(6045), 959–964.

Diamond, A., Barnett, W.S., Thomas, J., & Munro, S. (2007). Preschool program improves cognitive control. *Science*, 318(5855), 1387–1388.

Diamond, A., Briand, L., Fossella, J., & Gehlbach, L. (2004). Genetic and neurochemical modulation of prefrontal cognitive functions in children. *American Journal of Psychiatry*, 161(1), 125–132. https://doi.org/10.1176/appi.ajp.161.1.125.

Diamond, A., Prevor, M.B., Callender, G., & Druin, D.P. (1997). Prefrontal cortex cognitive deficits in children treated early and continuously for PKU. *Monographs of the Society for Research in Child Development*, 62(4), i–208.

D'Mello, A.M., & Stoodley, C.J. (2015). Cerebro-cerebellar circuits in autism spectrum disorder. *Frontiers in Neuroscience*, 9, article 408. doi:10.3389/fnins.2015.00408.

Driscoll, I., Hamilton, D.A., Petropoulos, H., Yeo, R.A., Brooks, W.M., Baumgartner, R.N., & Sutherland, R.J. (2003). The aging hippocampus: Cognitive, biochemical and structural findings. *Cerebral Cortex*, 13(12), 1344–1351. https://doi.org/10.1093/cercor/bhg081.

Dunn, E.C., Soare, T.W., Zhu, Y., Simpkin, A.J., Suderman, M.J., Klengel, T., Smith, A.D.A.C., Ressler, K.J., & Relton, C.L. (2019). Sensitive periods for the effect of childhood adversity on DNA methylation: Results from a prospective, longitudinal study. *Biological Psychiatry*, 85(10), 838–849. https://doi.org/10.1016/j.biopsych.2018.12.023.

Dyer, C.A. (1999). Pathophysiology of phenylketonuria. *Mental Retardation and Developmental Disabilities Research Reviews*, 5(2), 104–112. https://doi.org/10.1023/a:1024190429920.

East, P., Doom, J.R., Blanco, E., Burrows, R., Lozoff, B., & Gahagan, S. (2021). Iron deficiency in infancy and neurocognitive and educational outcomes in young adulthood. *Developmental Psychology*, 57(6), 962–975. https://doi.org/10.1037/dev0001030.

Edelman, G.M. (1987). *Neural Darwinism: The theory of neuronal group selection*. Basic Books.

Edin, F., Macoveanu, J., Olesen, P., Tegnér, J., & Klingberg, T. (2007). Stronger synaptic connectivity as a mechanism behind development of working memory-related brain activity during childhood. *Journal of Cognitive Neuroscience*, 19(5), 750–760. https://doi.org/10.1162/jocn.2007.19.5.750.

Eisenberg, N., Fabes, R.A., & Spinrad, T.L. (2006). Prosocial development. In N. Eisenberg, W. Damon, & R.M. Lerner (Eds.), *Handbook of child psychology: Social, emotional, and personality development* (pp. 646–718). Wiley.

Eisenberg, N., Valiente, C., & Champion, C. (2004). Empathy-related responding. In A. G. Miller (Ed.), *The social psychology of good and evil* (pp. 386–415). Guildford Press.

Eisenberg, N., Fabes, R.A., Murphy, B., Karbon, M., Maszk, P., Smith, M., O'Boyle, C., & Suh, K. (1994). The relations of emotionality and regulation to dispositional and situational empathy-related responding. *Journal of Personality and Social Psychology*, 66, 776–797.

Ekman, P. (1992). Facial expressions of emotion: New findings, new questions. *Psychological Science*, 3(1), 34–38. doi:10.1111/j.1467-9280.1992.tb00253.x.

Ekman, P., Sorenson, E.R., & Friesen, W.V. (1969). Pan-cultural elements in facial displays of emotion. *Science*, 164(3875), 86–88.

El Zaatari, W., & Maalouf, I. (2022). How the Bronfenbrenner bio-ecological system theory explains the development of students' sense of belonging to school? *SAGE Open*, 12(4). https://doi.org/10.1177/21582440221134089.

Engel, M.L., & Gunnar, MR. (2020). The development of stress reactivity and regulation during human development. *International Review of Neurobiology*, 150, 41–76.

Engelhardt, L.E., Briley, D.A., Mann, F.D., Harden, K.P., & Tucker-Drob, E.M. (2015). Genes unite executive functions in childhood. *Psychological Science*, 26(8), 1151–1163. https://doi.org/10.1177/0956797615577209.

Erikson, E. (1968). *Identity, youth and crisis*. Norton.

Eriksson, P.S., Perfilieva, E., Björk-Eriksson, T., Alborn, A.M., Nordborg, C., Peterson, D.A., & Gage, F.H. (1998). Neurogenesis in the adult human hippocampus. *Nature Medicine*, 4(11), 1313–1317. https://doi.org/10.1038/3305.

Fahie, C.M., & Symons, D.K. (2003). Executive functioning and theory of mind in children clinically referred for attention and behavior problems. *Journal of Applied Developmental Psychology*, 24(1), 51–73.

Fay-Stammbach, T., Hawes, D.J., & Meredith, P. (2014). Parenting influences on executive function in early childhood: A review. *Child Development Perspectives*, 8(4), 258–264.

Feldman, R. (2007). Parent–infant synchrony: Biological foundations and developmental outcomes. *Current Directions in Psychological Science*, 16(6), 340–345.

Ferguson, H.J., Brunsdon, V.E.A., & Bradford, E.E.F. (2021). The developmental trajectories of executive function from adolescence to old age. *Scientific Reports*, 11, 1382. https://doi.org/10.1038/s41598-020-80866-1.

Fernández García, L., Merchán, A., Phillips-Silver, J., & Daza González, M.T. (2021). Neuropsychological development of cool and hot executive functions between 6 and 12 years of age: A systematic review. *Frontiers in Psychology*, 12, Article 687337.

Fischer, K.W., & Bidell, T.R. (2006). Dynamic development of action and thought. In R.M. Lerner & W. Damon (Eds.), *Handbook of child psychology: Theoretical models of human development* (pp. 313–399). Wiley.

Fischer, K.W., & van Geert, P. (2014). Dynamic development of brain and behavior. In P.C.M. Molenaar, R.M. Lerner, & K.M. Newell (Eds.), *Handbook of developmental systems theory and methodology* (pp. 287–315). Guilford Press.

Fivush, R., & Nelson, K. (2004). Culture and language in the emergence of autobiographical memory. *Psychological Science*, 15(9), 573–577. www.jstor.org/stable/40064143.

Flavell, J.H., Flavell, E.R., & Green, F.L. (1983). Development of the appearance–reality distinction. *Cognitive Psychology*, 15, 95–120. doi:10.1016/0010-0285(83)90005-1.

Font, S.A., & Gershoff, E.T. (2020). Foster care: How we can, and should, do more for maltreated children. *Social Policy Report*, 33(3), 1–40.

Forehand, R., & McKinney, B. (1993). Historical overview of child discipline in the United States: Implications for mental health clinicians and researchers. *Journal of Child and Family Studies*, 2, 221–228.

Fox, N.A., Henderson, H.A., Marshall, P.J., Nichols, K.E., & Ghera, M.M. (2005). Behavioral inhibition: Linking biology and behavior within a developmental framework. *Annual Review of Psychology*, 56, 235–262.

Frankel, L., & Sampige, R. (2022). Supporting families: Lessons learned from the COVID-19 pandemic. *Human Development*, 66(3), 163–166.

Friedman, L.A., & Rapoport, J.L. (2015). Brain development in ADHD. *Current Opinion in Neurobiology*, 30, 106–111.

Friedman, N.P., Miyake, A., Young, S.E., DeFries, J.C., Corley, R.P., & Hewitt, J.K. (2008). Individual differences in executive functions are almost entirely genetic in origin. *Journal of Experimental Psychology: General*, 137(2), 201–225. https://doi.org/10.1037/0096-3445.137.2.201.

Frye, D., Zelazo, P.D., & Palfai, T. (1995). Theory of mind and rule-based reasoning. *Cognitive Development*, 10(4), 483–527.

Fuster J.M. (2002). Frontal lobe and cognitive development. *Journal of Neurocytology*, 31(3-5), 373–385.

Gabel, S., & Peters, S. (2004). Presage of a paradigm shift? Beyond the social model of disability toward resistance theories of disability. *Disability & Society*, 19(6), 585–600. https://doi-org.proxy.lib.csus.edu/10.1080/0968759042000252515.

Gaigg, S.B., Bowler, D.M., & Gardiner, J.M. (2014). Episodic but not semantic order memory difficulties in autism spectrum disorder: Evidence from the historical figures task. *Memory*, 22(6), 669–678. doi:10.1080/09658211.2013.811256.

García, O., & Torres-Guevara, R. (2021). Monoglossic language education policies and Latinx students' language. In E.G. Murillo Jr, D. Delgado Bernal, S. Morales, L. Urrieta Jr, E. Ruiz Bybee, J.S. Muñoz, V.B. Saenz, D. Villanueva, M. Machado-Casas, & K. Espinoza (Eds.), *Handbook of Latinos and education* (2nd ed.; pp. 93–102). Routledge.

García Coll, C., Crnic, K., Lamberty, G., Wasik, B.H., Jenkins, R., Vázquez García, H., & McAdoo, H.P. (1996). An integrative model for the study of developmental competencies in minority children. *Child Development*, 67(5), 1891–1914.

García Coll, C., & Szalacha, L.A. (2004). The multiple contexts of middle childhood. *Future of Children*, 14(2), 81–97. https://doi.org/10.2307/1602795.

Gaskins, S., & Alcalá, L. (2023). Studying executive function in culturally meaningful ways, *Journal of Cognition and Development*, 24, 260–279. doi:10.1080/15248372.2022.2160722.

Gathercole, S.E. (1998). The development of memory. *Journal of Child Psychology and Psychiatry*, 39(1), 3–27. https://doi.org/10.1017/S0021963097001753.

Gergely, G., & Watson, J.S. (1996). The social biofeedback model of parental affect-mirroring. *International Journal of Psychoanalysis*, 77(6), 1181.

Ghetti, S., & Alexander, K.W. (2004). If it happened, I would remember it: Strategic use of event memorability in the rejection of false autobiographical events. *Child Development*, 75, 542–561.

Ghetti, S., Lyons, K.E., Lazzarin, F., & Cornoldi, C. (2008). The development of metamemory monitoring during retrieval: The case of memory strength and memory absence. *Journal of Experimental Child Psychology*, 99(3), 157–181. https://doi.org/10.1016 /j.jecp. 2007.11.001.

Gilligan, C. (2011). *Joining the resistance*. Polity Press.

Ginet, M., & Py, J. (2001). A technique for enhancing memory in eye witness testimonies for use by police officers and judicial officials: The cognitive interview. *Le Travail Humain*, 642(2), 173–191.

Goddings, A.-L., Roalf, D., Lebel, C., & Tamnes, C.K. (2021). Development of white matter microstructure and executive functions during childhood and adolescence: A review of diffusion MRI studies. *Developmental Cognitive Neuroscience*, 51, Article 101008. https://doi.org/10.1016/j.dcn.2021.101008.

Gogtay, N., Giedd, J.N., Lusk, L., Hayashi, K.M., Greenstein, D., Vaituzis, A.C., Nugent, T.F., Herman, D.H., Clasen, L.S., Toga, A.W. et al. (2004). Dynamic mapping of human cortical development during childhood through early adulthood. *Proceedings of the National Academy of Sciences*, 101, 8174–8179.

Goldman-Rakic P.S. (1995). Cellular basis of working memory. *Neuron*, 14(3), 477–485. https://doi.org/10.1016/0896-6273(95)90304–90306.

Goosens, K.A., & Sapolsky, R.M. (2007). Stress and glucocorticoid contributions to normal and pathological aging. In D.R. Riddle (Ed.), *Brain aging: Models, methods, and mechanisms* (pp. 305–322). Taylor & Francis. https://doi-org.proxy.lib.csus.edu/10.1201/9781420005523.ch13.

Gottlieb, G. (2007). Probabilistic epigenesis. *Developmental Science*, 10(1), 1–11.

Grabell, A.S., Olson, S.L., Miller, A.L., Kessler, D.A., Felt, B., Kaciroti, N., Wang, L., & Tardif, T. (2015). The impact of culture on physiological processes of emotion regulation: A comparison of US and Chinese preschoolers. *Developmental Science*, 18 (3), 420–435.

Granic, I., Lobel, A., & Engels, R.C.M.E. (2014). The benefits of playing video games. *American Psychologist*, 69(1), 66–78. https://doi.org/10.1037/a0034857.

Gray, J.A. (1990). Brain systems that mediate both emotion and cognition. *Cognition & Emotion*, 4(3), 269–288.

Greenough, W.T., Black, J.E., & Wallace, C.S. (1987). Experience and brain development. *Child Development*, 58(3), 539–559.

Gueron-Sela, N., Camerota, M., Willoughby, M.T., Vernon-Feagans, L., Cox, M.J., & The Family Life Project Key Investigators (2018). Maternal depressive symptoms, mother-child interactions, and children's executive function. *Developmental Psychology*, 54(1), 71–82. https://doi.org/10.1037/dev0000389.

Gunnar, M.R., & Quevedo, K.M. (2007). Early care experiences and HPA axis regulation in children: A mechanisms for later trauma and vulnerability. *Progress in Brain Research*, 167, 137–149. doi:10.1016/S0079-6123(07)67010-1.

Gunnar, M.R., Brodersen, L., Nachmias, M., Buss, K., & Rigatuso, J. (1996). Stress reactivity and attachment security. *Developmental Psychobiology*, 29(3), 191–204.

Gutiérrez, K.D., & Rogoff, B. (2003). Cultural ways of learning: Individual traits or repertoires of practice. *Educational Researcher*, 32(5), 19–25.

Hackman, D.A., Gallop, R., Evans, G.W., & Farah, M.J. (2015). Socioeconomic status and executive function: developmental trajectories and mediation. *Developmental Science*, 18(5), 686–702. https://doi.org/10.1111/desc.12246.

Haft, S.L., Duong, P.H., Ho, T.C., Hendren, R.L., & Hoeft, F. (2019). Anxiety and attentional bias in children with specific learning disorders. *Journal of Abnormal Child Psychology*, 47(3), 487–497. https://doi.org/10.1007/s10802-018-0458-y.

Hall, H.K., Millear, P.M.R., Summers, M.J., & Isbel, B. (2021). Longitudinal research on perspective taking in adolescence: A systematic review. *Adolescent Research Review*, 6, 125–150. https://doi.org/10.1007/s40894-021-00150-9.

Harris, K.R., Graham, S., Mason, L., McKeown, D., & Olinghouse, N.G. (2018). Self-regulated strategy development in writing: A classroom example of developing executive function processes and future directions. In L. Meltzer (Ed.), *Executive function in education: From theory to practice* (2nd ed.; pp. 326–356). Guilford Press.

Hart, N., Fawkner, S., Niven, A., & Booth, J.N. (2022). Scoping review of yoga in schools: Mental health and cognitive outcomes in both neurotypical and neurodiverse youth populations. *Children*, 9(6), 849.

Harter, S. (2012). Emerging self-processes during childhood and adolescence. In M.R. Leary & J.P. Tangney (Eds.), *Handbook of self and identity* (pp. 680–715). Guilford Press.

Hendry, A., Jones, E.J.H., & Charman, T. (2016) Executive function in the first three years of life: Precursors, predictors and patterns. *Developmental Review*, 42, 1–33.

Henning, C., Summerfeldt, L.J., & Parker, J.D. (2022). ADHD and academic success in university students: The important role of impaired attention. *Journal of Attention Disorders*, 26(6), 893–901.

Herbert, M.R., Ziegler, D.A., Makris, N., Filipek, P.A., Kemper, T.L., Normandin, J.J., Sanders, H.A., Kennedy, D.N., & Caviness, V.S., Jr. (2004). Localization of white matter volume increase in autism and developmental language disorder. *Annals of Neurology*, 55(4), 530–540. https://doi.org/10.1002/ana.20032.

Herlenius, E., & Lagercrantz, H. (2004). Development of neurotransmitter systems during critical periods. *Experimental Neurology*, 190(1), S8–S21. https://doi.org/10.1016/j.expneurol.2004.03.027.

Hodel A.S. (2018). Rapid infant prefrontal cortex development and sensitivity to early environmental experience. *Developmental Review*, 48, 113–144. https://doi.org/10.1016/j.dr.2018.02.003.

Hodges, H., Fealko, C., & Soares, N. (2020). Autism spectrum disorder: definition, epidemiology, causes, and clinical evaluation. *Translational Pediatrics*, 9(1), S55–S65. https://doi.org/10.21037/tp.2019.09.09.

Hofer, M.A. (1994). Hidden regulators in attachment, separation, and loss. *Monographs of the Society for Research in Child Development*, 59(2-3), 192–207.

Holingue, C., Volk, H., Crocetti, D., Gottlieb, B., Spira, A.P., & Mostofsky, S.H. (2021). Links between parent-reported measures of poor sleep and executive function in childhood autism and attention deficit hyperactivity disorder. *Sleep Health*, 7 (3), 375–383. https://doi.org/10.1016/j.sleh.2020.12.006.

Holmes, C.J., Kim-Spoon, J., & Deater-Deckard, K. (2016). Linking executive function and peer problems from early childhood through middle adolescence. *Journal of Abnormal Child Psychology*, 44, 31–42.

hooks, b. (1994). *Teaching to transgress: Education as the practice of freedom.* Routledge.

Hostinar, C.E., & Miller, G.E. (2019). Protective factors for youth confronting economic hardship: Current challenges and future avenues in resilience research. *American Psychologist*, 74(6), 641.

Hubel, D.H., & Wiesel, T.N. (1962). Receptive fields, binocular interaction and functional architecture in the cat's visual cortex, *Journal of Physiology*, 160, 106–154. doi:10.1113/jphysiol.1962.sp006837.

Hughes, C. (2023). Executive functions: Going places at pace. *Journal of Cognition and Development*, 24, 296–306. doi:10.1080/15248372.2023.2187636.

Hughes, C., & Devine, R.T. (2019). For better or for worse? Positive and negative parental influences on young children's executive function. *Child Development*, 90(2), 593–609.

Huttenlocher P.R. (1979). Synaptic density in human frontal cortex - Developmental changes and effects of aging. *Brain Research*, 163(2), 195–205. https://doi.org/10.1016/0006-8993(79)90349-4.

Huttenlocher P.R. (1990). Morphometric study of human cerebral cortex development. *Neuropsychologia*, 28(6), 517–527. https://doi.org/10.1016/0028-3932(90)90031-i.

Huttenlocher, P.R., & Dabholkar, A.S. (1997). Regional differences in synaptogenesis in human cerebral cortex. *Journal of Comparative Neurology*, 387(2), 167–178. https://doi.org/10.1002/(sici)1096-9861(19971020)387:2<167:aid-cne1>3.0.co;2-z.

International Human Genome Sequencing Consortium (2004). Finishing the euchromatic sequence of the human genome. *Nature*, 431(7011), 931–945. https://doi.org/10.1038/nature03001.

Ip, K.I., Felt, B., Wang, L., Karasawa, M., Hirabayashi, H., Kazama, M., Olson, S., Miller, A., & Tardif, T. (2021). Are preschoolers' neurobiological stress systems responsive to culturally relevant contexts? *Psychological Science*, 32(7), 998–1010.

Ip, K.I., Miller, A.L., Karasawa, M., Hirabayashi, H., Kazama, M., Wang, L., Olson, S. L., Kessler, D., & Tardif, T. (2021). Emotion expression and regulation in three cultures: Chinese, Japanese, and American preschoolers' reactions to disappointment. *Journal of Experimental Child Psychology*, 201, Article 104972.

Iyer, R.V., Kochenderfer-Ladd, B., Eisenberg, N., & Thompson, M. (2010). Peer victimization and effortful control: Relations to school engagement and academic achievement. *Merrill-Palmer Quarterly*, 56(3), 361–387.

Izard, C.E. (1994). Innate and universal facial expressions: Evidence from developmental and cross-cultural research. *Psychological Bulletin*, 115(2), 288–299. https:// doi.org/10.1037/0033-2909.115.2.288.

Jenkins, C., Geisthardt, C., & Day, J.K. (2023). Supporting children and families in medical settings: Insights from child life specialists during the COVID-19 Pandemic. *Journal of Child and Family Studies*, 1–18. Advance online publication. https://doi. org/10.1007/s10826-023-02537-9.

Jenuwein, T., & Allis, C.D. (2001). Translating the histone code. *Science*, 293(5532), 1074–1080. https://doi.org/10.1126/science.1063127.

Johnson, M.H. (1990). Cortical maturation and perceptual development. In H. Bloch & B.I. Bertenthal (Eds.), *Sensory-motor organizations and development in infancy and early childhood* (pp. 145–162). Kluwer Academic Press. https://doi.org/10. 1007/978-94-009-2071-2_11.

Johnson, M.H. (2011). Interactive specialization: A domain-general framework for human functional brain development? *Developmental Cognitive Neuroscience*, 1(1), 7–21. https://doi.org/10.1016/j.dcn.2010.07.003.

Johnson M.H. (2012). Executive function and developmental disorders: The flip side of the coin. *Trends in Cognitive Sciences*, 16(9), 454–457. https://doi.org/10. 1016/j.tics.2012.07.001.

Jones, B., & Phillips, F. (2016). Social work and interprofessional education in health care: A call for continued leadership. *Journal of Social Work Education*, 52(1), 18–29.

Jones, V. (2020). Challenging race neutral rhetoric: Black student leaders' counter-narratives of racial salience in PWI student organizations. *Journal of Diversity in Higher Education*, 13(1), 23–32. https://doi.org/10.1037/dhe0000105.

Jones Harden, B., Duncan, A.D., Morrison, C.I., Panlilio, C., & Clyman, R.B. (2015). Compliance and internalization in preschool foster children. *Children and Youth Services Review*, 55, 103–110.

Jordan, M.R., Amir, D., & Bloom, P. (2016). Are empathy and concern psychologically distinct? *Emotion*, 16(8), 1107.

Joseph, G.G., Reddy, V., & Searle-Chatterjee, M. (1990). Eurocentrism in the social sciences. *Race & Class*, 31(4), 1–26. https://doi.org/10.1177/030639689003100401.

Judd, N., Klingberg, T., & Sjöwall, D. (2021). Working memory capacity, variability, and response to intervention at age 6 and its association to inattention and mathematics age 9. *Cognitive Development*, 58, Article 101013.

Kagan, J. (2007). *What is emotion? History, measures, and meanings*. Yale University Press.

Kagan, J. (2022). Temperamental and theoretical contributions to clinical psychology. *Annual Review of Clinical Psychology*, 18, 1–18.

Kagan, J., Snidman, N., Kahn, V., & Towsley, S. (2007). The preservation of two infant temperaments into adolescence. *Monographs of the Society for Research in Child Development*, 72(2). https://doi-org.proxy.lib.csus.edu/10.1111/j.1540-5834.2007.00431.x.

Kail, R., & Bisanz, J. (1982). Information processing and cognitive development. *Advances in Child Development and Behavior*, 17, 45–81. https://doi.org/10.1016/s0065-2407(08)60357-2.

Karpinski, A.C., & Scullin, M.H. (2009). Suggestibility under pressure: Theory of mind, executive function, and suggestibility in preschoolers. *Journal of Applied Developmental Psychology*, 30(6), 749–763. https://doi.org/10.1016/j.appdev.2009.05.004.

Kearsley, G.P., & Royce, J.R. (1977). A multifactor theory of sensation: Individuality in sensory structure and sensory processing. *Perceptual and Motor Skills*, 44(3), 1299–1316. https://doi.org/10.2466/pms.1977.44.3c.1299.

Keenan, J.P., Gallup, G.G., & Falk, D. (2003). *The face in the mirror: The search for the origins of consciousness*. HarperCollins.

Khan, M.S. (2020). Paid family leave and children health outcomes in OECD countries. *Children and Youth Services Review*, 116, Article 105259.

Kibby, M.Y., Lee, S.E., & Dyer, S.M. (2014). Reading performance is predicted by more than phonological processing. *Frontiers in Psychology*, 5, 960. https://doi.org/10.3389/fpsyg.2014.00960.

Kim-Spoon, J., Deater-Deckard, K., Calkins, S.D., King-Casas, B., & Bell, M.A. (2019). Commonality between executive functioning and effortful control related to adjustment. *Journal of Applied Developmental Psychology*, 60, 47–55. https://doi-org.proxy.lib.csus.edu/10.1016/j.appdev.2018.10.004.

King Jr, M.L. (1963). Letter from Birmingham Jail. *Atlantic Monthly*, 212(2), 78–88.

King Jr, M.L. (1968). The role of the behavioral scientist in the civil rights movement. *Journal of Social Issues*, 24, 1–12.

Klawetter, S., Glaze, K., Sward, A., & Frankel, K.A. (2021). Warm connections: Integration of infant mental health services into WIC. *Community Mental Health Journal*, 57, 1130–1141.

Klingberg, T. (2008). *The overflowing brain: Information overload and the limits of working memory*. Oxford University Press.

Kochanska, G., Murray, K.T., & Harlan, E.T. (2000). Effortful control in early childhood: Continuity and change, antecedents, and implications for social development. *Developmental Psychology*, 36(2), 220–232. https://doi-org.proxy.lib.csus.edu/10.1037/0012-1649.36.2.220.

Kochanska, G., Murray, K., Jacques, T.Y., Koenig, A.L., & Vandegeest, K.A. (1996). Inhibitory control in young children and its role in emerging internalization. *Child Development*, 67(2), 490–507. https://doi.org/10.2307/1131828.

Koeske, G.F., & Koeske, R.D. (1990). The buffering effect of social support on parental stress. *American Journal of Orthopsychiatry*, 60(3), 440–451.

Kolb, B., & Gibb, R. (2011). Brain plasticity and behaviour in the developing brain. *Journal of the Canadian Academy of Child and Adolescent Psychiatry*, 20(4), 265–276.

Kolb, B., Mychasiuk, R., Muhammad, A., Li, Y., Frost, D.O., & Gibb, R. (2012). Experience and the developing prefrontal cortex. *Proceedings of the National Academy of Sciences*, 109 (2), 17186–17193. https://doi.org/10.1073/pnas.1121251109.

Korom, M., Goldstein, A., Tabachnick, A.R., Palmwood, E.N., Simons, R.F., & Dozier, M. (2021). Early parenting intervention accelerates inhibitory control development among CPS-involved children in middle childhood: A randomized clinical trial. *Developmental Science*, 24(3), e13054. https://doi.org/10.1111/desc.13054.

Kozak, K., Greaves, A., Waldfogel, J., Angal, J., Elliott, A.J., Fifier, W.P., & Brito, N. H. (2021). Paid maternal leave is associated with better language and socioemotional outcomes during toddlerhood. *Infancy*, 26(4), 536–550.

Kramsch, C. (2014). Teaching foreign languages in an era of globalization: Introduction. *The Modern Language Journal*, 98, 296–311. https://doi.org/10.1111/j.1540-4781.2014.12057.x.

Lakes, K.D., & Hoyt, W.T. (2004). Promoting self-regulation through school-based martial arts training. *Journal of Applied Developmental Psychology*, 25(3), 283–302.

Laurita, A.C., Hazan, C., & Spreng, R.N. (2019). An attachment theoretical perspective for the neural representation of close others. *Social Cognitive and Affective Neuroscience*, 14(3), 237–251.

Lecce, S., & Bianco, F. (2018). Working memory predicts changes in children's theory of mind during middle childhood: A training study. *Cognitive Development*, 47, 71–81.

Leclère, C., Viaux, S., Avril, M., Achard, C., Chetouani, M., Missonnier, S., & Cohen, D. (2014). Why synchrony matters during mother-child interactions: A systematic review. *PloS One*, 9(12), e113571. https://doi.org/10.1371/journal.pone.0113571.

Legare, C.H., Dale, M.T., Kim, S.Y., & Deák, G.O. (2018). Cultural variation in cognitive flexibility reveals diversity in the development of executive functions. *Scientific Reports*, 8(1), Article 16326. https://doi.org/10.1038/s41598-018-34756-2.

Lerner, R.M. (2006). Developmental science, developmental systems, and contemporary theories of human development. In R.M. Lerner & W. Damon (Eds.), *Handbook of child psychology: Theoretical models of human development* (pp. 1–17). Wiley.

Lester, F.K. (Ed.). (2007). *Second handbook of research on mathematics teaching and learning*. Information Age Publishing.

Leung, R.C., Vogan, V.M., Powell, T.L., Anagnostou, E., & Taylor, M.J. (2016). The role of executive functions in social impairment in Autism Spectrum Disorder. *Child Neuropsychology*, 22(3), 336–344.

Lewis, M., & Brooks-Gunn, J. (1979), Toward a theory of social cognition: The development of self. *New Directions for Child and Adolescent Development*, 4, 1–20. https://doi.org/10.1002/cd.23219790403.

Lewkowicz, D.J. (2010). Infant perception of audio-visual speech synchrony. *Developmental Psychology*, 46(1), 66–77. https://doi.org/10.1037/a0015579.

Lin, L.C., Qu, Y., & Telzer, E.H. (2018). Cultural influences on the neural correlates of intergroup perception. *Culture and Brain*, 6, 171–187.

Lloyd, M., Doydum, A., & Newcombe, N. (2009). Memory binding in early childhood: Evidence for a retrieval deficit. *Child Development*, 80, 1321–1328. https://doi.org/10.1111/j.1467-8624.2009.01353.x.

Lo, C.K.-M., & Cho, Y.W. (2021). Community-based interventions to reduce child maltreatment. *Research on Social Work Practice*, 31(6), 621–633. https://doi.org/10.1177/1049731520986968.

Logie, R.H., & Pearson, D.G. (1997). The inner eye and the inner scribe of visuospatial working memory: Evidence from developmental fractionation. *European Journal of Cognitive Psychology*, 9(3), 241–257. https://doi.org/10.1080/713752559.

Logue, S.F., & Gould, T.J. (2014). The neural and genetic basis of executive function: Attention, cognitive flexibility, and response inhibition. *Pharmacology, Biochemistry, and Behavior*, 123, 45–54. https://doi.org/10.1016/j.pbb.2013.08.007.

Lozoff, B., Beard, J., Connor, J., Barbara, F., Georgieff, M., & Schallert, T. (2006). Long-lasting neural and behavioral effects of iron deficiency in infancy. *Nutrition Reviews*, 64(5 Pt 2), S34–S91. https://doi.org/10.1301/nr.2006.may.s34-s43.

Luciana, M., & Nelson, C.A. (1998). The functional emergence of prefrontally-guided working memory systems in four- to eight-year-old children. *Neuropsychologia*, 36 (3), 273–293. https://doi.org/10.1016/s0028-3932(97)00109-7.

Lupien, S.J., McEwen, B.S., Gunnar, M.R., & Heim, C. (2009). Effects of stress throughout the lifespan on the brain, behaviour and cognition. *Nature Reviews Neuroscience*, 10(6), 434–445.

Luria, A.R. (1961). *The role of speech in the regulation of normal and abnormal behavior*. Liveright.

MacDonald, D.J., Côté, J., & Deakin, J. (2010). The impact of informal coach training on the personal development of youth sport athletes. *International Journal of Sports Science & Coaching*, 5(3), 363–372.

MacWhinney, B. (2015). Language development. In L.S. Liben, U. Müller, & R.M. Lerner (Eds.), *Handbook of child psychology and developmental science: Cognitive processes* (pp. 296–338). Wiley. https://doi.org/10.1002/9781118963418.childpsy208.

Maister, L., Simons, J.S., & Plaisted-Grant, K. (2013). Executive functions are employed to process episodic and relational memories in children with autism spectrum disorders. *Neuropsychology*, 27(6), 615–627. https://doi.org/10.1037/a0034492.

Mandler, J.M. (1998). Representation. In W. Damon (Ed.), *Handbook of child psychology: Vol. 2. Cognition, perception, and language* (pp. 255–308). Wiley.

Markant, J.M., & Thomas, K.M. (2013). Postnatal brain development. In P.D. Zelazo (Ed.), *Oxford handbook of developmental psychology* (pp. 129–163). Oxford University Press.

Markowitz, F.E. (2003). Socioeconomic disadvantage and violence: Recent research on culture and neighborhood control as explanatory mechanisms. *Aggression and Violent Behavior*, 8, 145–154.

Marulis, L.M., Baker, S.T., & Whitebread, D. (2020). Integrating metacognition and executive function to enhance young children's perception of and agency in their learning. *Early Childhood Research Quarterly*, 50(Part 2), 46–54. https://doi.org/10.1016/j.ecresq.2018.12.017.

Mary, A., Slama, H., Mousty, P., Massat, I., Capiau, T., Drabs, V., & Peigneux, P. (2016). Executive and attentional contributions to theory of mind deficit in attention deficit/hyperactivity disorder. *Child Neuropsychology*, 22(3), 345–365.

Maslach, C., Schaufeli, W.B., & Leiter, M.P. (2001). Job burnout. *Annual Review of Psychology*, 52(1), 397–422.

Masten, A.S. (2018). Resilience theory and research on children and families: Past, present, and promise. *Journal of Family Theory & Review*, 10(1), 12–31.

McAdams, D. P., & Zapata-Gietl, C. (2015). Three strands of identity development across the human life course: Reading Erik Erikson in full. In K. C. McLean & M. Syed (Eds.), *The Oxford handbook of identity development* (pp. 81–94). Oxford University Press.

McAuley, T., & White, D.A. (2011). A latent variables examination of processing speed, response inhibition, and working memory during typical development. *Journal of Experimental Child Psychology*, 108(3), 453–468. https://doi.org/10.1016/j.jecp.2010.08.009.

McClelland, M.M., & Cameron, C.E. (2019). Developing together: The role of executive function and motor skills in children's early academic lives. *Early Childhood Research Quarterly*, 46, 142–151.

McClelland, M.M., Geldhof, G.J., Cameron, C.E., & Wanless, S.B. (2015). Development and self-regulation. In W.F. Overton, P.C.M. Molenaar, & R.M. Lerner (Eds.), *Handbook of child psychology and developmental science: Theory and method* (pp. 523–565). John Wiley & Sons, Inc. https://doi.org/10.1002/9781118963418.childpsy114.

McCormack, H.M., MacIntyre, T.E., O'Shea, D., Herring, M.P., & Campbell, M.J. (2018). The prevalence and cause(s) of burnout among applied psychologists: A systematic review. *Frontiers in Psychology*, 9, 1897.

McEwen, B.S. (2007). Physiology and neurobiology of stress and adaptation: Central role of the brain. *Physiological Reviews*, 87(3), 873–904.

McGaugh J.L. (2000). Memory–A century of consolidation. *Science*, 287(5451), 248–251. https://doi.org/10.1126/science.287.5451.248.

Melton, A.W. (1963). Implications of short-term memory for a general theory of memory. *Journal of Verbal Learning and Verbal Behavior*, 2, 1–21. http://hdl.handle.net/2027.42/32209.

Meltzoff, A., & Borton, R. (1979). Intermodal matching by human neonates. *Nature*, 282, 403–404. https://doi.org/10.1038/282403a0.

Meltzoff, A.N., & Moore, M.K. (1983). Child Development, 54(3), 702–709. https://doi.org/10.2307/1130058.

Mesman, J., Van Ijzendoorn, M.H., & Sagi-Schwartz, A. (2016). Cross-cultural patterns of attachment. In J. Cassidy & P.R. Shaver (Eds.), *Handbook of attachment: Theory, research, and clinical applications* (3rd ed.; pp. 852–877). Guilford Press.

Miller, G.A. (1956). The magical number seven, plus or minus two: Some limits on our capacity for processing information. *Psychological Review*, 63(2), 81–97. https://doi.org/10.1037/h0043158.

Miller, P.H. (2016). *Theories of developmental psychology*. Macmillan Higher Education.

Mitchell, R.L., & Phillips, L.H. (2007). The psychological, neurochemical and functional neuroanatomical mediators of the effects of positive and negative mood on executive functions. *Neuropsychologia*, 45(4), 617–629.

Miyake, A., & Friedman, N.P. (2012). The nature and organization of individual differences in executive functions: Four general conclusions. *Current Directions in Psychological Science*, 21(1), 8–14. https://doi.org/10.1177/0963721411429458.

Moffitt, T.E., Arseneault, L., Belsky, D., Dickson, N., Hancox, R.J., Harrington, H.A., & Caspi, A. (2011). A gradient of childhood self-control predicts health, wealth, and public safety. *Proceedings of the National Academy of Sciences*, 108(7), 2693–2698.

Monterrosa, E.C., Frongillo, E.A., Drewnowski, A., de Pee, S., & Vandevijvere, S. (2020). Sociocultural influences on food choices and implications for sustainable healthy diets. *Food and Nutrition Bulletin*, 41(2), 59S–73S. https://doi.org/10.1177/0379572120975874.

Morales, J., Calvo, A., & Bialystok, E. (2013). Working memory development in monolingual and bilingual children. *Journal of Experimental Child Psychology*, 114(2), 187–202. https://doi.org/10.1016/j.jecp.2012.09.002.

Morelli, G., & Lu, L. (2021). Pluralities and commonalities in children's relationships. In R.A. Thompson, J.A. Simpson, & L.J. Berlin (Eds.), *Attachment: The fundamental questions*. Guilford Press.

Moriña, A., & Biagiotti, G. (2022). Academic success factors in university students with disabilities: A systematic review. *European Journal of Special Needs Education*, 37(5), 729–746.

Müller, U., & Kerns, K. (2015). The development of executive function. In L.S. Liben, U. Müller, & R.M. Lerner (Eds.), *Handbook of child psychology and developmental science: Cognitive processes* (pp. 571–623). Wiley. https://doi.org/10.1002/9781118963418.childpsy214.

NelsonIII, C.A., Thomas, K.M., & de Haan, M. (2006). Neural bases of cognitive development. In D. Kuhn, R.S. Siegler, W. Damon, & R.M. Lerner (Eds.), *Handbook of child psychology: Cognition, perception, and language* (pp. 3–57). Wiley.

O'Hara, K.M.D. (2002). *Emotion regulation and frontal asymmetry: Relations with temperament and attachment.* Doctoral dissertation, University of California, Davis.

Olson, K.R., & Dweck, C.S. (2008). A blueprint for social cognitive development. *Perspectives on Psychological Science*, 3(3), 193–202. https://doi.org/10.1111/j.1745-6924.2008.00074.x.

Ortiz, R., & Sibinga, E.M. (2017). The role of mindfulness in reducing the adverse effects of childhood stress and trauma. *Children*, 4(3), 16. doi:10.3390/children4030016.

Osher, D., Cantor, P., Berg, J., Steyer, L., & Rose, T. (2020). Drivers of human development: How relationships and context shape learning and development. *Applied Developmental Science*, 24(1), 6–36. https://doi.org/10.1080/10888691.2017.1398650.

Otgaar, H., Howe, M.L., Muris, P., & Merckelbach, H. (2019). Associative activation as a mechanism underlying false memory formation. *Clinical Psychological Science*, 7(2), 191–195.

Ozier, E.M., Taylor, V.J., & Murphy, M.C. (2019). The cognitive effects of experiencing and observing subtle racial discrimination. *Journal of Social Issues*, 75(4), 1087–1115.

Ozonoff, S., Pennington, B.F., Rogers, S.J. (1991). Executive function deficits in high-functioning autistic individuals: Relationship to theory of mind. *Journal of Child Psychology and Psychiatry*, 32(7), 1081–1105.

Palomino, C.I., & Brudvig, A. (2022). Examining the role of demographic characteristics, attachment, and language in preschool children's executive function skills. *Early Child Development and Care*, 192, 1967–1981. doi:10.1080/03004430.2021.1958803.

Park, H.R., Lee, J.M., Moon, H.E., Lee, D.S., Kim, B.N., Kim, J., Kim, D.G., & Paek, S.H. (2016). A short review on the current understanding of autism spectrum disorders. *Neurobiology*, 25(1), 1–13. https://doi.org/10.5607/en.2016.25.1.1.

Park, M., Brain, U., Grunau, R.E., Diamond, A., & Oberlander, T.F. (2018). Maternal depression trajectories from pregnancy to 3 years postpartum are associated with children's behavior and executive functions at 3 and 6 years. *Archives of Women's Mental Health*, 21, 353–363.

Parker, D.R., & Boutelle, K. (2009). Executive function coaching for college students with learning disabilities and ADHD: A new approach for fostering self-determination. *Learning Disabilities Research & Practice*, 24(4), 204–215.

Pearlin, L.I., & Kohn, M.L. (1966). Social class, occupation, and parental values: A cross-national study. *American Sociological Review*, 31(4), 466–479. https://doi.org/10.2307/2090770.

Perner, J. (1991). *Understanding the representational mind.* MIT Press.

Perner, J., & Lang, B. (2002). What causes 3-year-olds' difficulty on the dimensional change card sorting task? *Infant and Child Development*, 11(2), 93–105. https://doi.org/10.1002/icd.299.

Persson, J., Welsh, K.M., Jonides, J., & Reuter-Lorenz, P.A. (2007). Cognitive fatigue of executive processes: interaction between interference resolution tasks. *Neuropsychologia*, 45(7), 1571–1579. https://doi.org/10.1016/j.neuropsychologia.2006.12.007.

Petanjek, Z., Judaš, M., Šimic, G., Rasin, M.R., Uylings, H.B., Rakic, P., & Kostovic, I. (2011). Extraordinary neoteny of synaptic spines in the human prefrontal cortex. *Proceedings of the National Academy of Sciences*, 108(32), 13281–13286. https://doi.org/10.1073/pnas.1105108108.

Petersen, R., Lavelle, E., & Guarino, A.J. (2006). The relationship between college students' executive functioning and study strategies. *Journal of College Reading and Learning*, 36(2), 59–67.

Piccolo, L.R., Merz, E.C., Noble, K.G., & Pediatric Imaging, Neurocognition, and Genetics Study (2019). School climate is associated with cortical thickness and executive function in children and adolescents. *Developmental Science*, 22(1), e12719.

Petitto, L.A. (1997). In the beginning: On the genetic and environmental factors that make early language acquisition possible. In M. Gopnik (Ed.), *The inheritance and innateness of grammars* (pp. 45–69). Oxford University Press.

Piaget, J. (1954). *The construction of reality in the child*. Basic Books. https://doi.org/10.1037/11168-000.

Posner, M.I., & Rothbart, M.K. (2007). Research on attention networks as a model for the integration of psychological science. *Annual Review of Psychology*, 58, 1–23.

Proctor, R.W., & Proctor, J.D. (2021). Sensation and perception. In G. Salvendy & W. Karwowski (Eds.), *Handbook of human factors and ergonomics* (5th ed., pp. 57–90). Wiley.

Rakic, P. (1995). A small step for the cell, a giant leap for mankind: A hypothesis of neocortical expansion during evolution. *Trends in Neurosciences*, 18(9), 383–388. https://doi.org/10.1016/0166-2236(95)93934-p.

Ramzan, N., & Amjad, N. (2017). Cross cultural variation in emotion regulation: A systematic review. *Annals of King Edward Medical University*, 23(1).

Raver, C.C., Blair, C., & Willoughby, M. (2013). Poverty as a predictor of 4-year-olds' executive function: New perspectives on models of differential susceptibility. *Developmental Psychology*, 49(2), 292–304. https://doi.org/10.1037/a0028343.

Redlich, A.D., & Goodman, G.S. (2003). Taking responsibility for an act not committed: The influence of age and suggestibility. *Law and Human Behavior*, 27, 141–156.

Regueiro, S., Matte-Gagné, C., & Bernier, A. (2020). Patterns of growth in executive functioning during school years: Contributions of early mother–child attachment security and maternal autonomy support. *Journal of Experimental Child Psychology*, 200, Article 104934. https://doi-org.proxy.lib.csus.edu/10.1016/j.jecp.2020.104934.

Ristic, J., & Enns, J.T. (2015). The changing face of attentional development. *Current Directions in Psychological Science*, 24(1), 24–31. https://doi-org.proxy.lib.csus.edu/10.1177/0963721414551165.

Roberts, M., Tolar-Peterson, T., Reynolds, A., Wall, C., Reeder, N., & Rico Mendez, G. (2022). The effects of nutritional interventions on the cognitive development of preschool-age children: A systematic review. *Nutrients*, 14(3), 532. https://doi.org/10.3390/nu14030532.

Rodríguez, C. (2022). The construction of executive function in early development: The pragmatics of action and gestures. *Human Development*, 66(4-5), 239–259. https://doi-org.proxy.lib.csus.edu/10.1159/000526340.

Roediger, H.L. (1990). Implicit memory: Retention without remembering. *American Psychologist*, 45(9), 1043–1056. https://doi.org/10.1037/0003-066X.45.9.1043.

Rogers, L.O., & Way, N. (2021). Child development in an ideological context: Through the lens of resistance and accommodation. *Child Development Perspectives*, 15(4), 242–248.

Romer, D., Duckworth, A.L., Sznitman, S., & Park, S. (2010). Can adolescents learn self-control? Delay of gratification in the development of control over risk taking. *Prevention Science*, 11, 319–330. https://doi.org/10.1007/s11121-010-0171-8.

Rose, S.A., Feldman, J.F., & Jankowski, J.J. (2012). Implications of infant cognition for executive functions at age 11. *Psychological Science*, 23(11), 1345–1355. https://doi.org/10.1177/0956797612444902.

Rothbart, M.K., & Derryberry, D. (1981). Development of individual difference in temperament. In M.E. Lamb, & A.L. Brown (Eds.), *Advances in developmental psychology* (pp. 37–86). Erlbaum.

Rothstein, R. (2017). *The color of law: A forgotten history of how our government segregated America*. Liveright.

Rubin, K.H., Hemphill, S.A., Chen, X., Hastings, P., Sanson, A., Coco, A.L., Zappulla, C., Chung, O.-B., Park, S.-Y., Doh, H.S., Chen, H., Sun, L., Yoon, C.-H., & Cui, L. (2006). A cross-cultural study of behavioral inhibition in toddlers: East–West–North–South. *International Journal of Behavioral Development*, 30(3), 219–226. https://doi.org/10.1177/0165025406066723.

Ruffini, C., Osmani, F., Martini, C., Giera, W.K., & Pecini, C. (2023). The relationship between executive functions and writing in children: A systematic review. *Child Neuropsychology*, 1–59. Advance online publication. https://doi.org/10.1080/09297049.2023.2170998.

Russell, J.A. (1980). A circumplex model of affect. *Journal of Personality and Social Psychology*, 39(6), 1161.

Russell, J. (1996). *Agency: Its role in mental development*. Erlbaum.

Sabbagh, M.A., Xu, F., Carlson, S.M., Moses, L.J., & Lee, K. (2006). The development of executive functioning and theory of mind. A comparison of Chinese and U. S. preschoolers. *Psychological Science*, 17(1), 74–81. https://doi.org/10.1111/j.1467-9280.2005.01667.x.

Safford, K., & Drury, R. (2013). The 'problem' of bilingual children in educational settings: Policy and research in England. *Language and Education*, 27(1), 70–81.

Sagi, A., van IJzendoorn, M.H., Aviezer, O., Donnell, F., Koren-Karie, N., Joels, T., & Harl, Y. (1995). Attachments in a multiple-caregiver and multiple-infant environment: The case of the Israeli kibbutzim. *Monographs of the Society for Research in Child Development*, 60(2-3), 71–91. https://doi.org/10.2307/1166171.

Samango-Sprouse, C. (2007). Frontal lobe development in childhood. In Miller, B.L., & Cummings, J.L. (Eds.). *The human frontal lobes: Functions and disorders* (2nd ed.; pp. 576–593). Guilford Press.

Santucci, A.K., Silk, J.S., Shaw, D.S., Gentzler, A., Fox, N.A., & Kovacs, M. (2008). Vagal tone and temperament as predictors of emotion regulation strategies in young children. *Developmental Psychobiology*, 50(3), 205–216. https://doi.org/10.1002/dev.20283.

Sapolsky, R.M. (2012). Super humanity. *Scientific American*, 307(3), 40–43.

Sapolsky, R.M. (2015). Stress and the brain: Individual variability and the inverted-U. *Nature Neuroscience*, 18(10), 1344–1346. https://doi-org.proxy.lib.csus.edu/10.1038/nn.4109.

Sarsour, K., Sheridan, M., Jutte, D., Nuru-Jeter, A., Hinshaw, S., & Boyce, W.T. (2011). Family socioeconomic status and child executive functions: the roles of language, home environment, and single parenthood. *Journal of the International Neuropsychological Society*, 17(1), 120–132. https://doi.org/10.1017/S1355617710001335.

Scarr, S., & McCartney, K. (1983). How people make their own environments: A theory of genotype → environment effects. *Child Development*, 54(2), 424–435.

Schaaf, J.M., Alexander, K.W., & Goodman, G.S. (2008). Children's false memory and true disclosure in the face of repeated questions. *Journal of Experimental Child Psychology*, 100, 157–185.

Schacter, D.L. (1992). Understanding implicit memory: A cognitive neuroscience approach. *American Psychologist*, 47(4), 559–569. https://doi.org/10.1037/0003-066X.47.4.559.

Schacter, D.L. (2001). *The seven sins of memory: How the mind forgets and remembers.* Houghton Mifflin.

Scherer, K.R., & Moors, A. (2019). The emotion process: Event appraisal and component differentiation. *Annual Review of Psychology*, 70, 719–745.

Schirmbeck, K., Rao, N., & Maehler, C. (2020). Similarities and differences across countries in the development of executive functions in children: A systematic review. *Infant and Child Development*, 29(1), Article e2164. https://doi.org/10.1002/icd.2164.

Schore, A.N. (2001). Effects of a secure attachment relationship on right brain development, affect regulation, and infant mental health. *Infant Mental Health Journal*, 22(1-2), 7–66.

Senzaki, S., Wiebe, S.A., Masuda, T. & Shimizu, Y. (2018) A cross-cultural examination of selective attention in Canada and Japan: The role of social context. *Cognitive Development*, 48, 32–41. https://doi.org/10.1016/j.cogdev.2018.06.005.

Seth, A.K. (2013). Interoceptive inference, emotion, and the embodied self. *Trends in Cognitive Sciences*, 17(11), 565–573.

Setoh, P., Scott, R.M., & Baillargeon, R. (2016). Two-and-a-half-year-olds succeed at a traditional false-belief task with reduced processing demands. *Proceedings of the National Academy of Sciences*, 113(47), 13360–13365. https://doi.org/10.1073/pnas.1609203113.

Shoda, Y., Mischel, W., & Peake, P.K. (1990). Predicting adolescent cognitive and self-regulatory competencies from preschool delay of gratification: Identifying diagnostic conditions. *Developmental Psychology*, 26(6), 978.

Silk, J.S., Siegle, G.J., Lee, K.H., Nelson, E.E., Stroud, L.R., & Dahl, R.E. (2014). Increased neural response to peer rejection associated with adolescent depression and pubertal development. *Social Cognitive and Affective Neuroscience*, 9(11), 1798–1807. https://doi-org.proxy.lib.csus.edu/10.1093/scan/nst175.

Singer, T., Seymour, B., O'doherty, J., Kaube, H., Dolan, R.J., & Frith, C.D. (2004). Empathy for pain involves the affective but not sensory components of pain. *Science*, 303(5661), 1157–1162.

Sluzenski, J., Newcombe, N.S., & Kovacs, S.L. (2006). Binding, relational memory, and recall of naturalistic events: A developmental perspective. *Journal of Experimental Psychology: Learning, Memory, and Cognition*, 32(1), 89.

Snell-Rood, E.C. (2013). An overview of the evolutionary causes and consequences of behavioural plasticity. *Animal Behaviour*, 85(5), 1004–1011.

Snyder, M. (1981). On the self-perpetuating nature of social stereotypes. In D.L. Hamilton (Ed.), *Cognitive processes in stereotyping and intergroup behavior* (pp. 183–213). Taylor & Francis.

Sobeh, J., & Will Spijkers (2013). Development of neuropsychological functions of attention in two cultures: A cross-cultural study of attentional performances of Syrian and German children of pre-school and school age. *European Journal of Developmental Psychology*, 10, 318–336. doi:10.1080/17405629.2012.674761.

Soto, E.F., Irwin, L.N., Chan, E.S.M., Spiegel, J.A., & Kofler, M.J. (2021). Executive functions and writing skills in children with and without ADHD. *Neuropsychology*, 35 (8), 792–808. https://doi.org/10.1037/neu0000769.

Sowell, E.R., Thompson, P.M., Tessner, K.D., & Toga, A.W. (2001). Mapping continued brain growth and gray matter density reduction in dorsal frontal cortex: Inverse relationships during post-adolescent brain maturation. *Journal of Neuroscience*, 21(22), 8819–8829. https://doi.org/10.1523/JNEUROSCI.21-22-08819.2001.

Sowell, E.R., Thompson, P.M., Holmes, C.J., Jernigan, T.L., & Toga, A.W. (1999). In vivo evidence for post-adolescent brain maturation in frontal and striatal regions. *Nature Neuroscience*, 2(10), 859–861. http://dx.doi.org/10.1038/13154.

Spangler, G., & Grossman, K. (1993). Biobehavioral organization in securely and insecurely attached infants. *Child Development*, 64(5), 1439–1450. doi:10.1111/j.1467-8624.1993.tb02962.x.

Spangler, G., & Grossman, K. (1999). Individual and physiological correlates of attachment disorganization in infancy. In J. Solomon & C. George (Eds.), *Attachment disorganization* (pp. 95–124). Guilford Press.

Spencer, J.P. (2020). The development of working memory. *Current Directions in Psychological Science*, 29(6), 545–553. https://doi.org/10.1177/0963721420959835.

Sperling, G. (1960). The information available in brief visual presentations. *Psychological Monographs: General and Applied*, 74(11), 1–29. https://doi.org/10.1037/h0093759.

Spiegel, J.A., Goodrich, J.M., Morris, B.M., Osborne, C.M., & Lonigan, C.J. (2021). Relations between executive functions and academic outcomes in elementary school children: A meta-analysis. *Psychological Bulletin*, 147(4), 329.

Squire, L.R. (2004). Memory systems of the brain: A brief history and current perspective. *Neurobiology of Learning and Memory*, 82(3), 171–177. doi:10.1016/j.nlm.2004.06.005.

Stein, B.E., Stanford, T.R., & Rowland, B.A. (2014). Development of multisensory integration from the perspective of the individual neuron. *Nature Reviews Neuroscience*, 15(8), 520–535. https://doi.org/10.1038/nrn3742.

Steinberg, L. (2008). A social neuroscience perspective on adolescent risk-taking. *Developmental Review*, 28(1), 78–106.

Stiles, J., & Jernigan, T.L. (2010). The basics of brain development. *Neuropsychology Review*, 20(4), 327–348. https://doi.org/10.1007/s11065-010-9148-4.

Stiles, J., Brown, T.T., Haist, F., & Jernigan, T.L. (2015). Brain and cognitive development cognitive processes. In L. Liben, U. Müller, & R. Lerner (Eds.), *Handbook of child psychology and developmental science* (vol. 2, 7th ed.; pp. 1–54). Wiley. doi:10.1002/9781118963418.childpsy202.

Storz G. (2002). An expanding universe of noncoding RNAs. *Science*, 296(5571), 1260–1263. https://doi.org/10.1126/science.1072249.

Studer, M. (2007). Rehabilitation of executive function: To err is human, to be aware—divine. *Journal of Neurologic Physical Therapy*, 31(3), 128–134.

Swadener, B. (2012). "At risk" or "at promise"? From deficit constructions of the "other childhood" to possibilities for authentic alliances with children and families. *International Critical Childhood Policy Studies*, 3, 7–29.

Szatmari, P. (2018). Risk and resilience in autism spectrum disorder: A missed translational opportunity? *Developmental Medicine & Child Neurology*, 60(3), 225–229.

Tajik-Parvinchi, D., Farmus, L., Tablon Modica, P., Cribbie, R.A., & Weiss, J.A. (2021). The role of cognitive control and emotion regulation in predicting mental health problems in children with neurodevelopmental disorders. *Child: Care, Health and Development*, 47(5), 608–617.

Taumoepeau, M. (2019). Culture, communication and socio-cognitive development: Understanding the minds of others. In T. Tulviste, D.L. Best, & J.L. Gibbons (Eds.), *Children's social worlds in cultural context* (pp. 41–54). Springer. https://doi.org/10.1007/978-3-030-27033-9.

Telzer, E.H., Fuligni, A.J., Lieberman, M.D., Miernicki, M.E., & Galván, A. (2015). The quality of adolescents' peer relationships modulates neural sensitivity to risk taking. *Social Cognitive and Affective Neuroscience*, 10, 389–398. https://doi.org/10.1093/scan/nsu064.

Thelen, E., & Smith, L.B. (2006). Dynamic systems theories. In R.M. Lerner & W. Damon (Eds.), *Handbook of child psychology: Theoretical models of human development* (pp. 258–312). Wiley.

Thomas, A., & Chess, S. (1977). *Temperament and development*. Brunner/Mazel.

Thomason, M.E., Race, E., Burrows, B., Whitfield-Gabrieli, S., Glover, G.H., & Gabrieli, J.D. (2009). Development of spatial and verbal working memory capacity in the human brain. *Journal of Cognitive Neuroscience*, 21(2), 316–332. https://doi.org/10.1162/jocn.2008.21028.

Thompson, A., & Steinbeis, N. (2020). Sensitive periods in executive function development. *Current Opinion in Behavioral Sciences*, 36, 98–105. https://doi.org/10.1016/j.cobeha.2020.08.001.

Thompson, R.A. (2015). Relationships, regulation, and early development. In M.E. Lamb, C. Garcia Coll, & R.M. Lerner (Eds.), *Handbook of child psychology and developmental science: Social and emotional development* (vol. 3, 7th ed.; pp. 201–246). Wiley.

Thompson, R.A. (2021). Attachment networks and the future of attachment theory. *New Directions for Child and Adolescent Development*, 2021(180), 149–156.

Tousignant, B., Eugène, F., & Jackson, P.L. (2017). A developmental perspective on the neural bases of human empathy. *Infant Behavior and Development*, 48, 5–12.

Tronick, E. (2007). *The neurobehavioral and social-emotional development of infants and children*. Norton.

Tschannen-Moran, M., & Hoy, A.W. (2007). The differential antecedents of self-efficacy beliefs of novice and experienced teachers. *Teaching and Teacher Education*, 23 (6), 944–956.

Tucker-Drob, E.M., Briley, D.A., & Harden, K.P. (2013). Genetic and environmental influences on cognition across development and context. *Current Directions in Psychological Science*, 22(5), 349–355. https://doi.org/10.1177/0963721413485087.

Tulving, E. (1972). Episodic and semantic memory. In E. Tulving & W. Donaldson (Eds.), *Organization of memory* (pp. 381–403). Academic Press.

Tulving, E. (1993). What is episodic memory? *Current Directions in Psychological Science*, 2(3), 67–70. https://doi.org/10.1111/1467-8721.ep10770899.

Turiel, E. (2003). Resistance and subversion in everyday life. *Journal of Moral Education*, 32(2), 115–130.

Ungar, M. (2013). Resilience, trauma, context, and culture. *Trauma, Violence, & Abuse*, 14(3), 255–266. https://doi.org/10.1177/1524838013487805.

Vallotton, C.D. (2008). Signs of emotion: What can preverbal children "say" about internal states? *Infant Mental Health Journal*, 29(3), 234–258. https://doi.org/10.1002/imhj.20175.

Vélez-Agosto, N.M., Soto-Crespo, J.G., Vizcarrondo-Oppenheimer, M., Vega-Molina, S., & García Coll, C. (2017). Bronfenbrenner's bioecological theory revision: moving culture from the macro into the micro. *Perspectives on Psychological Science*, 12(5), 900–910. https://doi.org/10.1177/1745691617704397.

Vygotsky, L.S. (1978). *Mind in society: The development of higher psychological processes.* Harvard University Press.

Vygotsky, L.S. (1981). The genesis of higher mental functions. In J.V. Wertsch (Ed.), *The concept of activity in Soviet psychology* (pp. 144–188). Sharpe.

Vygotsky, L.S. (1987). *The collected works of L.S. Vygotsky*, Vol. 1. *Problems of general psychology.* Plenum Press.

Waddington, C. (1942). Canalization of development and the inheritance of acquired characters. *Nature*, 150, 563–565. https://doi.org/10.1038/150563a0.

Walden, T.A., & Smith, M.C. (1997). Emotion regulation. *Motivation and Emotion*, 21, 7–25.

Walker, R.F., & Murachver, T. (2012). Representation and theory of mind development. *Developmental Psychology*, 48(2), 509–520. https://doi.org/10.1037/a0025663.

Wang, E.A., Riley, C., Wood, G., Greene, A., Horton, N., Williams, M., Violano, P., Brase, R.M., Brinkley-Rubinstein, L., Papachristos, A.V., & Roy, B. (2020). Building community resilience to prevent and mitigate community impact of gun violence: Conceptual framework and intervention design. *BMJ open*, 10(10), e040277.

Wang, Z., Devine, R., Wong, K., & Hughes, C. (2015). Theory of mind and executive function during middle childhood across cultures. *Journal of Experimental Child Psychology*, 149, 6–22. doi:10.1016/j.jecp.2015.09.028.

Waxman, S.G. (1980). Determinants of conduction velocity in myelinated nerve fibers. *Muscle Nerve*, 3, 141–150.

Webb, S.J., Monk, C.S., & Nelson, C.A., (2001). Mechanisms of postnatal neurobiological development: Implications for human development. *Developmental Neuropsychology*, 19(2), 147–171. https://doi.org/10.1207/S15326942DN1902_2.

Weisz, V., Beal, S.J., & Wingrove, T. (2013). The legal system experiences of children, families, and professionals who work with them. In M.K. Miller & B.H. Bornstein (Eds.), *Stress, trauma, and wellbeing in the legal system* (pp. 63–88). Oxford University Press.

Welsh, M.C., & Pennington, B.F. (1988). Assessing frontal lobe functioning in children: Views from developmental psychology. *Developmental Neuropsychology*, 4, 199–230.

White, R.E., Prager, E.O., Schaefer, C., Kross, E., Duckworth, A.L., & Carlson, S.M. (2017). The "Batman Effect": Improving perseverance in young children. *Child Development*, 88(5), 1563–1571.

Whitehurst, G., & Lonigan, C. (2008). Child development and emergent literacy. *Child Development*, 69, 848–872. doi:10.1111/j.1467-8624.1998.tb06247.

Williams, D.L. (2018). Executive function and complex processing models. In J.L. Johnson, G.S. Goodman, & P.C. Mundy (Eds.), *Wiley handbook of memory, autism spectrum disorder, and the law* (pp. 53–69). Wiley. https://doi.org/10.1002/9781119158431.ch3.

Williamson, J.M., & Lyons, D.A. (2018). Myelin dynamics throughout life: An ever-changing landscape? *Frontiers in Cellular Neuroscience*, 12, 424. https://doi.org/10.3389/fncel.2018.00424.

Witherspoon, D.P., Bámaca-Colbert, M.Y., Stein, G.L., & Rivas-Drake, D. (2020). Hidden populations: Uncovering the developmental experiences of minoritized populations across contexts. *Developmental Psychology*, 56(8), 1425–1430. https://doi.org/10.1037/dev0001055.

Wong, T.Y., Chang, Y.T., Wang, M.Y., & Chang, Y.H. (2023). The effectiveness of child-centered play therapy for executive functions in children with attention-deficit/hyperactivity disorder. *Clinical Child Psychology and Psychiatry*, 28(3), 877–894. doi:10.1177/13591045221128399.

Woodard, K., Pozzan, L., & Trueswell, J.C. (2016). Taking your own path: Individual differences in executive function and language processing skills in child learners. *Journal of Experimental Child Psychology*, 141, 187–209. https://doi.org/10.1016/j.jecp.2015.08.005.

Worthman, C.M., Dockray, S., & Marceau, K. (2019). Puberty and the evolution of developmental science. *Journal of Research on Adolescence*, 29(1), 9–31.

Wu, Q., & Xu, Y. (2020). Parenting stress and risk of child maltreatment during the COVID-19 pandemic: A family stress theory-informed perspective. *Developmental Child Welfare*, 2(3), 180–196. doi:10.1177/2516103220967937.

Yakovlev P.L., & Lecours A.R. (1967). The myelogenetic cycles of regional maturation of the brain. In A. Minkowski (Ed.), *Regional development of the brain in early life* (pp. 3–70). Blackwell.

Yosso, T.J. (2005). Whose culture has capital? A critical race theory discussion of community cultural wealth. *Race Ethnicity and Education*, 8, 69–91. doi:10.1080/1361332052000341006.

Zelazo, P.D., & Carlson, S.M. (2012). Hot and cool executive function in childhood and adolescence: Development and plasticity. *Child Development Perspectives*, 6(4), 354–360.

Zelazo, P.D., & Carlson, S.M. (2020). The neurodevelopment of executive function skills: Implications for academic achievement gaps. *Psychology & Neuroscience*, 13(3), 273–298. https://doi.org/10.1037/pne0000208.

Zelazo, P.D., Carlson, S.M., & Kesek, A. (2008). The development of executive function in childhood. In C.A. Nelson & M. Luciana (Eds.), *Handbook of developmental cognitive neuroscience* (pp. 553–574). Boston Review.

Zhou, V., & Wilson, B.J. (2022). A cross-sectional study of inhibitory control in young children with autism spectrum disorder. *Early Child Development and Care*, 192, 1045–1055. doi:10.1080/03004430.2020.1835880.

Author Index*

Subject Index

Page numbers in *italic* indicate illustrations

For Product Safety Concerns and Information please contact our EU
representative GPSR@taylorandfrancis.com
Taylor & Francis Verlag GmbH, Kaufingerstraße 24, 80331 München, Germany